The Spirit of Buffalo Women

Prominent Women who called WNY their Home

The women profiled in this book contributed to the development of WNY as social benefactors, community leaders, politicians, educators, entertainers, authors, journalists, artists, philanthropists, business owners and management executives.

RICK FALKOWSKI

Published by
Rick Falkowski
Williamsville, NY 14231
buffalomusichistory.com
rickfalkowski@aol.com
Buffalohistorybooks.com
Facebook: Historic & Influential People from Buffalo & WNY

The Spirit of Buffalo Women: Prominent Women who called WNY their Home

ISBN number: 979-8-9869824-2-7

1. Buffalo, NY
2. Local History
3. Historic People, Nonfiction

Edited by: Mike Buckley, Catherine Flickinger Schweitzer
Layout and Design: Nancy Wise-Reid
Proof Readers: Marsha Falkowski, Mike Reid, Nancy Wise-Reid
Photo enhancement and optimization: Nancy Wise-Reid, Steve Loncto
Front Cover Digital Painting: Paul Marko/Download Design

First Edition: November 2023
First Printing: November 2023
Printed in the U.S.A.

TABLE OF CONTENTS

TABLE OF FIGURES

Front cover:

Digital painting - Paul Marko/Download Design

Back Cover:

Author Photo - photo credit - Marsha Falkowski

INTRODUCTION & ACKNOWLEDGEMENTS

When I began writing books about Buffalo history I quickly realized that the contributions by area women were often not properly acknowledged and women were usually referred to by Mrs. their husband's name. This was an inequity that I felt had to be rectified.

In my previous books I attempted to include the accomplishment of WNY Women where possible. That resulted in a separate presentation titled Influential Buffalo Women. I began giving talks about women from the WNY area and at the end of the presentation people often asked if I had a book that included the information from the lecture. I advised the information came from all of my books and some that was not included in any of the books. Rather than having to purchase all three books, these people were interested in a book just about the people that were discussed in the presentation. A Prominent Women of WNY book was needed.

When I was writing Profiles Volume III: Historic & Influential People from Buffalo & WNY – the Late 1900s, in late 2022, I encountered several issues that would not allow the book to be completed for the November 15, 2023 scheduled release date. The book release was already scheduled at the Buffalo History Museum, so I decided to complete the Women's book first. It was also already in progress and could be published in time for the November release date.

As the book was being completed, my editor Mike Buckley said he felt the cover should look different than the Influential People books. A title of The Spirit of Buffalo Women was proposed and Mike thought of the Spirit of Niagara poster from the Pan-American Exposition. He inquired if that look could be updated and incorporated as the book cover. Several graphic artists were consulted, and Paul Marko of Download Design submitted a proposal. His suggested cover depicted an android Artificial Intelligence appearance that includes women of all races and nationalities. Exactly the Spirit of Buffalo Women that we wanted to convey.

Time constraints and getting COVID in August put me behind in completing this book by the required deadline. Mike Buckley stepped up by creating abridged versions of some of the women who were included in previous publications. Catherine Flickinger Schweitzer offered her assistance in researching some of the women that were to be covered and adding information to the completed profiles. Catherine also wrote a couple of the profiles in the book, identified in Source

Notes, which allowed The Spirit of Buffalo Women to be completed just in time for publication.

Without the assistance of Mike and Catherine this book would not have been completed in 2023. Nancy Wise-Reid contributed by devising a system to layout the book as it was being written. I figured out how to enhance the photos to 300 dpi and Nancy was able to clear up some pictures, so all did not have to be sent to Steve Loncto in North Carolina for optimization. Steve still offered his expertise in enhancing some of the more difficult pictures.

There were many other people that assisted in this project. Following is a listing of some of the names and I apologize to anyone that I missed.

- Alan Bozer
- Andree Renee Simpson
- Anthony Greco
- Amie Whitemore
- Barbara Buckley
- Barbara Nevergold
- Barbara Buckley
- Buffalo Billy Greco
- Carolyn Clement Clark
- Christine Ziemba
- Doris Jones
- Evelyn Merriweather
- Gina Marie Browning Lattuca
- Heather Gring
- John DiSciullo
- Julie Reinstein
- Justin Higner
- Karen Pusateri
- Kelsey Reed
- Mark Woodward
- McKinley Falkowski
- Penny Wolfgang
- Rebecca Justinger
- Richard Fustino
- Sara Larkin
- Susan McCartney

JOAN BAEZ

Folk Singer and 1960s Activist

Joan Baez was born in Staten Island to Albert Baez and Joan Chandos Bridge Baez. Her father was born in Mexico but moved to Brooklyn where his Methodist minister father obtained a post at a Spanish speaking congregation. Her mother was born in Scotland, the daughter of an English Anglican priest who claimed to be descended from the Dukes of Chandos. Joan's father considered becoming a minister but decided to study mathematics and physics, earning a PhD from Stanford University.

Due to her father's employment, the family continually moved. Joan and her two sisters Pauline Thalia Baez Bryan and Margarita Mimi Baez Farina lived in various countries and U.S. states, including one year in Iraq. When Joan was 7 and 8 years old, in

Figure 1 Joan Baez

1948 and 1949, the family lived in Clarence Center while her father worked at an armament industry plant in the defense industry in Buffalo. She took piano lessons while living in WNY but was not yet playing guitar or writing songs.

Baez recalls that she and her sisters would climb one of the trees on their property to watch the only television in town at the brick house across the street from her home. In a 2011 interview she said they wanted to watch "Kukla, Fran and Ollie." While in Clarence her father started attending Quaker meetings. This exposure affected Joan's attitude, igniting her interest in pacifism and civil rights. After a year of meetings her father decided to stop working in the defense industry and took a position as a professor at the University of Redlands in California for one half the pay of his defense industry job.

The segregation attitude of America in the late 1940s affected Joan for the rest of her life. Being a Mexican resulted in people thinking she was Black. While living in Clarence Center she experienced racial slurs and was called the N word by someone in town. She remembers replying, "You ought to see me in the

1

summertime." This discrimination resulted in Baez refusing to perform during the 1960s at any colleges that were segregated and only play at schools where all races were welcome. The result was that she only played at Black colleges in the south during this time.

Dr. Baez took a position at Stanford University, that afforded Joan the opportunity of having a permanent home for her high school years, graduating from Palo Alto high school in 1958. A friend of her father gave Joan a ukulele and taught her how to play basic chords. When she was 13 years old her aunt took her to a Pete Seeger concert and Joan started learning to play his songs. When she was 17 Joan purchased a Gibson acoustic guitar to accompany her singing of folk songs. While still in California she recorded a demonstration album, but it did not garner any record company interest.

Shortly after her high school graduation, Joan's father took a job at MIT in Boston.

Baez briefly attended Boston University but left to concentrate on her singing career. In 1958 she played her first job at a coffee house in Cambridge where she became a favorite of Harvard University students. At the Club 47 in Cambridge, she met Bill Wood who hosted a WRUB Harvard Radio Balladeers program. They started performing together and in 1959 released an album *Folksingers 'Round Harvard Square* on Veritas Records. Later in 1959 Baez was invited by Albert Grossman to perform at the Gate of Horn nightclub in Chicago. There she met Bob Gibson and Odetta, prominent folk and gospel vocalists. Baez considered Odetta, Marian Anderson and Pete Seeger as her influences, and it was Bob Gibson that asked her to sing two songs with him at the 1959 Newport Folk Festival.

Figure 2
Joan Baez performing early in career

The guest appearance with Gibson at Newport bolstered her career. During 1960 she was signed by Vanguard Records, made her NYC Debut at the 92nd Street Y, was invited back to Newport as a solo performer and released her first album *Joan Baez*. In 1961 she met Bob Dylan at Gerde's Folk City, released her second album *Joan Baez Volume Two* and embarked on her first U.S. tour. In 1962 she became more involved in civil rights, released her third album *Joan Baez in Concert* and was on the cover of Time Magazine in November 1962.

2

The music career and civil rights involvement of Joan Baez are intertwined, both being equally important in her life. 1963 was a seminal year of her career as she appeared at the Monterey Folk Festival with Bob Dylan, introduced Bob Dylan at the Newport Folk Festival, was the headliner at the Newport Folk Festival and she sang "We shall Overcome" by Pete Seeger at the March on Washington when Martin Luther King Jr. gave his "I Have a Dream" speech. This led to singing and participating in various Civil Rights events and causes.

Baez became an outspoken critic of the Vietnam War beginning in 1964 and was involved in the Berkley Free Speech Movement and with Cesar Chavez United Farm Workers. She also campaigned for the End of the Death Penalty, Prison Reform, LGBTQ+ Rights, Voting Rights, Environmental Issues and spoke out against the War in Iran.

Some of the awards received and achievements of Joan Baez include 1969 performing 14 songs at Woodstock, 1985 opening Live Aid Philadelphia concert, 2007 Lifetime achievement award at Grammys, 2009 performed at Barack Obama's inauguration, 2011 inducted into Grammy Hall of Fame, 2011 Amnesty International inaugural Joan Baez Human Rights Award, 2014 ASCAP Centennial Award, 2017 inducted into Rock and Roll Hall of Fame and 2020 Kennedy Center Award, but due to COVID received at the May 2021 Award Ceremony.

Figure 3 Joan Baez sitting on the steps of her childhood home in Clarence Center
Photo credit Shirley Walker

Joan first met Bob Dylan in 1961 and in 1963 she returned Bill Gibson's favor by introducing Bob Dylan at the 1963 Newport Folk Festival. They had a relationship that ended in 1965 but they remained friends and toured together in the Rolling Thunder Revue 1975/6 and in 1984 along with Carlos Santana. Joan married draft resister David Harris in 1968 and had a son Gabriel who was Joan's touring drummer and percussionist. She dated Steve Jobs from Apple; he was in his mid-20s and Baez in her early 40s. Jobs wanted to get married but Joan declined and they remained friends until the end of Jobs' life.

The house where Baez lived in Clarence Center was at 6095 Railroad Street. The home that Flight 3407 crashed into was 6038 Long Street, only two blocks away. In November 2011, two and a half years after the tragedy when Baez was booked to play a concert at Kleinhans Music Hall, she was invited by Clarence town historian Mark Woodward to visit her previous home and the crash site memorial. She was greeted by town supervisor Scott Bylewski and Erie County Historian Douglas Kohler for the ceremonies in Clarence before her concert.

In addition to the Joan Baez connections to Buffalo mentioned, Buffalo guitarist and vocalist Grace Stumberg was Joan's tour guitar tech and assistant, singing backup at performances. Joan's tour manager was Buffalo resident Blair Woods who began his music career as tour manager for Buffalo duo John & Mary (John Lombardo and Mary Ramsey) and later worked with 10,000 Maniacs. During her entire career, Joan kept in touch with friends she made in Clarence Center by inviting them backstage at concerts and even writing the song "Lily" about one of her childhood acquaintances.

Figure 4 Home where Joan Baez lived on Railroad Street in Clarence Center
Photo courtesy Sara Larkin

LUCILLE BALL

Star of I Love Lucy and Executive at Desilu Productions

Lucille Ball was born on August 6, 1911 at 69 Stewart Street in Jamestown, N.Y., delivered by her grandmother Flora Belle Hunt. Her mother was Desiree "DeDe" Evelyn Hunt Ball and her father was Henry Durrell Ball. After Lucy was born, the family moved to Montana where Henry was a lineman for the telephone company. Lucy originally said she was born in Butte, Montana because she thought it sounded more glamorous than Western New York.

Lucy and her mother returned to Jamestown NY, after her father passed away. They moved in with her mother's parents, Fred and Flora Belle Hunt, at their small

Figure 5 Lucille in 1934

apartment on Buffalo Street. However, Lucy's mother DeDe became depressed and it was decided she should go to California for a change. While she was gone, Lucy went to live with her aunt Lola, DeDe's little sister.

About three years later, DeDe married Ed Peterson who was good to Lucy but not a father figure. In fact, he asked that Lucy call him Ed. DeDe and Ed moved to Detroit for work. Lucy stayed with Ed Peterson's parents who believed in a strict Puritan upbringing for children. They taught Lucy hard work, discipline and a perfectionist attitude.

When DeDe and Ed returned to Jamestown, Grandpa Fred Hunt bought a home for the extended family at 59 8th Street in Celeron NY, near the Celeron Amusement Park. The park had midway rides, but Lucy was attracted to the stage plays, bandshell music performances and outdoor movie screen which showed, The Perils of Pauline melodrama film serial and other releases. With her friend Marion Strong, she went to dances at the Celeron Pier Ballroom to see big bands like Harry James, Glenn Miller, Duke Ellington and Benny Goodman. Lucy worked as a short order cook in the hamburger stand and later at the ice cream stand.

As an adolescent, Lucy began getting into trouble. She got into fights at school, threw a typewriter at her typing teacher, ran away often and pulled regular teenage antics like leaving class to get a drink of water and exiting the building. Her eighth-grade principal, Mr. Bernard Drake, was the first person to label her exuberant feelings as talent and urged her to get on stage. As a high school freshman, Lucy was encouraged by teacher Miss Lilliam Appleby to channel her urge to express herself into acting. With her friend Pauline Lopus, their first production was Charley's Aunt where they charged 25-cents a ticket and made a profit of $25.00 which was donated for a ninth-grade party. They used the wicker furniture from Lucy's living room for the stage set. DeDe worked at clothing stores including Marcus & Company on Main St. in Jamestown and was a good seamstress. She assisted with other school plays, sewing the costumes and encouraging her daughter. Lucy tried out for all available plays in Jamestown and during the performance of The Scottish Rite Revue, she was so enthusiastic about her dance that she fell into the Palace Theatre orchestra pit, pulling her arm out of its socket. The Jamestown Post Journal hailed her as a new discovery. During the summer before her sophomore year of high school, Lucy entered the Miss Celoron bathing beauty contest, judged by Miss America 1927. DeDe sent her to photographer-T. Henry Black, to take a photo for the Jamestown newspaper. Her photo did not appear in the paper because, according to Mr. Black, "It's difficult to get a satisfactory picture of Miss Ball because the lady is just not photogenic!"

At age 17 with DeDe's support, Lucy enrolled at the John Murray Anderson–Robert Milton theater school in Manhattan. Of the 70 students in the class, only 12 continued after the first semester with the school writing DeDe to advise her that Lucy did not have what it takes to be an actress and she would be wasting her money if she continued. One student in Lucy's class that excelled was Bette Davis; but even though Lucy was asked to leave, she is listed with Bette Davis as the two most successful alumni from the school.

Lucy remained in New York, and found a paying job modeling coats. Her luck improved when Lucy obtained a job as a model with Hattie Carnegie's dress shop in NYC where the rich society women and movie stars purchased $1,000 dresses and $40,000 sable coats. For $35.00 a week, Lucy modeled 30 to 40 evening gowns and suits a day. Not taking care of herself, Lucy became ill and contracted rheumatoid arthritis. She returned to the family home, now in the Wilcox Apartments in Jamestown, and participated in an experimental treatment of horse serum injections. While recuperating in 1930, she was visited by Bill Bemus who cast her as Aggie Lynch in Within the Law with the Jamestown Players. The play was also a success at the Chautauqua Institution and bolstered Lucy's confidence in her acting.

Returning to NYC, she obtained a job at Jackson's first-class clothing house near Times Square. A painter named Ratterman did an oil portrait of Lucy wearing a flowing chiffon dress that was sold to Chesterfield cigarettes. Overnight, Lucy was on billboards across NYC and she was called the new Chesterfield girl. This got her a part in the Goldwyn Studios Eddie Canter movie, Roman Scandals, as one of twelve well-known poster girls. The Goldwyn contract paid her transportation to Hollywood and $125 a week for six weeks of filming at United Artists studio. The six-week filming of Roman Scandals was extended to six months as a Goldwyn Girl. That was followed by a $75.00 a week stock contract with Columbia and a three-month contract at RKO, that stretched into seven years. She was making enough money to have her mother, grandfather and brother move to Hollywood and live with her.

By 1938, Lucy was receiving small parts in A movies and larger parts in B movies, along with working on a radio show. It was on the radio that she honed her comedy skills. Since her contract was annually picked up with automatic increases in salary, a 28-year-old Lucy was making $1,000 a week plus income from the radio shows. Lucy was told that RKO bought the rights to a successful Broadway play, Too Many Girls, and she was being considered for the starring role.

The movie, Too Many Girls, changed Lucy's life. One of her co-stars was a 22-year-old Cuban, Desiderio Alberto Arnaz y de Acha III (Desi Arnaz). Desi's father was mayor of Santiago Cuba for ten years, a member of the Cuban House of Representatives, owned three ranches and a palatial mansion and vacation home on a private island in Santiago Bay. His mother's father was an executive at the Bacardi Rum Company. During the Cuban Revolution of 1933 when Batista seized power, Desi's father was imprisoned and his property confiscated. He fled to Miami with little more than the shirt on his back. Desi joined him in Miami and after establishing a reputation as a performer, Desi was given the lead of the Broadway play and

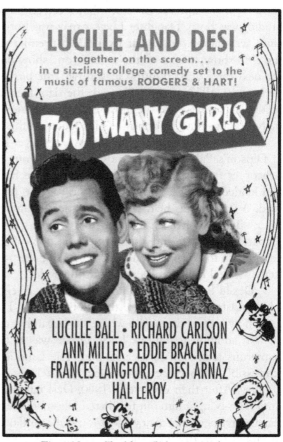

Figure 6 Lucy - Too Many Girls promotional poster

7

included in the Too Many Girls movie cast. Desi's handsome Latin appearance, talent and charm bewitched Lucy, and they were married in November 1940. Lucy claimed it was not love at first sight, it took five minutes.

In the spring of 1950, after ten years of marriage they formed a corporate legal partnership called Desilu Productions Inc. to promote themselves as a team. They created a Mr. and Mrs. Vaudeville act with Desi singing and playing the bongo drums and Lucy trying to butt into his nightclub act. The act was a success but went off the road when Lucy had a miscarriage and had one more movie to fulfill her Columbia contract. In 1951, CBS said they were interested in a pilot for a Lucy/Desi TV Show. With the assistance of writers from Lucy's radio show, My Favorite Husband, a pilot based off their vaudeville act, was accepted. However, there were two problems. Lucy was again pregnant, and the sponsor wanted a live weekly show filmed in NYC.

Since they did not want to move to New York, the filming was resolved by Lucy and Desi taking a $1,000 per show cut in pay and agreeing to produce the shows at their expense. In return they received ownership of the show, and Desilu Studios was born. Daughter Lucie Arnaz was born on July 17, 1951, and the first show was filmed on August 15, 1951. It premiered on October 15, 1951, and by the 20th show, they were the number one show on television, a position held for the next three years. During season two, the birth of Little Ricky was telecast on January 19, 1953, to coincide with the date Desi Jr. was delivered by caesarean section. That show was the most watched television show up to that date, receiving higher ratings than Eisenhower's inauguration the following day.

In 1956 the premier of their movie, Forever Darling, was held in Jamestown at Dipson's Palace Theatre, now the Reg Lenna Civic Center. They arrived by helicopter from Buffalo, after they toured the Bell Aircraft plant in Wheatfield, and landed during a blinding rainstorm at the Jamestown High School football field. A parade was held with 25,000 people lining the streets to greet Desi and Lucy. They visited Lucy's former home, Jamestown Hospital, Bigelow's Department Store and the former location of Celeron Amusement Park. In addition to the movie premier, Lucy held a reception for her Celeron classmates in the Crystal Ballroom of the Jamestown Hotel.

Desilu Productions continued to grow. Eventually, Desilu owned a total of 33 soundstages, eleven more than 20th Century Fox and four more than MGM. Lucy now owned the studio where she began her career.

In addition to I Love Lucy, Desilu was responsible for the production of numerous television series including The Untouchables, Star Trek and Mission Impossible. It became the number one television production company in the country. After their divorce in 1960, Desi remained involved with the company until Lucy bought him out for three million dollars in 1962. This made her the first female president of a major television studio and one of the most powerful women in Hollywood. In 1967, she sold Desilu to Gulf+Western for seventeen million dollars or $130 million current dollars.

In 1989, the city of Jamestown approached Lucy about starting a comedy festival and opening a comedy museum. She gave permission for the use of her name but said she would like to see a national comedy museum honoring all forms of comedy rather than one dedicated to her accomplishments alone. The Lucille Ball Comedy Festival was started in 1991. The Lucille Ball Desi Arnaz Museum opened in 1996 and preserves the career of The First Couple of Comedy with exhibits and a re-creation of Ricky Ricardo's Tropicana Room from the I Love Lucy Show. In 2018, the 37,000 square foot National Comedy Center opened with 50 immersive exhibits that take visitors on an interactive journey through the history of comedy. It was voted the Best New Museum by the readers of USA Today in 2020. Celeron Park where Lucy danced to big bands at the Pier Ballroom and experienced vaudeville and theatrical shows, is now Lucille Ball Memorial Park. It is home to two Lucille Ball statues, Scary Lucy and Lovely Lucy.

Figure 7 Promotion photo of the I Love Lucy show cast

Lucy died on April 26, 1989 at the age of 77. In October 2002 her remains were moved from Hollywood to Lakeview Cemetery in Jamestown where she was buried with her family.

CHRISTINE BARANSKI

Award-winning Actress of Stage, Television and Movies

C hristine Baranski was born on May 2, 1952 in Buffalo and raised in the Polish neighborhood of Cheektowaga on the east side border of the city of Buffalo. She has appeared in Broadway plays, television shows and movies, being nominated for 15 Emmy Awards.

Her grandmothers were both involved with entertainment and the Polish-American theater scene in WNY. Maternal grandmother Stella Mazurowska sang on WGR radio in the 1920s and her paternal grandmother Janina Baranska hosted a show on WWOL in the late 1940s and early 1950s. She recalls that when she was young, after her Nana would put her and her older brother Michael to sleep, Nana and her lady friends would be in the living room, getting drunk, singing songs and dancing. Like many

Figure 8 Christine Baranski in Villa Maria High School yearbook

other baby boomers, she had fond memories of a Polish upbringing in Buffalo.

Baranski's father was the advertising manager of *Dziennik Dla Wszystkich*, a Polish language daily newspaper published in Buffalo from 1907 to 1957 and translated as *Everybody's Daily*. She attended Villa Maria Academy a private Roman Catholic all girl's secondary school on Pine Ridge Road in Cheektowaga. At school she played on the basketball team (Christine is 5'9"), and was class president and salutatorian of her 1970 graduating class.

While still a high school student, Christine became involved with performing on the stages of the Buffalo area as a member of the Buffalo Theater Workshop and Company of Man. A 1969 review in the UB Spectrum described her as a "versatile young lady." The article continued, "Christine Baranski, who is reportedly a high school senior, establishes herself as one of the most versatile young actresses I have seen anywhere in recent years."

After graduation from Villa, she attended the NYC Julliard School, receiving a BFA in 1974. Upon completing her studies, she began her acting career in theater, appearing with various theater companies. She made her Broadway and

Off-Broadway debuts in 1980. In that year she also came back to Buffalo's Studio Arena for the world premiere of *Lady of the Diamond*. During her acting career she won two Tony Awards on Broadway for *The Real Thing* in 1984 and *Rumors* in 1989. She also won two Drama Desk Awards and in 2018 was inducted into the American Theater Hall of Fame.

Concentrating her success on the stage, Baranski only made a few television appearances. She made the transition to television in 1995 when she was cast as Cybill Shepherd's hard drinking friend, Maryann Thorpe, in the sitcom Cybill,

Figure 9 Baranski on Studio Arena stage in Diamonds in the Ruff Photo Buff State 1980

winning an Emmy Award as Best Supporting Actress. The series ran until 1998 and Christine appeared on many other television series including a multiple year, 16-episode guest starring role of Dr. Beverly Hofstadter, mother of Leonard Hofstadter, in *The Big Bang Theory*. She also starred as Diane Lockhart on *The Good Wife* (2009-2016) and its spinoff *The Good Fight* (2017-2022) in which Baranski was also the producer. In total, Baranski has received 15 Emmy nominations, only winning the Emmy for Cybill in 1995.

In addition to stage and television, Baranski has starred in many movies including but not limited to, *Lovesick* (1983), *9½ Weeks* (1986), *Addams Family Values* (1993), *The Ref* (1994), *The Birdcage* (1996), *The Odd Couple II* (1998), *How the Grinch Stole Christmas* (2000), *Mama Mia* (2008), *Into the Woods* (2014) and *A Bad Moms Christmas* (2017).

Baranski was married to actor and playwright Matthew Cowles from 1983 until his death in 2014. They prohibited their young daughters from watching television because they disapproved of the sexual content and violent depictions on shows. Their daughters are attorney/actress Isabel Cowles born in 1984 and actress Lily Cowles born in 1987.

In 2000, six years before Baranski's alma mater Villa Maria Academy closed, she was invited to give the graduation commencement speech. This was the 40th anniversary of her 1970 salutatorian speech. In her address Christine emphasized that she wanted the young women of the graduating class to understand that life wasn't about awards, fame and money. She told them "Follow the path that gives you the most joy. In other words, follow your heart."

Baranski grew up a Buffalo Bills fan and lived through four Super Bowl losses. She told The Late Show host Stephen Colbert that she loves her Bills and has a t-shirt that says "Buffalo – a drinking town with a football problem." The fortunes of the team have changed for the better and Christine's support never waned, she remains a self-described very "loud" Buffalo Bills fan.

TERESSA BELLISSIMO

Created Buffalo Chicken Wings

Figure 10 Teressa & Frank Bellissimo

Teressa Bellissimo added a new dish to the culinary delights of the world when she placed some chicken wings under the broiler, sprinkled them with hot sauce and added some celery sticks with blue cheese dressing on the side. Modern-day chicken wings, now referred to worldwide as Buffalo Wings, were unveiled.

Born in Sicily in 1900, Teressa Guzzo Bellissimo immigrated to Buffalo. She and her husband Frank opened the original location of the Anchor Bar near the harbor in downtown Buffalo in 1935. It was where Buffalo Memorial Auditorium was to be built, so in 1940 they moved to 1047 Main Street at High Street, its present site. The Anchor Bar became a popular Italian restaurant, and they also became known for presenting quality live jazz entertainment.

On March 4, 1964, her son Dominic Bellissimo was tending bar late on a Friday night at The Anchor Bar. Several of his friends stopped in for a drink and said they were starving. Teressa did not have any prepared food left in the restaurant. She found some chicken wings she was saving for a broth, added some hot sauce, fried the wings up in butter and placed them under the broiler. Adding celery and blue cheese dip, Dominic's friends loved them. The next day they were added to the menu. This is the story that has been adopted for the spur of the moment creation of chicken wings.

Another story is when the order Frank and Teressa placed for chicken parts was received it was only chicken wings. At this time chicken wings were basically throw-away parts of the chicken. Teressa decided that Thursday to return the shipment to their supplier. She woke up in the middle of the night, decided to do something with the wings and wrote out a recipe before going back to sleep. The next day Teressa experimented with the dish and planned to sample them with Dominic's friends who usually showed up just before midnight. She invited the group to the back room, asking them to sample a new snack she is considering adding to the menu. The entire dish of wings was quickly devoured.

The next day Frank started giving them away for free at the bar, in place of peanuts or pretzels. Suddenly everyone wanted the wings and some people stopped ordering lunch, just eating the free wings. Frank decided to stop serving them until he could figure out how to present them as a dish that can be sold. He added the idea of including celery sticks on the side with blue cheese dip and put them on the menu.

Figure 11 Early photo of The Anchor Bar

If you believe the spontaneous idea or planned recipe inception of chicken wings, one thing is common in both versions, Teressa is the person that invented the dish. Even if Frank tried to take credit for the added side condiments, Teressa came up with the idea. She was successful in making the chicken wing an important part of the bird and increased chicken production in the U.S.

Of course, there are others that claim the rights of serving the first chicken wings. In 1961, John Young opened his first restaurant at Jefferson and Carlton, about a twenty-minute walk from the Anchor Bar. His menu offered ribs, chicken wings, steak, eggs, bacon, grits and sausage. In 1964 when Teressa invented her wings, Young moved to Jefferson and High Street. Two years later, in 1966, he relocated to Jefferson and West Utica. At this location he named his restaurant John Young's Wings and Things, registering that name in the Erie County Clerk's Office.

Young advertised "Ten whole chicken wings for one dollar." He had crowds out the door and musicians on tour in Buffalo always stopped to try John Young's wings. After visiting Wings and Things, Young claims that Joe Tex wrote and recorded his 1969 hit record "Chicken Crazy."

He contended that although Teressa claimed she served the first chicken wings in 1964, he started selling them in 1961, continued serving the same wings at his restaurant and finally registered the Wings name in 1966. The difference between the John Young and Anchor Bar wing, is that Young served the entire wing while the Anchor Bar cut them into drum and flat with the tip discarded. The Young wing was breaded and served in mumbo sauce, a sweet and spicy ketchup-esque condiment. Young got the idea for the wings and restaurant name from Wings 'N' Things, a Washington DC restaurant owned by Chinese and run by African-Americans that opened in 1962. Mumbo Sauce was invented by Argia Collins from Indianola Mississippi who debuted the sauce in Chicago in 1950. It was a barbecue sauce that included tomato paste, vinegar, spices, garlic powder, onion powder, paprika, hickory smoke flavor and lemon juice. Regardless if Young

13

or someone else was first, Teressa is the person that created drum and flat hot sauce wings that are called Buffalo Wings.

Teressa used Frank's Hot Sauce in her original Anchor Bar chicken wing recipe, as did Duff's who started selling wings in 1969. These two establishments argue over the bragging rights for offering the best wings in Buffalo and now both market their own chicken wing sauce. Frank's Hot Sauce now markets Franks Buffalo Sauce. The Hot Sauce consists of a blend of cayenne pepper, vinegar and salt; the Buffalo Sauce adds butter and other ingredients. La Nova also markets their barbeque chicken wing sauce worldwide.

At first other restaurants refused to offer chicken wings because it was considered an Anchor Bar product. However, by the mid-70s, nickel wing night (and later ten cent chicken wing night) became a tradition at sports bars across WNY, and the rest of the country by the mid-1980s. They became staples at national chains like TGI Fridays, McDonalds and Pizza Hut. The Wing King, Drew Cerza, feels the growth was spearheaded by the Super Bowl success of the Buffalo Bills, appearing in four straight Super Bowls in the early 1990s. Sports fans saw Bills Mafia eating chicken wings at events across Buffalo. The food looked like fun to eat and became associated with football. Now some people will not watch the Super Bowl without pizza and wings.

Buffalo Mayor Stan Makowski proclaimed July 29, 1977 National Chicken Wing Day and July 29 is now celebrated as Chicken Wing Day across the country. In 2002 Drew Cerza founded the Buffalo Wing Festival held Labor Day weekend. It was held at the Buffalo downtown Dunn Tire Park (now Sahlen Field) baseball stadium and moved to the Buffalo Bills Highmark Stadium in Orchard Park. The festival benefits local charities and features wing tasting from restaurants worldwide, wing eating contests, a mullet competition and live music. It averages 50,000 attendees and for its 20th Anniversary in 2022, twenty tons of chicken wings were delivered for consumption. They had to get even more delivered before the festival ended.

Thanks to Teressa Bellissimo Buffalo Wings are on restaurant menus across the U.S. Here in Buffalo, the location of the invention does not have to be identified, so they are just wings.

Figure 12 Teressa in Anchor Bar advertisement

ZORAH BERRY

Classical Concert Promoter

Z orah Brake was born in Toledo, Ohio in 1889. Her father was a Methodist minister and singer who encouraged Zorah to attend Oberlin College in Toledo as a vocal major. A throat ailment derailed her singing career, but she met fellow music student William J. Berry at the college. They married and relocated to Detroit.

In Detroit Zorah and William Berry became involved with the Philharmonic Concert Company. In 1922, the Berrys moved to Buffalo where William was associated with his brother-in-law Edward H, Mueller, an architect, lawyer and realtor. After William died in 1923, Zorah obtained a position selling tickets for a concert series at the Masonic Consistory. The following year she became the Buffalo representative for the Philharmonic Concert Company.

In 1925, Zorah was named local manager of the concert series and The Philharmonic Concert Company booked

Figure 13 Zorah Berry 1935
Photo PD

performing artists in Detroit, Lansing, Flint, Kalamazoo, Grand Rapids, Buffalo and Toronto. By offering multiple dates, they were able to secure dates by well-known artists at reduced fees. Berry booked classical, opera and dance artists, ensembles and orchestras at the Consistory. The series became known as the Buffalo Philharmonic Concert Company series, with Zorah Berry as booking agent and local manager and were presented through the 1932-3 season.

The concerts were rebranded as the Zorah Berry Philharmonic Concerts, the Zorah Berry concerts or Zorah Berry Presents beginning with the 1933-4 season. Berry opened an office in the Denton, Cottier and Daniels Music Store at 32 Court Street. Denton, Cottier and Daniels was the primary retailer of pianos, band instruments, orchestra instruments and sheet music in Buffalo. It was the natural location for Berry's offices which in 1933 sold individual concert tickets for $1.10 to $2.75 and season tickets for her eight concerts between $6.00 and $17.00, depending upon the seat location.

In 1933 the concerts presented by Zorah Berry were moved to the Elmwood Music Hall, at the corner of Elmwood Avenue and Virginia Street. The building was designed by Buffalo's female architect Louise Bethune in 1885, as an armory for the 74th New York National Guard Regiment. However, the end of the 19th century was a time of building monumental armories and by 1899 the 74th regiment moved to the immense Connecticut Street Armory, vacating the 13-year-old Bethune designed structure. The city of Buffalo took possession of the facility and turned it into a convention center, seating 2,700 in folding chairs on the floor and another 350 on the balcony. Although not aesthetically attractive, not well heated and furnished with only wooden folding chairs, concert goers were delighted by the acoustics that carried the voices of the vocalists and intricacies of the soloists. Audiences even overlooked the outdoor screeching of trolley cars, to enjoy the symphonic concerts. The facility also housed the gigantic organ from the Pan-American Exposition at the Temple of Music, donated to the city of Buffalo by J.N. Adams for alternate Sunday recitals. The last concert before the Elmwood Music Hall was condemned was the Zorah Berry presented performance by theatre star Nelson Eddy.

Berry's 1933-4 concerts primarily featured soloists and smaller ensembles including soprano Lucrezia Bori, tenor Richard Crooks, pianist Ossip Gabrilowitsch, violinist Fritz Kreisler, soprano Lotte Lehmann, Rachmaninoff, the Vienna Boys' Choir and the Ballet Russe. She also presented Buffalo born opera soprano, Rose Bampton, who became a Metropolitan Opera star. In subsequent years, some of her dance presentations were held at Shea's Court Street Theatre and the Erlanger Theatre, across from the Statler Hotel at Delaware and Mohawk. When the Buffalo Philharmonic Orchestra, founded in 1934 and premiered in 1935 at the Elmwood Concert Hall, performed the first concert at Kleinhans Music Hall on October 19, 1940, Berry began presenting large scale performances in this new concert hall. She originally booked the Boston Symphony Orchestra at the Elmwood Concert Hall and moved her presentations back to the Consistory after it closed. When Kleinhans opened she expanded to scheduling larger orchestras. Beginning in 1940, Berry presented the Philadelphia Orchestra, Minneapolis Symphony Orchestra, Pittsburgh Symphony Orchestra and later in her career booked the Royal Philharmonic Orchestra of London, Boston Pops, New York Philharmonic, Concertgebouw Orchestra of Amsterdam and Vienna Philharmonic Orchestra.

The 30th anniversary of Zorah Berry Presents was celebrated in the 1955-6 season. Afterwards, she merged with the Buffalo Philharmonic Orchestra Society series and was given the title of the BPO Society's Supervisor of Sales, with tickets available at the BPO Office at Kleinhans or at Zorah Berry's 32 Court Street Office. She stated that her business was being turned over to the BPO "as a gift, for it has been my wish that when I retire the Zorah Berry Concerts will be handled in a dignified manner and the high standard I have maintained 31 years will continue." The association lasted for six seasons, through 1962-3 and was not renewed.

In 1963, Zorah Berry partnered with William D. MacPhearson, medical director and supervisor of the Niagara Lutheran Home for the Great Artists Series. The concerts were sponsored by Niagara Lutheran Home and all were held at Kleinhans

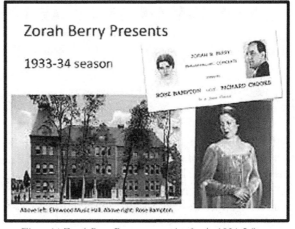

Figure 14 Zorah Berry Presents promotion for the 1934-5 Season

Music Hall. During the inaugural season, Berry now 74 years old, fell and broke her hip. After being hospitalized, she conducted the Great Artists Series business from Niagara Lutheran Home by telephone. The final Great Series Concert was on April 5, 1965 and featured Marian Anderson, renowned African-American vocalist and an important artistic figure in the civil rights movement, on her farewell tour.

Zorah Berry married William D Logan in 1929. They lived at 328 Summer Street and Logan died in 1945. Berry was also a member of the Zonta Club of Buffalo, serving as its first vice president in 1943. She died on March 3, 1969 at the age of 80, at the Niagara Lutheran Home and is buried at Forest Lawn Cemetery. In 1975, William D. MacPhearson, donated the Zorah Berry Collection to the Buffalo & Erie County Library music department. Her papers included her scrapbooks of news clippings on performances she presented over her 43-year career, a narrative and pictorial history of Buffalo concert life. It has been determined that from her first concert as local manager of the Philharmonic Concert Company in 1925, until her Great Artists series in 1965, she booked at least 186 different performing acts, representing 372 concerts over her 40-year career. Zorah Berry estimated that over one million people attended the concerts she presented. In 1953 she was named one of nine women of the year in Buffalo and in 1963, The Buffalo Evening News named her an Outstanding Citizen and called her a "brilliant force in the cultural development of the Niagara Frontier."

LOUISE BLANCHARD BETHUNE

The First Woman to practice as a Professional Architect in the United States

Jennie Louise Blanchard Bethune was born in Waterloo, NY, near Seneca Falls, in 1856 to a family of educators. Taught at home until the age of eleven, she attended high school in Buffalo. A "caustic remark" made to her in high school directed her attention to architecture, and "an investigation was begun in a spirit of playful self-defense, soon became an absorbing interest".

Kelly Hayes McAlonie, author of *Louise Blanchard Bethune: Every Woman Her Own Architect*, wrote, "There can be little doubt that while stubbornness may have led to a passion for the field, it was strength of character that enabled her to overcome obstacles placed in front of her becoming an architect."

Figure 15 Louise Bethune
Photo PD

Upon graduation in 1874 she prepared to enter the newly opened architecture program at Cornell University. Yet when offered an apprenticeship as a draftsman in 1876 at the office of Richard Waite, one of the most prominent architecture firms in Buffalo, she accepted. Rather than attending Cornell, her five-year apprenticeship and study (while also working part time at the office of F.W. Caulkins) allowed her to start her own firm in 1881. Later that year she married Canadian Robert Bethune, a colleague in the Richard Waite firm, who joined her in forming the architectural company Bethune & Bethune. William Fuchs joined the firm, in 1891.

Historian Austin Fox wrote "Louise grew up within the orbit of the women's rights movement When she opened her own architectural office in October 1881, she evidently timed the move to coincide with the Women's Congress being held here at that time."

In 1885 she applied for membership in the Western Association of Architects (WAA) and was unanimously and enthusiastically accepted as its first woman member based on her professional reputation, and setting a precedent for others. She was placed on the committee of state associations as the first and only member from New York State in the WAA.

The Pioneering Women of America website includes this interesting quote from two preeminent architects of the era about Louise Bethune's credentials: "Of particular note is the leadership exhibited by the executive committee, especially Daniel Burnham and Louis Sullivan, who were, respectively, the chairman and member of the board of directors at the time. When asked their opinion on the matter, Burnham said, "we are all agreed [that women should be admitted into the association]; we are very much in favor of it." The board stated, "If the lady is practicing architecture and is in good standing, there is no reason why she should not be one of us. . ... She has done work by herself and been very successful. She is unanimously elected a member."

The following year she organized the Buffalo Society of Architects (now AIA Buffalo/WNY) and served as vice president and treasurer. In 1888, Bethune was the first woman elected to the American Institute of Architects. When the WAA and the AIA merged in 1889, Bethune became the AIA's first woman fellow. Included in her AIA application was her design for the first floor of the former Buffalo Police Station No. 2.

Louise Bethune enjoyed educational design but did not specialize in it. She noted it was her duty as the first professional woman architect to demonstrate capacity in all facets of architectural practice. The portfolio of Bethune, Bethune & Fuchs included everything from small residential to institutional, commercial, and industrial work. Bethune designed 150 buildings of all styles in Buffalo and New England but concentrated on public buildings, especially schools. She designed 18 schools including Hamburg High School, Lockport High School and Buffalo Public Schools. Other examples include designs for Offerman Stadium and the first transformer building on Niagara Street which brought electricity from Niagara Falls to Buffalo in 1898. Two of her major projects were the 74th Armory, which became the Elmwood Music Hall, and the Hotel Lafayette. Her firm also designed the Denton, Cottier & Daniels store at Court & Pearl Street which was one of the first buildings designed in Buffalo utilizing poured concrete slabs and steel frame construction. She also designed the former Jehle's Grocery Store at Bryant & Ashland which became Just Pasta and is now Trattoria Aroma.

Figure 16 Elmwood Music Hall the former 74th Armory
Photo BPO

Bethune was active in women's rights and championed equal opportunities and pay for women. She refused to enter the architectural design competition for the Women's Building at the 1893 Chicago World's Fair because the prize offered to men was $10,000 but only $1,000 to women. She did not believe in competitions and felt women should be paid the same as men. In her view, "complete emancipation lies in 'equal pay for equal service.'"

Louise was a founding member of the Buffalo Women's Wheel and Athletic Club, just the second such club for women in the country. She was the first woman to own a bicycle in Buffalo at the cost of $150 in 1891. Women's rights advocate Susan B. Anthony stated that "Let me tell you what I think of bicycling. I think it has done more to emancipate women than anything else in the world. It gives women a feeling of freedom and self-reliance."

Bethune was also a member of the Buffalo Genealogy Club, the Buffalo Historical Society, and the Daughters of the American Revolution. Louise Blanchard Bethune died on December 18, 1913 and is buried in Forest Lawn Cemetery. Her obituary stated that she was particularly proud of her work at the Lafayette Hotel in Buffalo, praised as "one of the most perfectly appointed and magnificent hotels in the country" when it opened in 1904.

When the Hotel Lafayette, a building important in both Buffalo and American history, was handsomely restored in 2012, the legacy of a pioneer in the architectural profession and women's rights has been preserved.

To honor Bethune, in 1971 the University of Buffalo purchased the former Buffalo Meter Company Building and renamed it the Louise Blanchard Bethune Hall. It housed the Architecture Department, Art Department and portions of the university's Division of Continuing Education. The building is located at 2917 Main Street, next to Bennett High School and a block from the LaSalle light rail station. The University of Buffalo vacated the building in 1994 and it was subsequently purchased by Ciminelli Real Estate Corporation who refurbished the property into 87 loft apartments, known as Bethune Lofts.

Louise Bethune is also recognized and celebrated by the "Trailblazing Women Monument Project" in Buffalo as "a national leader in the architecture profession during the Gilded Age, a staunch advocate for equal pay for equal work" and her advocacy for "co-education and design excellence in educational design." Louise Bethune was inducted into the National Women's Hall of Fame in 2006.

Only three cities in the U.S. other than Buffalo have an Olmsted Park and buildings designed by Henry Hobson Richardson, Louis Sullivan and Frank Lloyd Wright who are considered the trinity of American architecture. Those three other cities are New York City, Chicago and St. Louis. The fact that the first female architect was from Buffalo, only further solidifies Buffalo's reputation as a historic architectural city.

AMANDA BLAKE

Miss Kitty on Gunsmoke, Animal Activist

Amanda Blake was raised in Buffalo as Beverly Louise Neill. She was born on February 20, 1929 to Jesse and Louise Puckett Neill at Millard Fillmore Hospital.

She began her education at Kenmore's Lindbergh Elementary School and lived on East Eden Road when attending Hamburg Junior High School. She attended Amherst High School but did not graduate in WNY because her father was transferred to California by his employer in 1946.

In California, Blake graduated from Claremont High School,

Figure 17 Miss Kitty - Amanda Blake

worked for a short time as a telephone operator and attended Pomona College. However, due to her participation in community and theater productions, she devoted herself full time to work on the stage. Amanda embarked on a full acting schedule including, summer stock in New England, theater performances and acting on radio programs back in her hometown of Buffalo. When acting in small theater she also painted backdrops and scenery.

While still a teenager, she signed a contract with M-G-M and was in her first movie *Stars in My Crown* in 1950. Several other movies followed until 1955. Her television debut was on a TV drama on the *Schlitz Playhouse of Stars*. While at CBS studios she heard that the popular radio show *Gunsmoke* was going to be made into a television show. In an interview she said, "I knew I had to have the part of Kitty so I hounded the producer until I got it."

Gunsmoke starred Jim Arness as Marshall Matt Dillon and Blake portrayed Miss Kitty Russell, the feisty madame and proprietor of Dodge City's Long Branch Saloon. She played Miss Kitty on *Gunsmoke* for 19 years, appearing in over 500 episodes. *Gunsmoke* was on the radio from 1952 to 1961 and on television from 1955 to 1975. It is the longest running prime time drama and second longest running prime time fictional program in U.S. television history.

Figure 18 PAWS co-founder, Pat Derby presenting Amanda Blake PAWS' Lifetime Achievement for Animal Welfare Award Circa 1987

Photo courtesy PAWSweb.org

Being on *Gunsmoke* took up almost all of Blake's acting time. After 1955 she did not film additional movies and only made sporadic television appearances, including seven guest starring roles on the Red Skelton Show between 1957 to 1963. After leaving the *Gunsmoke* series in 1974, she was considered semi-retired, just making a couple guest appearances on television shows and TV game shows.

Blake devoted most of her spare time to animals. While still filming *Gunsmoke* she sometimes brought her pet lion Kemo on the set. With her third husband Frank Gilbert, in 1971 she co-founded the Arizona Animal Welfare League, the oldest no-kill animal shelter in Arizona. She and Frank worked on an experimental breeding program for cheetahs. They were one of the first to successfully breed them in captivity and they raised seven successive generations of their mating pair. Blake was a one-time board member of the Humane Society of the United States.

In 1985 she was involved with Pat Derby and Ed Stewart in making donations, appearances and creating fundraisers for the Performing Animal Welfare Society (PAWS), a sanctuary for retired, neglected or abused performing animals in Galt California. Amanda met Pat, an animal trainer, on the set of the *Gunsmoke* series in 1967 and they became close friends. In 1986 PAWS opened the first elephant sanctuary in the US and Blake would travel to Africa on PAWS behalf. She was at the reserve in Galt for the birth of its first baby elephant and lived there later in life to be close to her animals. When Blake passed away in 1989, since she did not have any children or close relatives, she left the majority of her estate to PAWS.

Several years after her death, the Amanda Blake Memorial Wildlife Refuge offering sanctuary for free ranging African hoofed wildlife like emu, rhea, fallow deer, eland, Muntjac deer and a herd of scimitar-horned oryx, opened in Herald California. This sanctuary closed in 2022 with the animals going to a new PAWS facility in San Andreas. Items that were in the Amanda Blake Museum, Gunsmoke memorabilia and other items are being sold to benefit PAWS.

A two to three pack a day smoker, Amanda had oral cancer surgery in 1977. Afterwards she made appearances across the country for the American Cancer Society and in 1984 was the recipient of the society's annual Courage Award, presented by then U.S. President Ronald Reagan. In 1985 she received the American Cancer Society's Sword of Hope award.

Blake was a relative of Kate Barry, the American Revolutionary War heroine who was a voluntary scout, gathering American patriots and providing information to the forces of General Pickens. For her contributions she is referred to as the "Heroine of the Battle of Cowpens", a battle won by the American forces that drove the British out of South Carolina and towards their defeat at Yorktown. Blake visited Walnut Creek SC and donated a cameo sized portrait of Barry to a local history museum where it is still exhibited.

Figure 19 Amanda Blake with President Ronald Reagan at White House in 1984

After becoming a TV star, her first trip back to Buffalo was a promotional visit in 1960. She returned several times and kept in regular contact with some of her old friends and relatives. Her last visit to WNY was to attend the 40th high school reunion of her graduating class from Amherst High School in 1989. Shortly before her death she traveled to Virginia City Nevada and signed several hundred autographs in the costume of Kitty Russell. She died of cancer on August 16, 1989 at the age of 60.

Known for her trademark red hair and blue eyes, during an interview after she left Gunsmoke, she was quoted as saying, "Nineteen years is a hell of a long time for someone to be stuck behind a bar."

JOAN BOZER

Olmsted Parks Conservancy, Preservationist and County Legislator

The Women's Hall of Fame summed up the tremendous era-defining contributions Joan Bozer invested in her adopted hometown when she was inducted as their honoree in 2002. "Legislator, preservationist, environmentalist, and feminist, Joan Kendig Bozer's name is connected with almost everything that makes Erie County such a likable, livable place. Preserving Buffalo's Old Post Office building, saving Olmsted parks, creating the county's commission on women, working for sustainable energy, and building a Pan-American Women's Pavilion are just a few of the things she has done for us. And she does it all with élan, grace and great humor."

Her story in Buffalo began in 1950 when Joan Kendig arrived in town to meet the family of Dr. John

Figure 20 Joan Bozer in 2020
Photo courtesy Alan Bozer

Bozer, her future husband. During that visit she was not only introduced to John's family, but also introduced to the City of Buffalo. And Buffalo and WNY is a better place because of it.

Born May 13, 1928 to Tom and Ruth Kendig, Joan grew up in in the town of Pelham in Westchester County. Her mother was a librarian and her father owned a manufacturing company, Benton Manufacturing Co., a major manufacturer of leather index tabs, commonly used in date books. Machinery he invented continues to be the state of the art in the industry and he was also a major manufacturer of tea bag tabs. Pelham is adjacent to the Bronx and less than 30 minutes from Grand Central Station. Joan went to high school in Pelham, graduated from the Katherine Gibbs School, and attended Dean Junior College in Franklin Mass.

Her husband was born in Buffalo and he followed his father into the medical profession. John Bozer, graduated from Nichols School in 1945, earned a bachelor's degree from Harvard in 1948, and graduated from the College of Physicians and Surgeons at Columbia University in 1952. After returning to Buffalo for his internship and residency at Buffalo General Hospital, he joined the U.S. Navy and pursued a fellowship at Peter Bent Brigham Hospital in Boston, before returning to Buffalo to serve as chief resident in medicine at Buffalo General. He established a private practice in internal medicine and cardiology at Buffalo Medical Group, and was a clinical professor of Medicine at the University at Buffalo.

*Figure 21 Joan & John Bozer 1951 wedding
Photo courtesy Alan Bozer*

According to her son Alan, when Joan first came to Buffalo her husband drove down Genesee Street to Humboldt Park (now Martin Luther King Park), took Humboldt Parkway to Delaware Park, and passed through Agassiz Circle on the way to his parents' home. After her first visit to the City of Buffalo, Joan wrote to her parents that she had arrived in one of the most beautiful cities in the world. Joan and John were married in 1951 in Pelham Manor NY, but due to John's military service they traveled to various postings until finally settling in Buffalo.

Joan graduated from college later in life, receiving a bachelor's degree in history and government from Empire College. After completing her education, Joan actively participated in the Buffalo community by serving as President of the Junior League of Buffalo, the League of Women Voters Buffalo/Niagara, and the Buffalo Friends of Olmsted Park (now known as the Olmsted Parks Conservancy). She was also one of the founders of the National Association for Olmsted Parks (now the Olmsted Network), founder of the International Trade Council and chair of the National Conference of Christians and Jews (now NCCJ – National Conference for Community & Justice).

Her husband John was a cardiologist. He died in 2016 and they were married for 65 years. They had four sons Alan, Timothy, Thomas and Andrew and a daughter Elizabeth Augustus. John and Joan were patrons of the arts, supporters of the BPO to local theater and enjoyed season tickets for Bills, Sabres and Braves sporting events. When she ran for public office, John was known as the "King of Canvassers" by his wife's staff because he walked door to door daily to talk with constituents and ask for their votes during her campaigns.

Figure 22 Bozer at ECC job site during construction
Photo courtesy Alan Bozer

Joan was elected to the Erie County Legislature in 1976, and served nine terms or 18 years. She was known for organizing the right people to work together on projects, for her environmental conservation efforts, and was considered the matriarch of the Buffalo Olmsted Parks Conservancy. Bozer was also responsible for saving the Old Post Office from imminent demolition in 1980, and activating this distinctive historic landmark with a new mission as the downtown campus of Erie Community College, an accomplishment shared with Legislator Minnie Gillette. ECC created an award named for these leaders in 1998. The award celebrates the compassion, perseverance and dedication to the needs of women and children demonstrated by the careers of Gillette and Bozer. Criteria for the award includes, "…the ability to unite women despite difference in race, political orientation or economic status; and the ability to serve as a role model for other women desiring to move into non-traditional fields of influence."

Her distinguished community service and unique leadership has been recognized with numerous awards, beginning with the Buffalo News "Citizen of the Year" in 1978. The Buffalo History Museum honored her as the sole recipient of the prestigious Red Jacket Award in 1996. In 2006 she received the Landmarker

Figure 23 Bozer family in 1977
Photo courtesy Alan Bozer

Award from the Landmark Society. Zonta Club bestowed its highest honor, the Marian de Forest Service Award, to her in 2009. In 2011, the League of Women Voters established the perennial "Joan K. Bozer Leadership Award", a tribute to her life as a role model in the community and an honor to be awarded to deserving candidates in the years ahead. In 2014 she received the Lifetime Achievement Award from Preservation Buffalo Niagara in 2014.

Some other notable projects that benefited from Joan's support and public advocacy include the St. Mary of Sorrows Church that became the King Urban Life Center, the Central Terminal and Belt Line Railroad, assisting with The Turtle in Niagara Falls, and advocacy for a county ban on smoking in the workplace. Her prominent interests included the environment, urban sprawl, renewable energy, in addition to the preservation of historic buildings and women's activism, chairing The Trailblazing Women Speaker Series.

One of her last accomplishments was increasing public access to the Downtown Buffalo waterfront by bringing the solar powered Buffalo Heritage Carousel to Canalside. This 1924 Spillman Engineering Carousel was manufactured and the animals hand carved in North Tonawanda. The project included refurbishing the entire carousel and constructing the solar powered building through the WNY Sustainable Energy Association. Her long-time vision for this solar-powered public amenity was finally realized when the building opened in 2021.

At the age of 94 on May 4, 2023 Joan Bozer passed away, leaving a vital legacy of leadership for people of all ages to admire and emulate. Always gracious, full of energy, and relentlessly committed to projects that improved the livability and quality of life in our community, Joan Bozer was a role model for everyone. All of us are fortunate that Joan Bozer devoted her considerable talents, courageous leadership, intelligence, creativity, kindness, and grace to service in our community. Her investments in our quality of life will benefit us for generations to come. She will be especially remembered for the leadership she provided the Buffalo Olmsted Parks Conservancy, the historic preservation of area landmarks and architecture, protecting the environment and promoting sustainable energy.

Figure 24 Joan Bozer at the solar powered Buffalo Heritage Carousel in Canalside
Photo courtesy Alan Bozer

KATE MADDOX ROBINSON BUTLER

Buffalo News, WBEN Radio, Channel 4 TV

K ate Maddox Robinson was born on April 25, 1878 to Augustus M. Robinson and Jennie Maddox in Atlanta Georgia. In 1909 she moved to Buffalo where she married Edward Butler Jr. who became publisher/editor of the Buffalo Evening News upon the death of his father in 1914.

She attended Wesleyan Women's College in Macon Georgia, Gunston Hall for Girls in Washington DC and studied concert piano in Paris France. Kate was a member of the Colonial Dames of America, an organization of women descended from an ancestor who lived in British America (1607-1775) and who was of service to the American Colonies. Kate was eligible to become a member based off the ancestry of both her mother and father.

Figure 25 Kate Butler

In 1909 Kate married Edward H. Butler Jr., son of Edward H. Butler Sr. who founded the Buffalo Sunday News in 1873 and Buffalo Evening News in 1880.

Kate became a leading member of society, joining the UB University Council and being elected president of the Twentieth Century Club. She was also a member of the Buffalo Philharmonic Society and a life member of the Buffalo Fine Arts Academy.

After the death of Edward H, Butler Sr, in 1914, Kate and her husband moved into his Butler mansion at 672 Delaware Avenue. When Edward Sr. lived in the 40 room, 20,000 square-foot mansion, he had a 30-person staff with four chauffeurs to drive his 24 automobiles. Edward Jr. reduced the staff to 16 people.

The Butlers hosted numerous events at their mansion, entertaining presidents, diplomats, politicians, dignitaries, celebrities and other special guests. Their daughter, Kate Butler Righter, Wallis Wickham recalled that when she was growing up, "it seemed that no one of any distinction would pass through this area without visiting my father and staying at our home." During WWI Kate served as treasurer of Liberty Loan drives in Buffalo. She was one of the early supporters of the University of Buffalo, donating the Westminster clock in Hayes Hall on the Main Steet Campus. During WWII she contributed to the American Hospital in

Paris, French ambulance service and French Red Cross. The Butler Family entertained Bob Hope and his entire cast at their mansion when they were in Buffalo on Navy Relief Fund drives.

Kate had been educated in Paris. Before WWII, Kate and Edward Butler Jr. maintained a home in Paris whose furniture and artwork were seized by German General Goering and hidden in Goering's Salt Mine Collection. Their possessions were retrieved after the war by Andrew Richie, director of the Albright Art Gallery, and returned to the Butlers.

In addition to social activities, she was interested in sports, especially skiing, skeet, shooting and fishing. She maintained a ski lodge in the Adirondacks and often visited European ski lodges. Kate held the record for the largest bonefish caught off Marathon Florida and caught a 48-pound Wahoo.

Edward Butler Sr. started the Buffalo Sunday News in 1873 and upon the death of his father in 1914, Edward Butler Jr. took control of the Buffalo News at the age of 30-year-old. With the assistance of his senior editor Alfred H. Kirchofer (1927 – 1966), he started WBEN radio in 1930, WBEN-FM, the first FM station in WNY in 1946 and WBEN-TV the first Buffalo television station in 1948. For five years it was the only television station in WNY.

Kate assisted her husband in his activities operating the newspaper, radio and television stations. Upon the death of her husband in 1956, Kate assumed the presidency of The News, and after replacing her son-in-law James Righter, became publisher in 1971. At first she spent most of her time in Paris but after becoming the publisher, she was generally at the office 6 days a week. It was said she parked her Rolls Royce on the sidewalk in front of 218 Main Street, so the employees knew she was in the building.

Kate established the Edward H. Butler Foundation in 1966 to benefit religious, charitable, scientific, literary and educational purposes. It was Kate who approved the design and move of the Buffalo News to their new building on Washington & Scott Street. She was too ill to visit the inside of the completed building, but was able to take a car ride around the building as it neared completion to give it her seal of approval.

Kate retained Alfred Kirchhofer as editor of the Buffalo News. He started with the paper in 1915 at the age of 23. Alfred became managing editor in 1927, headed radio station WBEN (the BEN stood for Buffalo Evening News) beginning when its license was granted in 1929 and directed the television station from before it went on the air. He became editor upon the death of Edward Butler Jr.

Figure 26 Kate & Edward Butler Jr.

29

in 1956 and retired in 1966, serving 51 years with the newspaper and other Butler family interests.

Kate and Edward Butler Jr. had two children, a son Edward Hubert Butler III (1915-1919) and a daughter Kate Robinson Butler Righter Wallis Wickham, born in 1921. Edward died at the age of three. Kate Robinson attended grammar school in Buffalo and in Paris France where her parents had an apartment. In 1935 she enrolled at St. Catherine's School in Richmond VA, transferred to Foxcroft School in Middleburg VA and completed her studies at Hathaway Brown School in Cleveland in 1940. She became active in civic, cultural and educational organizations beginning in 1943 when she joined the Junior League of Buffalo and became a member of the Junior Board at Buffalo General Hospital.

Daughter Kate Robinson's primary interest was Buffalo State College where she joined the College Council in 1954 serving through 1983, and was instrumental in funding the Edward H. Butler Library on the Buffalo State campus. She was also associated with the Buffalo Philharmonic Orchestra Society, the board of Children's Hospital and served on NYS Governor Nelson Rockefeller's Committee for International Official Visitors. Kate was married three times: James H. Righter in 1943, Bruce E. Wallis in 1973 and Dr. Robert D. Wickham in 1997.

Kate's husband James H. Righter served as publisher after her father's death in 1956. But her mother removed him from the publisher's position in 1971. Her mother's 1974 will left the Buffalo News properties to Kate Robinson and her two children, Edward Righter and Katie Righter.

Kate Robinson Butler Wickham died at the age of 97 in 2018. From 1976 to 1986 she served as vice-chairman on the Buffalo News, the last Butler Family member to be involved with the newspaper. After the death of her mother, Kate Maddox Robinson Butler, Kate Robinson sold the newspaper to Warren Buffett's Blue Chips Stamps Company. The television station was sold to publisher Robert Howard of Howard Publications and the radios stations were sold to Larry Levite of Algonquin Broadcasting.

Figure 27 Butler Mansion
Photo credit Rick Falkowski

TAYLOR CALDWELL

New York Times Best Selling Author of over 40 novels

Janet Miriam Holland Taylor Caldwell was born in Manchester England on September 7, 1900 and moved to Buffalo with her family in 1907 at the age of six. A prolific writer, she wrote over 40 novels that sold over 30 million copies, over a career that lasted five decades.

While still living in England, beginning at age four she attended an academically rigorous school where she studied Latin, French, history and geography. At six she won a national gold medal for an essay on novelist Charles Dickens. Her childhood was filled with a long list of household chores, attending Sunday School religious instruction and church twice a day. Caldwell attributed her Spartan childhood into molding her as a rugged individualist.

Figure 28 Taylor Caldwell & her husband Marcus Reback Photo courtesy her granddaughter Drina Fried

She started writing stories when she was eight years old and completed her first novel *The Romance of Atlantis* when she was twelve, however it was not published until 1975. During a 1976 interview she recalled a childhood full of hard work and without displays of affection claiming, "I never had a childhood" and "I never had an adolescence."

Caldwell married her first husband William Fairfax Combs when she was 18 years old. Between 1918 and 1919 she served in the United States Navy Reserve and then worked as a court reporter in the New York State Department of Labor in Buffalo. From 1924 to 1931 she was a member of the Board of Special Inquiry at the Department of Justice in Buffalo while attending night school at the University of Buffalo and obtaining a bachelor's degree in 1931. From her first marriage she had a daughter Mary Margaret Fried.

In 1931 Caldwell divorced Combs and married her boss, Marcus Reback, an official with the United States Immigration and Naturalization Service in Buffalo.

This was a long and happy marriage that produced a second daughter Judith and ended with the death of Marcus Reback in 1970.

Figure 29 Dynasty of Death book cover

Her marriage to Reback allowed her to quit working and write full time. The unpublished manuscripts continued to pile up and in 1938, at the age of 38, she sold the novel *Dynasty of Death* to a major publisher. Her editor, Maxwell Perkins, who also discovered F. Scott Fitzgerald and Ernest Hemingway, suggested she use the name Taylor Caldwell because he felt the novel would be better received if people though it was written by a man. *Dynasty of Death* became a best seller in 1938 and was followed by *The Eagles Gather* in 1940 and *The Final Hour* in 1944. *This Side of Innocence* in 1946 was the top selling fiction of the year, listed on the New York Times bestseller list for six months, including nine weeks at number 1. There was a public stir when her readers found out Taylor Caldwell was a woman. Caldwell was also known by her pen names Marcus Holland and Max Reiner and by her married name of J. Mariam Reback.

The writing of Caldwell is best described as historical fiction. She created characters that resembled actual people or used historical people or places in fictionized stories. An example was her book *Captains & Kings* which was based on the Kennedy and Rockefeller families, along with Howard Hughes and adapted into a television mini-series. She would annually take worldwide cruises and travel to various destinations with her husband who collaborated with her on her books and assisted in researching and documenting the locations visited. A novel would then be written at a later date, utilizing an actual site they visited in a new story she created.

She wrote *Dear and Glorious Physician* about the life of St. Luke and *Great Lion of God* about the life and times of St. Paul. These books are among the best-selling religious novels of all time. Other

Figure 30 Captains and the Kings book cover

books were about historical figures, such as Cardinal Richelieu and Genghis Khan.

In 1970 Caldwell became interested in reincarnation and befriended occultist author Jess Stern. He suggested to Caldwell that the historic detail of her novels was from subconscious recollection of previous lives. She agreed to be hypnotized and undergo past life regression, which Stern explained in his book, *The Search for a Soul – Taylor Caldwell's Psychic Lives*. Stern worked with Caldwell to rewrite her novel *The Romance of Atlantis*, that she wrote at age twelve. That novel was finally published in 1975, over sixty years after it was written.

Caldwell was a bourbon-and-vodka-drinking, chain-smoking, outspoken conservative who preferred to write in the nude or in a sheer nightgown from midnight to 8:00 am. She lived in the exclusive brick mansion LeBrun neighborhood east of Grover Cleveland Golf Course, the original Buffalo Country Club. A neighbor related - every night she turned on her kitchen light at 11:00 pm, placed a bottle of spirits next to her typewriter and wrote until the bottle emptied at dawn. She held elegant parties at her grand home and enjoyed her life. Her granddaughter Drina Fried recalled her grandmother telling her. "I vehemently believe that we should have as much fun as is possible in our dolorous life if it does not injure ourselves or anyone else. The only thing is – be discreet. The world will forgive you anything but getting caught."

Politically, Caldwell was an outspoken conservative and was a founding member of the Conservative Party in New York State. She wrote for the John Birch Society's monthly Journal *American Opinion* and was associated with the Liberty Lobby. The John Birch Society honored her with a plaque describing her as a "Great American Patriot and Scholar." Caldwell earned a fortune from her writing and received many honors including the National League of American Pen Women gold medal in 1948, Buffalo Evening News Award in 1949 and Grand Prix Chatvain in 1950.

In 1965 Caldwell and her husband John Reback were beaten by intruders during a home invasion at their Buffalo mansion. She lost her hearing and remained deaf due to the encounter. However, she kept writing and released new successful novels on a regular basis. In 1979 she suffered a stroke and lost her ability to speak. Her last publishing agreement was signed after the first stroke in 1979 and was a two book, $3.9-million-dollar contract.

Taylor continued writing until she suffered a second debilitating stroke at the age of 80, that left her paralyzed. Her last novel *Answer as a Man* was published in 1981 and debuted on the New York Times bestseller list before its official publication date.

Her fourth husband Robert Prestie moved Caldwell away from Buffalo and her family to a home in Greenwich Connecticut. She died at the Greenwich home in 1985 and it took years for her family to regain the rights to the volumes of books she published.

EVELYN RUMSEY CARY

Artist, Women's Suffrage and Patron of the Arts

W hen Evelyn was born on February 25, 1855, her parents Bronson Case Rumsey and Eveline Hall Rumsey resided at 1 Park Place at Delaware Avenue. In 1862 Bronson purchased land on Delaware Avenue extending from Tracy to West Tupper Street. There he built a mansion at 330 Delaware and created what was known as Rumsey Park.

Rumsey Park became the playground for the children living in the mansions of what was called Millionaires Row. Members of the Rumsey, Wheeler, Goodyear, Spaulding, Wright, Laverack, Dart, Cary, Milburn and other affluent families created friendships that lasted

Figure 31 Evelyn Rumsey Cary

throughout their lifetimes, playing on the grounds that had a lake with a boathouse for swimming and boating in the summer and for ice skating or playing hockey in the winter. Evelyn's mother hosted the Waverly Balls at their 330 Delaware Avenue mansion. These were Buffalo social affairs that mirrored the Vanderbilt

Figure 32 330 Delaware Avenue - Evelyn's childhood home

and Astor balls in NYC. The Rumsey family was one of the most affluent families in Buffalo, originally making their fortune from the tanning business created by Evelyn's grandfather Aaron Rumsey. Evelyn's father Bronson and uncle Dexter sold the tannery to the United States Leather Company in 1896, each receiving ten million dollars. They wisely invested in railroads, banks and real

34

estate, at one time owning 23 of the 44 square miles that comprised the city of Buffalo.

Following her graduation from Buffalo Seminary High School, she married Dr. Charles Cary in 1879. Charles was the grandson of politician, Holland Land Company agent and bank president Trumbull Cary. Trumbull purchased the Holland Land Company holdings in Chautauqua County in 1835. Charles' father Dr. Walter Cary was the only child of Trumbull Cary and Margaret Brisbane Cary. After Walter married Julia Love (sister of Maria Love) he built Cary Castle at 184 Delaware Avenue at West Huron.

Dr. Charles Cary was a practicing medical doctor and respected sportsman. He led a polo team that included members of the Cary and Rumsey family, along with lumber baron James M. Scatcherd. They were considered one of the top polo teams in the U.S. Charles was also an early promoter of golf and was an organizer of the Aeronautical Club of America, the second oldest aviation club in the world.

In 1891 Evelyn exhibited her works at the first Buffalo Society of Artists annual show. For the founding of the Twentieth Century Club in 1894, she designed the club's coat of arms "Facta Probant" for one of the oldest and most historic private women's clubs in the U.S. She later donated her painting of Charlotte Mulligan, the club's founder, that continues to be exhibited at the Twentieth Century Club on Delaware Avenue.

When the Pan-American Exposition was announced, Evelyn submitted the Spirit of Niagara painting as the official emblem of the Pan-American Exposition. The painting portrays the Maid of the Mist appearing as the crest of the falls, with the skyline of the city of Buffalo behind her. 120,962 lithographed posters were printed, 1,022,036 four color 3 x 5 reproductions were produced and the image was on the cover of 357,000 booklets. That resulted in over 1.5 million prints being distributed.

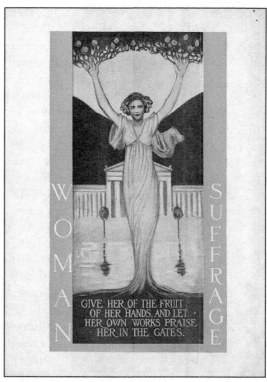

Figure 33 "Give her of the fruit" - Women's suffrage poster

35

In addition, at the Pan-Am, Cary decorated the Women Managers House, the former original location of the Buffalo Country Club. The Women's Building was the only recycled building on the Exposition Grounds. In was located on the Southwestern area of the Expo, surrounded by the Horticulture exhibit on land leased from the Rumsey family by the Country Club of Buffalo for golf and polo grounds.

She also painted the Women's Suffrage poster. "Give Her of the Fruit" in 1905. The poster was one of the most important visuals utilized in the women's suffrage movement. It depicts a female figure referencing classical antiquity, with sprouts from her fingertips and roots from her feet as Mother Nature, in front of a classical building, suggesting the importance of women in the country's most important institutions.

Cary contributed to the national suffrage movement with her art and also supported local female artists. She opened her home to young artists and assisted with their artistic training and development. Evelyn provided money for scholarships at the Albright Art School and was president of the Buffalo Society for Artists.

Figure 34 Pan-Am Spirit of Niagara 1901 poster

Evelyn influenced her brother Lawrence's daughter Eveyln Rumsey Lord and son Charles Cary Rumsey to become involved in the arts. Lawrence married Jennie Cary, the sister of Evelyn's husband Dr. Charles Cary. Evelyn Rumsey Lord was a portrait artist who established the Rumsey Award at the Art Department of UB, while Charles Cary Rumsey was a sculptor who created the frieze for the Manhattan Bridge, the Centaur in front of the Buffalo History Museum and the Three Graces Fountain for the Harriman Estate outside of NYC, a duplicate of which is in Forest Lawn Cemetery.

She continued to promote the city of Buffalo and artists from the city until her death in 1924, at the age of 69, in her 340 Delaware Avenue home within the Rumsey Park estate. After the death of Jennie Cary Rumsey, the Rumsey Park property was sold and commercially developed, now being the location of Child & Family Services and other businesses.

36

MARY R. CASS

Female Manufacturing Manager, F.N. Burt Company

Mary Cass was one of the first female general managers of a manufacturing facility in the U.S. Under her management the F.N. Burt Company completed several expansions and became one of the world's largest paper box manufacturers.

Cass was born on January 5, 1870 in Buffalo to James and Elizabeth Cass, who emigrated from England. After graduating from Central High School, she worked at Burdick Envelope Company and as a substitute teacher in Buffalo public schools. In 1891 she was hired by Frederick Northrup Burt of F.N. Burt, at a salary of five dollars a week. Her job description was a "do everything" worker in the one floor plant at 457 Washington Street. At this time F.N. Burt was an eight-employee print shop with only one press. They did not become involved with box making until 1896 when they manufactured their first soap boxes for the Larkin Company.

Figure 35 Mary Cass - business executive, golfer & avid motorist

The company moved to several different locations until 1901 when the company started building a 400,000 square foot box factory at 500 Seneca Street at Hamburg Street. This building was closer to the manufacturers in The Hydraulics neighborhood and was closer to the shipping depots near Exchange Street. Burt developed a technique to produce small oval and circle boxes which were their most successful product. New inventions also increased their set up box business at Main and Bryant. Investments in machinery and developing new patents gave F.N. Burt a near monopoly in the small and ornate box market. By 1909 they were making 98% of all cigarette boxes in the U.S. or a total of about 200 million per year.

When business founder Frederick Northrup Burt sold F.N. Burt Company to Moore Corporation Ltd. of Canada, a business forms company from Toronto in 1909, he retired from active management of the company and recommended that Mary Cass be named his replacement. In her years with the company, Mary had done most of the jobs available at the company and was promoted to vice president in 1906. When she was promoted to general manager in 1909, she became one of the highest paid female executives in the country.

Under the management of Cass, by 1921 F.N. Burt Company had 2,500 employees making over four million boxes a day and was the largest paper box manufacturer in the country, specializing in boxes for everything from mascara to face powder, facial creams, hair dye, candy, pencils, birthday candles, ribbon, ice cream, pharmaceuticals, cigarettes and many products of the nearby Larkin Company. She was not the first woman executive but certainly one of the most prominent.

Figure 36 F.N. Burt Company - 500 Seneca Street

In 1917, F.N. Burt Co. started making round, oval and oblong cosmetic boxes for the California Perfume Company, a predecessor to Avon Products, for whom they continued as their packaging supplier. The company also invented the paper cone cup for water coolers, a product line they sold to a competitor in 1925.

At a time when most men did not even know how to drive, Cass was an avid motorist. She also played golf with other business executives but enjoyed traditional womanly activities like dancing and going to the theater. She was a member of the Rotary and at her 30th Anniversary, Cass was the only woman at the event that was attended by businessmen from the WNY area and across the state.

Cass never married and took care of her widowed mother and assisted her relatives. She adopted a son, William D. Cass, and accepted the responsibility of providing support for her maid's daughter. Cass retired in 1935, after serving as general manager of F.N. Burt Co. for twenty-four years. During that time, she continued expanding the 500 Seneca Street facility until the complex included several buildings. The six-story main building still houses manufacturing businesses and the Hydraulic Loft Apartments. Cass was known for her altruistic management style with F.N. Burt Company being the first box company to establish a fully funded pension plan for its employees. If employee longevity is a measure of company success, half the workers at F.N. Burt Co. were employed for over 15 years, 15% were employed for over 25 years and a handful had 50 years seniority with the company.

She was also a founding member of Zonta, one of the most successful businesswomen in the country, an important figure in Buffalo's business history and she played a prominent role in the Women's Rights movement. Other members of the Women's movement are known for their political activism, but Cass is remembered for her achievements in business management where she proved to be equal to any man in industry. She died at the age of 75 on August 12, 1945 and is buried at Forest Lawn Cemetery.

Figure 37 Mary Cass executive office at F.N. Burt Company

SHIRLEY CHISHOLM

Assemblywoman, Congresswoman and Presidential Candidate

In 1868, Shirley Chisholm was the first African-American woman to be elected to Congress and in 1972, the first woman and African-American to seek the nomination for president of the U.S. in one of the two major political parties.

Figure 38 Chisholm campaign poster

Born in Brooklyn on November 30, 1924, Shirley was the oldest of four daughters born to Charles St. Hill, a factory worker from Guyana, and Ruby Seale St. Hill, a seamstress from Barbados. Shirley attended grammar school in a one room schoolhouse in Barbados while living there with her maternal grandmother from 1929 to 1934. Due to living in the Caribbean she always considered herself a Barbadian American and spoke with a West Indian accent throughout her life. She graduated from Brooklyn Girls' High in 1942 and cum laude from Brooklyn College in 1946. Her professors encouraged her to pursue a career in politics but she replied that she faced a double handicap as she was both "Black and female."

Chisholm began working as a nursery school teacher and earned her master's degree in early childhood education from Columbia University in 1951. She married private investigator Conrad Q. Chisholm in 1949 and by 1960 was a consultant to the New York City Division of Day Care. Chisholm was a member of the League of Women Voters, National Association for the Advancement of Colored People (NAACP), the Urban League and the Democratic Party in Bedford Stuyvesant Brooklyn. In 1960 she started the Unity Democratic Club, which was instrumental in mobilizing Black and Hispanic voters.

In 1964 she became the second African-American to be elected to the New York State Legislature. After her Bedford Stuyvesant neighborhood was redistricted, she ran for the seat in New York's Twelfth Congressional District in 1968. For the election she coined the campaign slogan, "Fighting Shirley Chisholm – Unbought and Unbossed." She won the election by a two to one vote margin. Chisholm was the first Black woman elected to Congress in 1968 and was the only female in the first-year class of newly elected Congress members that year.

She worked hard during her first term and was a founder of the Congressional Black Caucus in 1971. Chisholm worked to expand the Food Stamps Program and played a critical role in forming the Special Supplemental Nutrition Program for Women, Infants and Children (WIC). During her seven-term tenure in Congress she introduced 50 bills and was an advocate of the Equal Right Amendment, worked to improve opportunities for inner city residents, campaigned against discrimination against women, focused on gender and racial equality, fought for land rights for Native Americans, spoke out against the Vietnam War and the draft, was Secretary of the Democratic Caucus from 1977 to 1981, served on the Veterans Affairs Committee and the Education & Labor Committee.

In 1972 she announced her bid for the Democratic Nomination for President, resulting in her being the first African-American to run for a major party nomination. In her presidential announcement she described herself as a representative of the people, stating "I am not the candidate of Black America, although I am Black and proud. I am not the candidate of the women's movement of this country, although I am a woman and equally proud of that. I am the candidate of the people and my presence before you symbolizes a new era in American political history."

During the presidential nomination campaign, she received 2.7% of the total 16 million primary votes cast, finished in 7th place of all contenders and was the first woman to appear in a presidential debate. She received 152 first place votes in the convention for the presidential nomination, good for fourth place in the roll call tally.

Figure 39 Shirley Chisholm on Freedom Wall Mural

Chisholm met her second husband Arthur Hardwick Jr. of Buffalo in 1966 when they both served in the New York State Legislature. She received a divorce from her first husband in February 1977 and in November 1977 married Hardwick. The wedding took place at a suburban Buffalo hotel and was attended by prominent Democrats and Republicans, including Buffalo's Jack Kemp. After the marriage Chisholm spent more time in the Buffalo area, resulting in political criticism that she was inattentive to her home Brooklyn District. Hardwick was badly injured in a car accident in 1979 and Chisholm devoted more time taking care of him, resulting in her decision not to run for another Congressional term in 1983. That year she permanently moved to Williamsville. Although retired from politics, she maintained an interest in local education issues in WNY, supporting the Buffalo based Concerned Parents and Citizens for Quality Education. That organization was associated with the Uncrowned Queens Institute for Research and Education on Women, Inc. and she appeared on their weekly television program *Education in Review* and spoke at their public meetings.

Figure 40 Shirley Chisholm at White House with President Bill Clinton

While living in WNY, she accepted a teaching position at Mount Holyoke College and spoke at over 150 universities. Her husband died in 1986 and she moved to Florida in 1991. She was nominated by President Bill Clinton for the post of United States Ambassador to Jamaica in 1993 but turned it down due to health reasons. That year she was inducted into the National Women's Hall of Fame.

In 2015 Chisholm was awarded the Presidential Medal of Freedom by President Obama. Her portrait is one of 28 local and national Black Americans featured on the Freedom Wall at the intersection of Michigan Avenue and West Ferry Street in Buffalo.

In 2005 a documentary film *Shirley Chisholm '72: Unbought and Unbossed* was released and featured at the Sundance Film Festival and won a Peabody Award.

Shirley died on January 1, 2005 at the age of 80, did not have any children and is buried with her husband in the Birchwood Mausoleum at Forest Lawn Cemetery in Buffalo. Her gravesite is engraved "Unbought and unbossed." Her 1970 speech for the Equal Rights Amendment is ranked among the top 100 Speeches of the 20th Century by American Rhetoric.

CAROLYN JEWETT TRIPP CLEMENT

Civic Leader and Philanthropist, Donated Clement Mansion to American Red Cross

Carolyn was born in Buffalo on July 19, 1861, daughter of Augustus F. Tripp and Mary Mehitable Steele. Her father was a partner of Sidney Shepard in the firm Sidney Shepard & Company, later called the Republic Metalware Company. Augustus was related to Elam Jewett, publisher of the newspaper *The Commercial Advertiser*, owner of Willow Lawn (former Daniel Chapin farm) and traveling companion of former U.S. President Millard Fillmore. After graduating from the State Normal School, now Buffalo State College, Carolyn spent a year in Europe, studying piano and traveling.

She is credited with participating in the first local telephone conversation in Buffalo history.

Figure 41 Carolyn Clement
Photo courtesy Peter W. Clement

Carolyn was at the Sidney Shepard & Company store on Main Street and she spoke on the telephone to Mr. Shepard who was in the company's Clinton Street plant.

On March 2, 1884, Carolyn married Stephen M. Clement in the Tripp Mansion at 768 Delaware Avenue. Clement was president of Marine Bank and an officer or director of hydroelectric power, railway, lumber, shipping and iron/steel companies. Caroline and her husband lived in a home they built at 172 Summer Street at Oakland Place. When Stephen's father died in 1892, they moved to his former home at 737 Delaware Avenue. They also had a summer home known as Elmhurst and later named The Homestead in East Aurora. The Elmhurst Special Milk Company, located in an E.B. Green designed barn on the property, sold premium quality processed milk, prior to the later developments in pasteurization.

Stephen and Carolyn had six children: Norman Parsons (1885-1951), Edith Cochran (1886-1891), Stephen Merrell Jr. known as Merrell (1887-1943), Harold Tripp (1890-1971), Marion (1892-1918) and Stuart Holmes (1895-1974).

Figure 42 Clement & Grandchildren at 786 Delaware Avenue Mansion in 1928

When her father died in 1908, Carolyn inherited the Tripp family home at 768 Delaware Avenue, built by Erastus S. Prosser in 1855. Even though they were married at the Tripp House, they decided to demolish it and hired architect E.B. Green to design a palatial new mansion at the site. E.B. Green once commented on the Clement House: "Next to the Albright Home, the Clement House is the most extravagant home I ever built."

In 1911 Stephen suffered a heart attack while pitching hay on a hot July day at their East Aurora summer home/farm. He survived and vowed to forsake his hectic work schedule, divesting thirty percent of his Marine Bank holdings to Seymour Knox I and John Albright. Stephen sought relief from his heart disease in Baden-Baden, Germany, Atlantic City and other therapeutic destinations. Tragically, Stephen died on March 26, 1913, the day before his 29th wedding anniversary and before the new home was completed.

A widowed Carolyn Tripp Clement moved the Clement family into the 768 Delaware Avenue mansion in late 1913, devoting herself to raising her children and helping her community. She was very active in civic and community affairs as well as in her life-long devotion to Westminster Presbyterian Church. Carolyn Clement held many important positions and had great prestige and influence.

She was active at Westminster House, a social mission of her church, was president of the Westminster Women's Parish Society, an active supporter of the Westminster Hospital in Iran, served on the Council of the University of Buffalo, as a trustee of Buffalo General Hospital and State Teachers College, and was past president of the Twentieth Century Club.

In 1914 she donated land to Westminster Church to build a parish house adjacent to the church. Carolyn was a member of Westminster Church for most of her adulthood. That year she also endowed the Chair of Christian Methods at the Yale University's divinity school. In 1918, in memory of her daughter, she opened the Marion Clement Tener Vacation House, a summer camp for underprivileged children in Angola.

At the University of Buffalo, Carolyn served on the University Council from 1920 to 1941. Among several generous contributions to the University, she donated $80,000 to the school. The Carolyn Tripp Clement Hall, a 500-capacity dormitory, was dedicated in her memory by the university in 1964.

In May 1943, the American Association of University Women presented Carolyn Tripp Clement with their annual award, referring to her as "one who holds firmly to the basic thing of life, who has broad vision and intelligent, devoted sympathy for the people in the world who need help." To the award they added her firm belief that "the most important and vital thing in the world is the family group."

Carolyn's son Stuart Holmes Clement married Mary Livingston Bush, a daughter of Samuel Prescott Bush, the patriarch of the political Bush family. Mary was the aunt of U.S. President George H.W. Bush.

In 1941 Carolyn Tripp Clement made one of the largest donations in WNY history when she donated her house at 768 Delaware to the American Red Cross. For years it served as their regional blood center. Many Clement family members served in the armed forces, especially during World War II. The Red Cross was a vital partner with the military during times of conflicts and as urgent help for many during disasters. This gift was from her heart to benefit her greater community, an extension of "family". The 17,000 sq. ft. mansion was completed in 1914 at the cost of $300,000 or about $7 million at current value. After Carolyn moved from 768 Delaware, she lived in the Park Lane Apartments where she died in 1943 at the age of 82.

Figure 43 Carolyn Clement at her writing desk
Photo courtesy Peter W. Clement

The purpose of this building as a "home" lives on with the owners and organizations that followed the Clement Family. Mrs. Clement trained as a classical pianist, could play music by ear, and as an accomplished musician she played the organ as well as the harp. She designed the 1,040 square foot music room for two Steinway grand pianos, a harp, and a full-scale pipe organ, and a generous multi-

45

story interior to host concerts. She would be very pleased that the Buffalo Philharmonic Orchestra is now the owner and steward of the building. Concerts continue to be offered in that spectacularly elegant music room designed over a century ago.

Fortuitously, in 2017 the property at 768 Delaware Avenue was purchased for $2 million from the Buffalo Chapter of the American Red Cross by John Yurtchuk, former Calspan chairman and owner of Matrix Development. Afterwards Yurtchuk donated the building to the Buffalo Philharmonic Orchestra. The BPO occupies the 2nd floor and rents the 3rd floor to the Red Cross, at a price lower than its previous mortgage on the building. The first floor is shared by the BPO and American Red Cross. Most people still refer to the property as the Red Cross Building or Clement Mansion,

Figure 44 Painting of Carolyn Clement by Cecelia Beaux
Painting courtesy Peter W. Clement

admiring this beautiful mansion as it carries on the tradition of the Clement Family legacy of service to our community in many memorable ways.

Figure 45 Clement Mansion - 786 Delaware Avenue
Photo credit Rick Falkowski

FRANCES FOLSOM CLEVELAND

Only First Lady married to the President in The White House

Figure 46 Frances Folsom Cleveland

Frances Folsom was the daughter of Emma C. Harmon and prominent Buffalo attorney, Oscar Folsom, who was Grover Cleveland's law partner. She married Cleveland to become the youngest American First Lady.

Oscar Folsom was Cleveland's partner in the law firm Lanning, Cleveland & Folsom. With about twenty of their friends, they formed the Beaver Club on Grand Island with Cleveland remaining president of the club during its existence. The club members enjoyed fishing and duck hunting, along with socializing. Oscar often brought his wife and daughter Frances to the Beaver club. After Frances was born on July 21, 1864, Cleveland purchased a baby carriage as a gift. He held her in his arms when she was just a couple weeks old. Young Frances called him Uncle Cleve. As a child Frances was called Frank. They continued referring to each other by these names during their lifetime.

When Oscar Folsom died in a carriage accident on July 23, 1873, Cleveland assumed responsibility for Folsom's widow and nine-year-old daughter after being appointed administrator of Folsom's estate. The Folsom family lived at 168 Edward Street and Cleveland guided Frances' education. She attended Central High School in Buffalo and Medina High School, before enrolling at Wells College on Cayuga Lake in the New York Fingers Lakes region.

Cleveland entered the presidency as a bachelor on March 2, 1885 and his scholarly sister Rose Elizabeth Cleveland served as her brother's hostess for the first 15 months of his first term in office. When he entered the office, there was speculation about when and whom Cleveland would marry.

The Folsoms missed the inauguration but visited later in the spring and that is when Grover asked her to marry him. Frances graduated from Wells College in spring of 1885 and already had accepted Cleveland's proposal of marriage, but they decided not to announce it. Grover wanted her to see Europe and be exposed to the continent's more formal customs. Frances and her mother Emma departed in fall 1885 and upon returning on May 27, 1886 the press besieged the ship to question Emma regarding a possible marriage to the president. The White House had to issue a statement, President Cleveland was going to marry 21-year-old Frances Folsom, not her mother Emma.

Figure 47 Cleveland Wedding in the Blue Room of the White House in 1886

On June 2, 1886, President Cleveland married Frances in the Blue Room at the White House. There was a 27-year difference in age, he was 48 she was 21. Grover was the second president to be married while in office but their nuptials were the first and only wedding of a president ever held in the White House.

The guest list to the ceremony was limited to family, close friends, plus cabinet members and wives, a total of 31 guests. Grover's Buffalo associate Wilson Bissell was among the guests. The minister at the wedding ceremony was Grover's brother Reverend William Cleveland and John Philip Sousa led the Marine Band in a rendition of the Wedding March at the reception. Journalists were refused access to cover the wedding but still talked about it in the press like it was a European royal wedding. Following a one-week honeymoon in Deer Park Maryland, the couple had two receptions at the White House, one for the Diplomatic Corps and another for the general public. At these events Frances wore her wedding gown, the White House was decorated as for the wedding and the press was welcomed at these ceremonies. Later several informal receptions were also held at the Presidential Mansion.

After the wedding Frances was affectionately adopted by the press who wrote about all she did. They called her Frankie – which she despised. Frances received thousands of fan letters, was mobbed at presidential events and Cleveland feared for her safety. Businesses placed her image without permission or endorsement on an array of products including candy, perfume, liver pills, ashtrays, plates, handkerchiefs, playing cards, napkins and even

Figure 48 Folsom home on Edward Street in Buffalo

48

undergarments. The government tried to pass a law that would not allow the use of the image of any women without her written permission, but the law did not pass.

After their marriage, the Clevelands purchased a 17-acre working farm in the Georgetown Heights section of Washington, now referred to as Cleveland Park. The house was called Oak View but Frances called it Red Top because its roof was painted red. They sold the home for considerable profit after his first term. During his second term they rented a home called Woodley. They only lived at the White House during the active social season, November to December and February to April.

Grover and Frances Cleveland had five children. Their daughter Ruth was born between presidential terms on October 3, 1891 when they were living in New York City. She was called Baby Ruth. It was said the Baby Ruth candy bar was named after her. She died of diphtheria at the age of twelve. Their daughter Esther was born on September 9, 1893 and is the only child of a president that was born in the White House. Esther's daughter was philosopher Phillippa Foot. Marion was born on July 7, 1895 in Massachusetts. They had two sons that were born after Cleveland served his second term, attorney Richard born on October 28, 1897 and actor Francis born on July 18, 1903.

After leaving the presidency, Cleveland retained ill feelings for Buffalo residents because they brought up the Halpin affair, a story of Cleveland or Oscar Folsom fathering a child out of wedlock with Maria Halpin. Cleveland refused to return to WNY and they settled in Princton New Jersey. In 1897 they purchased a home called Westland in Princeton. He became involved in town matters and was a trustee of the university. Frances remained at the home after his death.

When Grover died on June 24, 1908 Frances took her children to Europe for an eight month stay from September 1909 to May 1910. She married her second husband, Professor Thomas Jex Preston Jr. on February 10, 1913, moved to London for a year in April 1914, and returned to the US when WWI started. Preston was a professor of archeology and member of the Princeton University community. Frances moved back to Aurora NY where she was a trustee member at Wells College and she also remained active in Princeton affairs until 1946.

Frances died on October 29, 1947 and is buried in Princeton, with Grover Cleveland. She remains the youngest first lady in U.S. history and was one of the first presidential wives adored by the general public.

Figure 49 Frances with the wives of the President Cleveland Cabinet Photo PD

49

LUCILLE CLIFTON

Poet, Author, Educator

Lucille Clifton (1936 – 2010) was an accomplished and nationally-recognized poet and author, college professor and teacher, and mother of six children whose life and career began in western New York. Clifton's poetry is easily identified because of the purposeful lack of capitalization and proper punctuation.

Lucille Clifton was one of the most distinguished, decorated and beloved poets of her time. She was a staff poet of the Community of Writers for nearly twenty years, first in 1991 and returning regularly until her death in 2010. She won the National Book Award for Poetry for *Blessing the Boats: New and Selected Poems 1988-2000* and was the first African-American female recipient of the Ruth Lilly Poetry Prize for lifetime achievement from the Poetry Foundation. Ms. Clifton received many additional honors throughout her career, including the Discovery Award from the New York YW/YMHA Poetry Center in 1969 for her first collection *Good Times*, a

Figure 50 Lucille Sayles Clifton at age 13

1976 Emmy Award for Outstanding Writing for the television special "Free to Be You and Me," a Lannan Literary Award in 1994, and the Robert Frost Medal from the Poetry Society of America in 2010. She was named a Literary Lion by the New York Public Library in 1996, served as a Chancellor of the Academy of American Poets from 1999 to 2005, and was elected a Fellow in Literature of the American Academy of Arts and Sciences. In 1987, she became the first author to have two books of poetry – Good Woman *and* Next – chosen as finalists for the Pulitzer Prize in the same year. She was also the author of twenty children's books, and in 1984 received the Coretta Scott King Award from the American Library Association for her book *Everett Anderson's Good-bye*. Her memoir, *Generations, A Memoir*, was published posthumously in 2021.

Clifton's free verse lyrics — spare in form — often concern the importance of family and community in the face of economic oppression. Though rooted in folktales and a strong tradition of storytelling, many of Clifton's poems are spirited, sometimes spiritual, explorations of race and gender. The New York Times Book Review praised Lucille Clifton as a "passionate, mercurial writer, by turns angry, prophetic, compassionate, shrewd, sensuous, vulnerable and funny…". Her widely respected poetry focuses on social issues, expressing the painful history of the Black American experience, and the female identity. The central message of her work is the celebration of African-American heritage and the endurance, strength, and beauty of Black women.

Clifton said, "One of the things that people tell me I do – and I think it is true – is that I say the "unsayable", to speak for those who are not yet able to speak for themselves, and also to say, "You are not alone." She said "With my poetry, I hope to comfort the afflicted and afflict the comfortable."

Clifton's family figures prominently in her poetry, from her six children to the African ancestors who were brought to America as slaves. Her great-grandmother, Lucille (for whom she is named),

Figure 51 Clifton with her children in Baltimore

killed the white father of her children and earned the "dignity" of being the first Black woman legally hanged in Virginia.

In addition to her many poetry collections, Clifton wrote twenty children's books as well. One of her best-known series featured a young Black boy, Everett Anderson, which included: *Some of the Days of Everett Anderson* (1970), *Everett Anderson's Goodbye* (1983), and *One of the Problems of Everett Anderson* (2001). She also wrote *My Friend Jacob*, about a disabled child's friendship.

Lucille Clifton was born as Thelma Lucille Sayles in 1936 in Depew, New York to Samuel, a steelworker, and Thelma, a laundress. During her childhood in Buffalo, she grew up on Purdy Street near East Ferry and Jefferson Avenue, Clifton listened to oral histories told by her mother, grandmothers and aunts. Though Thelma had received only a primary school education, she aspired to be a poet. Her ambitions were thwarted by Samuel who forbade his wife from writing poetry.

Figure 52 Clifton as a child in the 1940s

Clifton later addressed Thelma's frustrations in the poem "fury," which is dedicated to her mother. Clifton would also later credit Reverend Thomas J. Merriweather, the pastor at Macedonia Baptist Church in Buffalo, with developing her appreciation for the spoken word. The combination of these early influences inspired Clifton to begin writing verse at age 10. Thelma encouraged her daughter's early efforts which imitated the works of Edna St. Vincent Millay and Emily Dickinson.

Clifton attended Fosdick-Masten High School in Buffalo where she was an A student and the first person in her family to graduate from high school. In 1953, at age 16, her academic achievements won her a full scholarship to Howard University where she majored in Drama. At Howard, Clifton was mentored by Sterling A. Brown who taught a poetry seminar that he invited Clifton to join. Clifton befriended poet LeRoi Jones (later, Amiri Baraka), singer Roberta Flack, and future ambassador and Howard Law School dean Patricia Roberts Harris.

A year after leaving Howard, Lucille attended and completed her studies at Fredonia State Teacher's College. Through her old friend, Ishmael Reed whom she had known since they were teenagers, she met Fred James Clifton.

Fred, a Kentucky native and Korean War veteran, was a graduate student at the University of Buffalo. He was also a sculptor whose carvings depicted African faces. Clifton was smitten with Fred, remarking that he was the handsomest man she had ever seen. Her father, Samuel, was unfazed by Fred's charms and denounced his studies in the humanities as useless and impractical. To avoid her father's interference, Clifton and Fred eloped on May 10, 1958. Clifton was 21 and her husband was two years her senior. Eventually, the Cliftons had six children together—all born between 1960 and 1965. The family moved to Baltimore in 1967.

Lucille Clifton's first volume of poetry, *Good Times: Poems*, was published in 1969. Her friend, Ishmael Reed, first shared Clifton's work with Langston Hughes in 1966, Impressed, Hughes later included her poems in the major anthology *The Poetry of the Negro*.

In the late-1960s, Clifton sent some of her work to Robert Hayden. Hayden shared Clifton's poems with fellow poet, Carolyn Kizer, who was also serving as the first director of literary programs at the recently formed National Endowment for the Arts. Kizer then passed Clifton's work along to her associates at the 92nd Street Y in New York, leading to Clifton winning the community center's Discovery Award in 1969. In celebration of her win, Clifton and her husband attended a dinner at the New York City apartment of movie star Claudette Colbert. At the dinner party, Clifton met an editor from Random House who requested to see a manuscript of her poems. The 37 poems that Clifton offered were published in her début collection, *Good Times* (1969). The New York Times named the collection one of the year's best books.

In the following year, Clifton became poet-in-residence at Coppin State College in Baltimore—a position that she would hold for three years. She subsequently obtained a visiting professorship at Columbia University and at George Washington University. She also taught literature and creative writing at the University of California at Santa Cruz and at St. Mary's College of Maryland, and was Maryland's Poet Laureate from 1974 to 1985, becoming the second woman and the first African-American to hold the title.

Clifton went on to publish ten additional volumes of poetry, including *Two-Headed Woman* (1980), *Quilting* (1991), *The Book of Light* (1992), *The Terrible Stories* (1996), *Blessing the Boats: New and Selected Poems*, 1988-2000 (2000), *Mercy* (2004), and *Voices* (2008), as well as 22 children's books.

In the mid-1970s, she reunited with fellow Howard University alum, Toni Morrison, who was then an editor at Random House, to produce *Generations*. *Generations* is Clifton's sole work of prose. It explores themes of ancestry and domesticity that Clifton frequently explored in her poetry. The book examines Clifton's family history, going back to her Dahomeyan great-great grandmother, Caroline Donald Sale, and ends with the story of her father who had recently died.

Generations perpetuates Clifton's poetic convention of using family ties, including domestic dysfunction, as a theme. She wrote elegies for her younger brother Sammy ("august") who died of heart failure at 55 after a lifetime of struggling with drug and alcohol dependency, and for her older half-sister, Josephine ("here rests") who had become a prostitute but returned home to care for their father in his final days. In her poem "sisters," dedicated to her younger and closest sibling, Elaine, she describes the healthy interdependency that the pair developed as a defense against poverty and loneliness ("me and you / be scared of rats / be stepping on roaches").

Clifton's husband, Fred, died of lung cancer in 1984 at age 49. By then, Clifton was a respected and reputable poet and had recently accepted a teaching position at the University of California, Santa Cruz. In 1988, she was a finalist for the Pulitzer Prize for *Good Woman: Poems and a Memoir*, 1969-1980 (1987). In 2001, she won the National Book Award for *Blessing the Boats*. Clifton made another first when she became the first Black woman to win the Ruth Lilly Poetry Prize in 2007. Her poems have appeared in over 100 anthologies. Clifton spent her final years in Columbia, Maryland. She died in Baltimore at age 73 and spent 32 of those years in Buffalo.

Figure 53 Lucille with her husband Fred Clifton

KATHARINE CORNELL

The First Lady of American Theater

K atharine Cornell was born in Berlin, Germany in 1893 to Alice Plimpton and Peter Cortelyou Cornell. Her mother and father were from Buffalo, but Peter was in Berlin pursuing graduate medical studies. Upon completing his medical training, the family returned to Buffalo and resided at 174 Mariner Street, in the Allentown section of the city.

Katharine Cornell's grandfather was S. Douglas Cornell. S. Douglas was born in Buffalo and graduated from Hobart College where he excelled in dramatics. After graduation and a fruitful hiatus as a very successful gold mine operator in Colorado, he returned to Buffalo to run the family business. He managed Cornell Lead Works and in 1894 had a mansion built at 484

Figure 54 Katharine Cornell

Delaware Avenue. The Delaware Avenue home featured a theater, complete with a stage, lighting and seating. In 1872, S. Douglas was involved in forming the Buffalo Amateurs, a theatrical group consisting of members from Buffalo's elite families. They usually put on four plays a year during the late 1890s and early 20th century.

Katharine grew up in Buffalo and attended private schools in the city. She observed the plays that were performed at her grandfather's home theater and participated in outdoor plays presented at the summer home the Cornell family had in Cobourg, Ontario, Canada. After attending Maude Adams' Peter Pan at her father's Star Theatre, Katharine decided to devote her life to theater. As a young girl, she participated in productions of the Buffalo Studio Club at 508 Franklin Street where plays were presented in the living room. She was also active in athletics, being a runner-up in the city championship for tennis and an amateur swimming champion. Katharine was a member of the Garret Club where she participated in club theatrical presentations. After completing her early education in Buffalo, Katharine went to Oaksmere School, in Mamaroneck New York where she participated in many theatrical productions.

Her mother died in 1915 and left Katharine enough money to move to NYC where she became an apprentice with the Washington Square Players, that would later become the Theatre Guild. She was allowed to sit in on rehearsals and when the actress playing the bit part of the mother in *Bushido: A Japanese Tragedy* failed to show up, Cornell was given her one-line part, considered her New York debut. After two seasons of small roles in other Washington Square Players productions, Cornell joined Jessie Bonstelle's stock company. The repertory company divided its summers between Detroit and Buffalo. Cornell toured the East Coast with various theater companies and in 1920 she went to London, England to play Jo in Buffalo author Marian de Forest's stage adaption of Louisa May Alcott's novel *Little Women*. Her performance was praised by the London press and upon returning to New York she made her Broadway debut with a small part alongside Tallulah Bankhead in the play *Nice People*. Her first major Broadway role was as Sydney Fairfield in *A Bill of Divorcement* in 1921.

Katharine became acquainted with former actor, Guthrie McClintic, who she met when working for the Washington Square Players. They married in the summer home of Cornell's aunt at the American enclave in Cobourg, Ontario, Canada. It was generally acknowledged that McClintic was gay and Cornell was a lesbian, with their union being a lavender marriage. After their marriage they purchased a townhouse at 23 Beekman Place in Manhattan and independently established themselves as an actress and director. They decided to embark on a joint career, with McClintic producing all of Cornell's subsequent plays. Cornell and McClintic also formed a production company, M.C. & C. which gave them complete artistic

Figure 55 Cornell with husband Guthrie McClintic

freedom in choosing and producing the plays they presented. Katharine also served on the board of The Rehearsal Club, a place where young actresses could stay while looking for work and McClintic sometimes found roles for them in his plays. Their M.C. & C. company was responsible for launching the careers of numerous actors, giving them their first or most prominent roles on Broadway. They also introduced many English and Shakespearean actors to the American

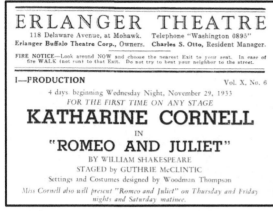

Figure 56 Ad for Katherine Cornell play at Buffalo's Erlanger Theater

stage and produced a number of plays by Shakespeare and George Bernard Shaw, making them popular with American audiences.

In 1924, Cornell played the title role in George Bernard Shaw's Candida, a role she would revive several times. After several years of performances in melodramas, the public was looking for Cornell to appear in different roles. McClintic and Cornell found the vehicle in the Barretts of Wimpole Street, the romance between two of England's great poets – Elizabeth Barrett and Robert Browning. Cornell would be identified with this role for the rest of her career. The play also established the couple as successful producers.

Once a standard practice, the tradition of great stars bringing their productions across the country had gone out of style. McClintic and Cornell decided to revive this practice and devoted the entire 1933-34 season to a cross country tour. They chose Candida and the Barretts of Wimpole Street for this tour, along with their first Shakespearian production – Romeo and Juliet. After a rocky start, Cornell was hailed as the best Juliet in a generation.

Cornell was very patriotic and supported the U.S. war effort. She took a company of actors abroad for a tour of military bases, performing The Barretts of Wimpole Street with Brian Aherne and original cast members. The company performed in Italy, France, the Netherlands and England. After the war, Cornell co-chaired the Community Players, a successor to the American Theatre Wing, to assist war veterans and their families. During her career, Cornell only appeared in one Hollywood film, *Stage Door Canteen*. The movie was a 1943 American WWII morale booster production featuring performances for serviceman on leave at a recreation center. Cornell played herself in the film.

After the death of her husband in 1961, feeling a lack of connection to the current theater community and without the partner who helped shape her career for 40 years, Katharine decided to retire from theater at the age of 70. She moved to a home in Martha's Vineyard where she lived with Nancy Hamilton, her companion and partner since the 1930s. Cornell died from pneumonia at 81 years old on June 9, 1974.

Katharine Cornell received many awards during her lifetime including the first Drama Club Award in 1935, the first Tony Award in 1937 and Eleanor Roosevelt presented her with the Chi Omega sorority's National Achievement Awards at a White House reception in 1937. The Katharine Cornell Foundation was funded from profits from Barretts of Wimpole Street and when dissolved in 1963 the assets were distributed to the Museum of Modern Art, to honor Cornell's close friend from Buffalo and museum president, A. Conger Goodyear. She received the Chancellor's Award from UB in 1935 and the Katharine Cornell Theatre in the Ellicott Complex on the North Campus is named after her. In 1972 Katharine Cornell was one of the original members elected to the American Theatre Hall of Fame and she is considered "The First Lady of the Theatre."

Figure 57 Katherine Cornell painting at Buffalo AKG Art Gallery

Figure 58 Cornell Mansion on Delaware Avenue
Photo credit Rick Falkowski

MADELINE DAVIS

LGBTQ+ Community Teacher, Stage Performer, Author & Historian

Madeline Davis was a trailblazer in the LGBTQ+ Community as a teacher, stage performer, author and historian. She played a leading role in the WNY gay liberation movement and was one of its core educators.

She was born on July 7, 1940 in Buffalo and grew up on the East Side. Her father was an assembly line worker at Ford Motor Company and a union organizer. Her mother attended nursing school and worked in the Erie County social services department. Madeline was an honor student at Bennett High School where she worked on the yearbook for four years and graduated in 1958. While in high school she had a part time job at the North Jefferson Branch Library.

Attending UB on a scholarship, she worked on campus at Lockwood Library. While in college, Madeline began singing at coffee houses in Buffalo, NYC, Toronto,

Figure 59 Madeline Davis receiving 2016 honorary doctorate

Seattle and San Francisco. In the 1960s she was the lead singer in a jazz-rock group, the New Chicago Lunch and later with the Madeline Davis Group. She began by playing folk songs and later added gay liberation anthems to her repertoire.

After graduating from UB with a B.A. in English and Master's in Library Science, she began working at the Buffalo and Erie County Public Library. As chief conservator and head of preservation, she managed the arrival and repair of books and directed a department of 30 people.

During the 1960s Madeline was married to a man, Allen Romano. However, she acknowledged engaging with the lesbian community in 1957 and coming out in the '60s. She divorced her husband after three years of marriage and became actively involved with the LGBTQ+ community.

In 1971 as one of the founder members of the Mattachine Society of the Niagara Frontier (local chapter of the early gay rights organization) she spoke at the first gay rally in Albany. Back in Buffalo, she invited politicians to discuss issues with the gay community and challenged the Buffalo Police concerning entrapment and raids on gay bars. In 1971 she also started the magazine Fifth Freedom, the first gay community newspaper in WNY.

As a singer songwriter, in 1971 she released "Stonewall Nation" a tribute to 1969 uprising in New York that is credited with sparking the gay rights movement. The song is considered the first gay liberation record. During her career she wrote 45 songs, most with gay or lesbian themes and for many years she organized benefit concerts for the gay community, usually performing at these events.

Figure 60 Madeline Davis performance
Photo by Morgan Gwenwald - Lesbian History Archives

She was the first openly gay delegate at a major political convention, the 1972 Democratic National Convention in Miami FL. She petitioned the convention to include gay rights in its platform. Davis addressed that convention and according to a New York Times report she stated, "I am a woman and a lesbian, a minority of minorities." Later in the speech she proclaimed, "Now we are coming out of our closets and onto the convention floor."

Davis organized a Pride workshop in 1973 that evolved into PFLAG (Parents and Friends of Lesbians and Gays). This organization assists all of those who support LGBTQ+ people.

She founded and taught in the Women's Studies College at UB, the institutional ancestor of the Women's Studies Department, now the Global Gender and Sexuality Studies Department. In 1974 she designed and taught the first ever course on lesbianism in the U.S. – Lesbianism 101. A second class WSC 265 was a course in lesbian oral history in which students interviewed lesbian elders about the pre-Stonewall bar scene. That class furnished the material for the book *Boots of Leather, Slippers of Gold: The History of the Lesbian Community.*

The book published in 1993 was a groundbreaking oral history recollection for the gay community. It documented the vibrant working-class lesbian area culture dating back to the 1930s. Davis wrote this book with Elizabeth Lapovsky Kennedy, another founder of the Women's Studies Dept.

In 1994 she was one of the founding members of Hag Theater, the first all lesbian theater company in the U.S. In addition, Davis was associated with Buffalo United Artists, being nominated for an Artie Award in 1993 for her one-woman drama *Cookin' with Typhoid Mary.* That year she also co-formed the Black Triangle Women's Percussion Ensemble, later performing with the percussion group Drawing Down the Moon.

Davis originally met Wendy Smiley when performing in a café in 1974. Twenty years later they reconnected and became involved in a relationship.

Although it was not a legal wedding, they were married at Temple Beth Zion in 1995. It was the first same sex listing in the wedding section in the Buffalo News. Their second wedding was a hand fasting in the woods in accordance with Madeline's Wiccan beliefs. Their third wedding was a Vermont Civil Union and the fourth was in Niagara Falls Ontario, which was a wedding recognized by New York State. For their fifth wedding Madeline and Wendy returned to Temple Beth Zion to a ceremony that was legal in New York State. After five weddings they decided - no more.

As a librarian and archivist, Davis began collecting records, memorabilia and evidence of queer lives and struggles in 2001. The Lesbian, Gay, Bisexual, Transgender Archives of WNY was formed to retain the research data from the class and book. The collection became a foundation, the Dr. Madeline Davis LGBTQ+ Archive of WNY. These archives and personal archives of Davis filled 220 boxes that were transferred to the Butler Library at Buffalo State College in 2009. The Buffalo History Museum presented her with the Owen Augspurger Award for her contributions to Erie County in 2013. It is one of the largest and most comprehensive archives of American queer life.

Then State Senator Byron W. Brown arranged for proclamation of Medeline D. Davis Day in New York State on April 25, 2004 and she served as grand marshal of Buffalo's annual Pride Parade in 2009. Davis was the subject of a 2009 documentary film *Swimming with Lesbians* and was inducted into The Advocate magazine's Hall of Fame in 2012. She died at her Amherst home on April 28, 2021.

In 2016 Davis was given an honorary Doctorate from the State University of New York for her lifetime of work towards making the lives of the LGBTQ+ community better for all of us.

Figure 61 Davis being honored at the UB Law School Outlaw dinner March 2014

ANI DIFRANCO

Independent Recording Artist and Preservationist

Figure 62 A pre-teen Ani DiFranco with Michael Meldrum
Photo courtesy the Estate of Michael Meldrum

Ani DeFranco is the most successful independent recording artist in the country and she was instrumental in preserving the Delaware Asbury Methodist Church.

She was born in Buffalo on September 23, 1979 to Elizabeth and Dante DiFranco. Her parents met when both were students at Massachusetts Institute of Technology (MIT). Dante was a research engineer and her mother, who was raised in Montreal, was studying architecture. When characterizing her parents Ani said her father was cool, calm and collected, while her mother was a motorcycle riding firebrand unafraid of telling people exactly how she felt.

Ani grew up in what she described as a plain, nondescript house in Buffalo. Both parents were professional people, who beginning when Ani was eight years old, were rarely home when she returned from school. Being a latchkey kid was commonplace in the 1980s, but Ani used this opportunity to become independent and learned to do things on her own. This was an attitude that stayed with her and she expanded upon it to become an independent recording artist.

When Ani was nine years old, she got an acoustic guitar and without any lessons started teaching herself songs, like the Beatles Ob-La-Di, Ob-La-Da. A year later, she went to Carlone Music Studios at 69 Allen Street and signed up for lessons. She took lessons from Rich Fustino and others, being taught from the New Alfred guitar course book, learning Beatles songs and instruction on how to write music. There she met Michael Meldrum, a local musician, music teacher and promoter. He started booking dates with Ani at local bars and watering spots, with Meldrum considered her guardian, so she could perform where alcohol was being served. By the time Ani was 11 she was a seasoned veteran, performing before small crowds in intimate university settings, entertaining larger crowds at folk festivals and paying her dues at local dives before the normal group of unruly patrons.

Meldrum booked singers at the start of their careers and industry veterans at Buffalo venues and always needed a place for them to stay. With her parents' permission, performers like John Gorka, Rod Anderson, Christine Lavin, Cheryl Wheeler, Suzanne Vega and Michelle Shocked stayed at the DiFranco home. Ani recalled, "I got to know them way back when and I was hanging out with a bunch of singer-songwriters." Suzanne Vega remembered striking up a friendship with the precocious ten-year-old and worried that Ani was hanging around with a fast crowd.

At this time in her life, DiFranco was more interested in dance than performing music and attended the Buffalo Academy of Visual & Performing Arts, a Buffalo public high school. She majored in dance and graduated in 1987. Ani then attended Buffalo State College in 1988 and 1989, majoring in painting, and New School for Social Research, specializing in poetry, in NYC from 1990 to 1992.

When Ani again picked up a guitar during summer vacation at age 14, she could not remember any of the songs she had previously learned. The muse took over and she started writing and performing her own compositions. She played the songs for Meldrum, who started booking her at more concerts and events. She played in a variety of settings, from Holiday Inns to the Essex Street Pub, from coffee houses like the Calumet Café to night clubs like Nietzsche's. Her resume states she performed in other bars, nightclubs, dumps and dives throughout WNY.

When Ani was 15 years old, her parents divorced, with her mother moving to Connecticut and father remaining in Buffalo. Not to take sides with either parent, she proclaimed herself an emancipated minor and got her own apartment. To cover the costs, she worked odd jobs, such as a candy striper, a carpenter, housepainter and waitress to supplement her meager earnings as a performer. It was at a construction job that she met her future manager Scot Fisher, who was managing home renovation projects while attending law school.

Figure 63 DiFranco with early teacher Rich Fustino in 2015
Photo courtesy Rich Fustino

By the time she was 17 she played her own songs wherever she was given the opportunity and hosted a Saturday open mic at the Essex Street Pub for several years, making $20.00 a night and returning to work and/or school during the week. She decided it was time to record her original songs and send demo tapes to record companies. The major labels either turned her down or ignored her but she received some interest from small independent labels. One label sounded perfect, but when she received the recording contract, she found the company was just interested in making money and controlling the artist's material. She decided to control her own career and take the Do It Yourself (DIY) approach by starting her own label.

By 1989 Ani had written over 100 songs, each framed in personal lyricism and a strong sense of melody based on folk, punk and rock. She later incorporated funk, hip hop, jazz, soul and electronica in her music, but she was affectionately called the "Little Folksinger." In 1989 she entered Audio Magic Recording Studio on Military Road in the Black Rock section of Buffalo. The 12-song

Figure 64 Signed DiFranco concert ticket
Ticket courtesy Rich Fustino

recording featured Ani singing and accompanying herself on acoustic guitar was engineered by John Caruso, pressed by Eastern Standard Productions (who today continue to manufacture Righteous Babe CDs) and produced by Ani DiFranco and Dale Anderson. The first batch of tapes were sold out by Ani at her dates and more were released as Ani DiFranco on Righteous Babe Records-001, the first release on the label. Many people made bootlegs of Ani's shows and shared the tapes with their friends. Ani attributes this tape sharing instrumental in getting her dates in cities where tapes were not sold.

Dale Anderson, the Buffalo Evening News reporter who created the Gusto entertainment insert, first heard Ani sing at a talent contest in Niagara Falls. After he listened to her first tape, he interviewed her for The News and thought she was the best singer songwriter to come along since Bob Dylan. Starting in 1989 he became her manager, primarily to make sure she got a lawyer and was not taken advantage of by the record industry. For four years and her first five albums, Dale booked her appearances before signing her with a national agency, handled radio promotion, publicity, helped form Righteous Babe Records (originally planned to be named Righteous Records), oversaw sales, serviced stores and independent distributors. He engineered her breakthrough appearance at the 1991 Mariposa Folk Festival in Toronto that led to festivals across Canada and a showcase at the 1991 South by Southwest in Austin Texas. Dale and Ani parted ways in 1994.

Now an attorney, Scot Fisher became Ani's manager and president of Righteous Babe Records after Dale left in 1994. Scot was involved in area preservation and in 1999, Ani purchased the deteriorating Delaware Asbury Methodist Church at Delaware and West Tupper. After ten years and more than 10 million in public and private funds it became The Church, then Asbury Hall and later Babeville. It remains a first-class concert, special event venue and houses

Hallwalls Contemporary Arts Center. Many performers complement the venue during performances on its stage.

Ani confessed that she played in a band when she was 16 but preferred to perform solo. After her first recordings were released, she toured solo, selling her tapes from the trunk of her car. In the early 1990s she added a drummer and in 1996 a bass player joined her touring group. Later she toured with a drummer, bass player and keyboardist, occasionally joined by a horn section at concerts.

As stated above, Ani decided not to sign with a major record company and formed her own record label – Righteous Babe Records. The L.A. Times raved that she thwarted the corporate overhead by choosing to remain independent, thereby pocketing $4.25 per unit as opposed to the $1.25 made by Hootie & the Blowfish or the $2.00 made by Michael Jackson. This story was picked up and reprinted by the New York Times, Forbes, Ms. and the Financial News Network. She thought she was a folksinger but became a Fortune 500 young entrepreneur.

DiFranco is proud of the profitable record label she built but is more interested in what she has created than the retained per unit profit. She explained that her company has 15 employees and they provide stimulating business for local Buffalo printers and manufacturers. Being an independent artist, she also hires independent distributors, promoters, booking agents and publicists. Since 1999 she has released recordings by various other artists on the label. Through her Righteous Babe Foundation, she has backed grassroots cultural and political causes including abortion rights and LGBTQ+ visibility.

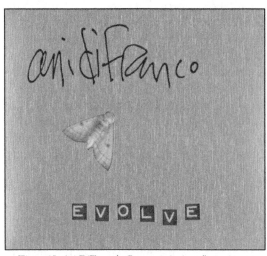

Figure 65 Ani DiFranco's Grammy winning album art cover

Ani was nominated for nine Grammy Awards. Four were for Best Recording Package and she won the grammy in that category in 2004 for the CD Evolve, which she shared with graphic artist Brian Brunert.

She has won various awards including Woman of Courage from the national Organization for Women, the Gay/Lesbian American Music Award for Female Artist of the Year, the Woody Guthrie Award, the prestigious Artistic Achievement Award at the 2013 Winnipeg Folk Festival, an honorary doctorate from the University of Winnipeg, the 2017 Lifetime Achievement Award from A2IM (the trade organization that represents independent record labels), Outstanding

Achievement for Global Activism from A Global Friendship and in 2021 was named a Champion for Justice by the National Center for Lesbian Rights. In addition, she collaborated with numerous organizations and has participated in many demonstrations, including performing before over 500,000 people at the 2004 March for Women's Lives in Washington DC.

During her career Ani has released 20 studio albums, along with numerous live recordings and compilations. In 2019 she also wrote her memoir No Walls and the Recurring Dream that reached the New York Times top 10 seller list.

Ani is extremely popular in the lesbian community and during her twenties proclaimed herself as bisexual. She has written songs about love and sex with men and women, addressing her sexuality in the 1992 song "In or out." She confided that she had abortions at the ages of 18 and 20, which inspired her 1990 composition "Lost Women Song." In 1998 Ani married her sound engineer Andrew Gilchrist and they divorced in 2003. In January 2007 she gave birth to a daughter Petah at her Buffalo home, marrying the child's father Mike Napolitano, her producer, in 2009. She gave birth to a son Dante in April 2013.

Since 2008 she has lived in the Bywater section of New Orleans and is involved in various community activities in that city. However, her Righteous Babe record company is still located in Buffalo and she is active at Babeville, the former Delaware Asbury Methodist Church.

Figure 66 Babeville - Delaware Asbury Methodist Church
Photo credit Rick Falkowski

JOANN FALLETTA

Conductor Buffalo Philharmonic Orchestra

When JoAnn Falletta was appointed Director of the Buffalo Philharmonic Orchestra in 1999, she became the first female conductor to lead a major American ensemble and has been credited with bringing the BPO to an unprecedented level of national and international prominence.

Falletta was born on February 27, 1954 and raised in an Italian-American household in the borough of Queens. At the age of seven she fell in love with music and began studying classical guitar. By the age of 12 she became interested in conducting and started studying orchestral scores. JoAnn graduated from St. Vincent Ferrer, a prep school for girls and decided to apply to music schools. Mannes College of Music was only a couple blocks away from St Vincent Ferrer's in NYC. JoAnn

Figure 67 JoAnn Falletta

Figure 68 JoAnne Falletta the guitarist
Photo courtesy JoAnne Falletta

wanted to pursue a dual major of guitar and conducting. Mannes enrolled her as a guitar student but allowed her to attend all conducting classes. To further her conducting skills, after graduating from Mannes she obtained an MA in orchestral conducting from Queens College. She completed her education, earning her master's and doctoral degrees from Juilliard, studying under Jorge Mester, Sixten Ehrling and Semyon Bychkov, including master's classes with Leonard Bernstein.

She began her performance career in her twenties as a guitar and mandolin player with the Metropolitan Opera and New York Philharmonic. Her first music director position was with the Jamaica Symphony Orchestra from 1977 to 1989, music director of the Queens

Philharmonic Orchestra, Ulster Orchestra, music director of the Denver Chamber from 1983 to 1992, associate conductor of the Milwaukee Symphony Orchestra from 1985-1988 (Lucas Foss was the music director), music director of the Bay Area Women's Philharmonic from 1986 to 1996, music director of the Long Beach Symphony Orchestra from 1989 to 2000 and music director of the Virginia Symphony Orchestra for 29 years from 1991 to 2021. These assignments lead to her appointment as BPO Music Director in 1999.

With Falletta as music director in 2018, the BPO commenced their first international tour in nearly three decades and performed at Warsaw's prestigious Beethoven Easter Festival where Falletta made history as the first American female conductor to lead an orchestra at the festival. Under the direction of Falletta, the BPO has again become performers at Carnegie Hall and they are a traveling symphony orchestra to other cities in the U.S. The BPO is also one of the most recorded orchestras of classical music.

As with many other music directors, Falletta holds several different jobs. She is the music director of the Buffalo Philharmonic and Virginia Symphony Orchestra, in addition to being artistic director of the Honolulu Symphony. That means traveling between Buffalo and Norfolk VA on a regular basis and the long flight to Hawaii three times a year. She and her husband Robert Alemany have been married since 1986. They call Buffalo their home, and own a condo on the Buffalo waterfront. They also own a condo in downtown Norfolk, but leave their car in Buffalo, renting one when they travel. Falletta loves that it is only a seven-minute drive from her condo to Kleinhans Music Hall. Alemany is a software engineer with IBM and with current technology works remotely from wherever his wife is working. He is also a member of her guitar trio.

Falletta has conducted over 100 orchestras in the U.S. and many of the most prominent orchestras in Europe, Asia and South America. Her guest conducting has included the orchestras of Philadelphia, Los Angeles, San Francisco, Detroit, Dallas, Houston, St. Louis, Toronto, Montreal, Seattle, San Diego, New Jersey and the National Symphony Orchestra. European appearances include the London Symphony Orchestra, Liverpool, and Manchester-BBC Philharmonics, RTE Concert Orchestra (Dublin), Scottish BBC Orchestra, Czech and Rotterdam

Figure 69 JoAnne Falletta with Leonard Bernstein in 1985
Photo courtesy JoAnne Falletta

Philharmonics, Orchestra National de Lyon, Mannheim Orchestra, Real Orquesta Sinfonica de Seville and the Lisbon Metropolitan Orchestra. Asian engagements include the Korean Broadcast Symphony Orchestra, Seoul Philharmonic, New Japan Philharmonic, China Symphony Orchestra, Beijing Symphony and the Shanghai Symphony. She has led the National Symphony in two PBS televised specials on New Years Eve and for the 50th Anniversary of the Kennedy Center

Her conducting style has been described by Gramophone Magazine as having "Toscanini's tight control over ensemble, Walter's affectionate balancing of inner voices, Stokowski's showmanship and a controlled frenzy worthy of Bernstein." Faletta is a strong advocate and mentor for student and young professional musicians, leading seminars for women conductors for the League of American Orchestras. In addition, Falletta instructs young musicians by conducting at conservatories such as The Julliard School, Curtis Institute of Music, Mannes, and Cleveland Institute of Music, and summer programs including the National Repertory Orchestra, National Orchestral Institute, Interlochen and Brevard Music Center. She established a collaboration between the BPO and Mannes College of Music to give up-and-coming conductors professional experience with a leading American orchestra.

Falletta was appointed to serve on the National Council on the Arts by President George W. Bush in 2008 and continued to serve under President Obama's administration until 2012. She is a member of the American Academy of Arts and Sciences and has introduced over 600 works by American composers, including over 150 world premieres.

The JoAnn Falletta International Guitar Concerto Competition, launched in 2004 by PBS member stations WNED-FM, WNED-TV and the Buffalo Philharmonic is considered one of the premier classical guitar performance competitions in the world. It is the world's first concerto competition for classical guitarists with accompaniment by a full symphony orchestra. The competition's goal is to identify and encourage young classical guitarists and help them in their musical journey. It brings international guitarists to Buffalo for a week of competitions for cash prizes, national and international broadcast exposure and a return engagement with the BPO.

Figure 70 JoAnne with her sister Luann
Photo courtesy JoAnne Falletta

Falletta has a discography of over 120 titles and the BPO has become one of the leading recording orchestras for Naxos, releasing 18 albums. Her Naxos recording of John Corigliano's Mr. Tambourine Man: Seven Poems of Bob Dylan with the BPO received two Grammys in 2008. JoAnn won her first individual Grammy in 2019 as conductor of the London Symphony Orchestra in the Best Classical Compendium category for *Spiritualist*. In 2021 she won the Grammy for Best Choral Performance as Conductor of the BPO in the world premier recording of *Richard Danielpour's "The Passion of Yeshua"*. Her 2020 recording of orchestral music of Florence Schmidt with the BPO received the prestigious Diapason d'Or Award. She recently released previously never-heard material to mark the 100th anniversary of William Walton's youthful masterpiece Façade, along with having additional recordings by the BPO and other orchestras in the process of being released.

ASCAP has called Falletta "a leading force for music of our time" and she was named Performance Today's Classical Woman of the Year. She has won two individual Grammy Awards and Gramophone Magazine named her "one of the Fifty Great Conductors, past and present."

Figure 71 JoAnne with her husband Robert Alemany

ABIGAIL POWERS FILLMORE

Changed the role of First Lady at White House

A bigail Powers met Millard Fillmore when he became her student in 1819 at an academy in New Hope NY near the town of Niles on Lake Skaneateles. She became his inspiration to further his education and to become an attorney. They married in 1826 and Fillmore became president of the U.S. in 1850.

She was born on March 13, 1798 in Stillwater NY, Saratoga County, the youngest of seven children born to Abigail Newland and Reverend Lemuel Powers, a leader of the First Baptist Church. Her father died when she was only two years old and her mother moved to Sempronius NY, to the home of Cyrus Powers, her oldest brother. Lemual left behind a large library of books which her mother, a former teacher, used to teach her how to read and appreciate her education.

Figure 72 Abigail Fillmore

Powers began working as a teacher when she was 16 years old at the Sempronius Village School and in 1819 was teaching at New Hope Academy where she met Millard Fillmore. They became engaged in 1819 but Abigail's family considered Fillmore the son of a dirt farmer and they discouraged their daughter from marrying him until he had the resources to support a family.

Millard Fillmore moved with his parents to East Aurora NY in 1821. There he took a job as a teacher and studied law in Buffalo. Abigail obtained various teaching positions in Central New York. While living apart establishing their careers, there was a three-year period of time where they did not even see each other. After Millard was accepted to the bar and became a practicing attorney, they married on February 5, 1826 at Abigail's brother's home in Moravia NY, south of Auburn.

After their marriage, they lived in a house Millard personally built on Main Street in East Aurora, across the street from his law office, now the location of Vidler's 5&10. Millard was the first resident attorney living in East Aurora. Normally female teachers were expected to resign after they married, but Abigail decided to keep teaching until she had children. Their son Millard Power Fillmore was born in east Aurora in 1828 and their daughter Mary Abigail Fillmore was born in 1832.

As Millard's law practice expanded, in 1831 they moved to a home at 180 Franklin Street in Buffalo. They joined the Unitarian Church and Abigail assisted in building the first Buffalo library, growing her personal library, originally started by her father, to over 4,000 books.

When Millard was elected to the New York State Assembly, Abigail remained in WNY. He was

Figure 73 Fillmore home in East Aurora built in 1826

first elected to the House of Representatives in 1832, but Abigail did not join him in Washington DC until his second term in Congress. She became interested in the cultural and academic institutions of the city. They moved back to Buffalo where Fillmore expanded his private law practice and Abigail became involved in the community. They moved to Albany when he was elected NYS Controller in 1847. When he was elected Vice President in 1848, Abigail initially stayed in Buffalo to take care of her sister. Upon the death of President Zachary Taylor, Fillmore became president on July 9, 1850.

When Fillmore became President, being a former teacher Abigail started the tradition of the First Lady being involved in educational issues. There was no library in the White House, so she lobbied to create one. Congress appropriated $2,000 (about $75,000 in current dollars) and Abigail personally selected the books for the White House Library, arranging them in the upstairs Oval Room. Abigail set up a music room and had three pianos installed in the White House, enjoying herself reading and listening to music, often performed by her daughter. She also started the tradition of inviting writers and entertainers to the White House, hosting Washington Irving, William Thackery, Charles Dickens, Anna Bishop and Jenny Lind. These meetings essentially created a salon in the library of the White House. Twelve of the original volumes selected by Fillmore remain in the White House Library and Abigail is considered the first librarian of the White House.

Abigail was very interested in political developments and often attended proceedings in Congress. Almost every night she and Millard discussed government affairs in the Oval Room library, which also served as the Fillmore's family room, reception room and music room. Abigail advised Millard that the signing of the Fugitive Slave Act would destroy him politically (which it did), she lobbied for the abolishment of flogging in the U.S. Navy and supported Women's Rights. She broke precedent by leaving the White House to attend functions, art exhibitions and concerts unaccompanied by her husband and traveled on her own to visit friends and family in other cities. In addition, Abigail had the first iron range and bath tub installed in the White House and oversaw the expansion of the White House heating system.

She suffered several ailments that prevented her from carrying out her duties as first lady, including an injured ankle that limited her mobility and prevented her from standing for hours in reception lines at White House events. Her daughter Mary Abigail Fillmore often filled in as hostess. Mary graduated from Buffalo Normal School, taught in Buffalo until her father became President, was fluent in French, conversant in Spanish, German and Italian and was an accomplished musician. Mary died at the early age of 22 on July 26, 1854 of cholera in East Aurora, only a year after her mother passed away.

Despite her poor health, Abigail stood beside her husband at the windy, snow driven outdoor inauguration of Fillmore's successor Franklin Pierce. She was chilled during the ceremony and returned to the Willard Hotel where her cold progressed to bronchial pneumonia and she passed away 26 days after the end of his term on March 30, 1853 at the age of 55.

Figure 74 The Franklin Street Fillmore home in Buffalo

Abigail is buried in her husband's plot in Forest Lawn Cemetery, along with her daughter Mary Abigail Fillmore and son Millard Powers Fillmore.

MARIAN DE FOREST

Founder of Zonta, Playwright & Journalist

In 2001, Marian de Forest was inducted into the National Women's Hall of Fame, but her impact goes well beyond any accolades. Marian de Forest was a successful playwright during the early 20th century, but her most successful creation, still running today, spotlights businesswomen instead of actors. She was a pioneering newspaper woman, theater critic, music promoter, and clubwoman. Not surprisingly, her motto was "work, work, work."

Her most ambitious and successful project had nothing to do with the theater. She saw a need for a club similar to the all-male Rotary Club where women in business professions could join together to support each other. In 1919, she called a meeting at the Statler Hotel in Buffalo to form a club as a service organization. Using a Lakota Sioux word meaning "honest" and "trustworthy," she named it the Zonta Club of Buffalo. Ms. De Forest

Figure 75 Marian de Forest
Photo courtesy Zonta Buffalo

described Zonta's mission as high ethical standards, good fellowship, and community service.

In one of her early speeches Ms. De Forest explained, "Zonta stands for the highest standards in the business and professional world...seeks cooperation rather than competition and considers the Golden Rule not only good ethics but good business."

She founded the Zonta Club of Buffalo to improve the status of women worldwide. Zonta was designed to represent as many different vocations as possible. Membership was limited to one woman for each category of business. Members were expected to spend at least 50% of their time in business at an executive level. Zonta's founding objective was to encourage friendship and dedication to the advancement of women in all professions.

The Zonta idea spread rapidly. By 1923, Zonta clubs had opened in New York City, Washington D.C. and other large cities. They joined forces to raise money for international charities, and by 1930, Zonta itself was international in scope, with clubs in Canada and Europe. In that year an international Confederation of Zonta Clubs dedicated its efforts to community service and further progress for women.

Marian de Forest was born in Buffalo on February 27, 1864 to Cyrus Hawley de Forest and Sarah Germain Sutherland. Her father came to Buffalo in 1827, established himself in furniture manufacturing and later in the coal industry. He was a community leader, serving as a Justice of the Peace, a trustee of the Buffalo Orphan Asylum and an elder at the First Presbyterian Church.

After suffering a serious eye injury as a young girl, Marian was kept in a darkened room for three years to avoid damaging her vision further. She received private tutoring through spoken lessons at home, and learned to memorize her lessons. "That's where she learned how to remember everything that people said. She could fill out a story with just about every detail that was in there because everything stuck in her head," explained Vivian Cody, Treasurer of the Zonta Club in Buffalo in 2023.

Attending the Buffalo Seminary for high school, Marian directed classmates in theatrical productions, was chosen editor of the school paper as a senior, and at graduation received the gold medal for highest scholarship, excellence in English literature and composition. After becoming the youngest person to graduate from the Buffalo Seminary in 1884, she became a journalist, one of the first women in the profession in WNY. Buffalo's numerous newspapers offered many opportunities for aspiring writers. De Forest eventually established herself as the drama critic and women's editor for the Buffalo Express for 20 years. Later, she became City Editor of the Buffalo Commercial newspaper.

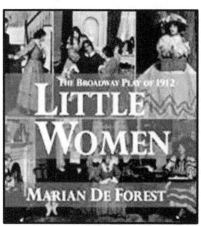

Figure 76 1912-Promo for the Little Women play

She was also a playwright best known for writing and producing Little Women, based on the Louisa May Alcott novel in 1911. Her play "Little Women: A Comedy in Four Acts" is said to have launched the career of Katharine Cornell, then a local actress.

De Forest wrote other plays, including "Erstwhile Susan," "The Lovers of Yesteryear" and "Mr. Man." When publicity for "Mr. Man" was slower than she wanted, she hired a plane, filled it with Zontians and dropped leaflets on the city. "She knew how to make a splash," said Cody.

Marian was one of the first women asked to join the writing group called the "Scribblers", founded by Charlotte Mulligan. Scribblers was a Buffalo club formed for women writers but was open to all citizens. Marian had encountered a wide variety of women's clubs from across the country as the executive secretary of the Board of Women Managers at Buffalo's ambitious 1901 Pan-American Exposition. Ideas for a club of her own were probably already stirring.

Figure 77 Marian de Forest
Photo courtesy Zonta Buffalo

Marian de Forest played an important role in Buffalo's cultural life. When the Buffalo Historical Society began to include women members in 1894, de Forest was one of the first women elected to their governing board. In 1922, she became president of a community theater group, the Buffalo Players. In 1924, she became a co-founder of the Buffalo Music Foundation, which brought a wider range of classical music to the city. During the Great Depression, she organized Pops concerts to give work to unemployed musicians and was a driving force behind the creation of the Buffalo Philharmonic Orchestra in 1934.

Devoted to animals, she served on the board of the SPCA for 14 years. She also served on the boards of the Buffalo Public Library, Executive Secretary on the Board of Women Managers, and she was elected to the Lyceum of London, a prestigious writer's society. Ms. De Forest was listed in the *Notable Women in American Theater* and *Who's Who in America*.

De Forest established the Buffalo Musical Foundation. With music loving citizens like Dr. Roswell Park and Edward H. Butler, she brought orchestras and the American Opera Company to town, including those from Boston, Cleveland and Detroit. She started a youth concert series with the Buffalo Public Schools, providing over 3,000 students annually a rare opportunity to hear great orchestras at the Elmwood Music Hall. Marian believed it was important for children to develop an appreciation of music and theater as these arts had brought so much joy to her own life.

William R. Ramsdell, former publisher of the *Buffalo Express*, wrote that she had "done so much to promote the best music in Buffalo available to all people, the city owes a great debt to Miss de Forest."

During her final illness, the Vienna Choir Boys paid tribute to her by going to the hospital to sing to her.

Colleagues described her as chatty, good-natured and a "ripping good dramatic critic." Zonta colleague Helen Z.M. Rogers wrote, "I think the outstanding characteristics of Marian were her great courage and humor. She met every new problem with gallant spirit, including the end of her own life. Her friends got the better part of her – better than the public."

Figure 78 Spirit of Womanhood sculpture in Delaware Park dedicated to DeForest by artist Larry Griffith

Marian de Forest died on February 17, 1935, just a few weeks shy of her 71st birthday, after a battle with cancer. She is buried in her family plot in Forest Lawn Cemetery alongside her partner Mai Davis Smith. One tribute said, "Her understanding of human nature was deep and sympathetic, her mind brilliant and analytical".

Despite her driving commitment as a journalist, playwright, major force in the progressive women's movement, and cultural leader, Ms. De Forest was always the personification of civic dedication and volunteerism, and was recognized as such in the media. Throughout her life, Marian de Forest served as a role model for working women. Her impact is still apparent today. She was, indeed, a remarkable woman, a woman among women who inspired, led, and made the impossible, possible.

Marian de Forest was inducted into the Western New York Women's Hall of Fame in 1998 and the National Women's Hall of Fame in Seneca Falls, NY in 2001. She was the first woman from Buffalo to be so honored. Marian de Forest was the inspiration behind the 1962 commission from the Buffalo Parks Department for the Larry Griffiths, Jr. statue "Spirit of Womanhood" in Delaware Park. She is prominently featured in the Women's Walkway, a cobblestone path commemorating 100 Women from Western New York.

Each year, Zonta International presents a Marian de Forest award, which honors someone doing good work in a field related to Marian, including journalism, theater, working with animals, and more.

MABEL GANSON DODGE LUHAN

Eccentric Buffalo Socialite, Writer and Patron of the Arts

Mabel Ganson was born in Buffalo on February 26, 1879. Her father was Charles Ganson and mother was Sara McKay Cook Ganson. She grew up in the family Gilded-Age mansion at 675 Delaware Avenue where her father despised her mother and her parents paid little attention to their only child.

Her father Charles was trained as a lawyer but never practiced the profession. Charles was an angry and unhappy man who was obsessed with flags. As an indication of his character, he created a personal flag and when his wife was out of town, he raised the flag at their house but when she returned, he lowered it to half-mast. He was the son of James M. Ganson, one of the founders of the Marine Bank at 7 Main Street, which evolved into Marine

Figure 79 Mabel Ganson and her infant son John Evans

Trust Company and Marine Midland. James lived at 396 Delaware Avenue, next to the Buffalo Club. Charles' mother Nancy Ganson outlived his father by 35 years and could often be seen knitting in her front window, waving to the men she knew that frequented the Buffalo Club. They all raised their hat to her in respect. Upon her death, she donated 396 Delaware Avenue to Trinity Church, located across the street from the mansion.

The father of Mabel's mother, Sara Cook, was also a successful banker. Sara kept busy by managing the household in accordance with long detailed letters received from her mother. Mabel's maternal grandmother basically ruled the roost of her daughter from afar. Mabel could not recall her mother ever kissing her or showing any affection. As a neglected child, Mable became the only resident of the third floor in the mansion and found solace in her books.

In *Intimate Memories: Background*, she wrote about growing up in Buffalo and her recollections of the people and places of Millionaires Row on Delaware Avenue. She also wrote how her parents, like others of the Victorian wealthy elite, left childrearing to the governesses and nursemaids, including how her parents unhappy, turbulent marriage and their lack of affection affected her life. On the bright side, her young friends in the elite neighborhood Row included members of the Laverack, Movius, Rumsey, Goodyear and Spaulding families. The hangout for this gang was Rumsey Park where on the pond they had boats in the summer and skated in the winter, along with playing on the many trails and lawns.

Figure 80 Mabel Ganson at 5 years old

Mabel attended St. Margaret's Episcopal School for Girls, located across the street from her home. At 16 years old her grandmother arranged for Mabel to attend Miss Graham's School in NYC. At school she befriended Mary Shillito, another affluent girl who had a lonely and unhappy family life. Mary was from Paris, France and told Mable stories of her sophisticated and cosmopolitan sister Violet. After the first school year, Mabel spent the summer in Paris where she fell in love with Violet and developed her persona as a friend and facilitator to the smart set.

The Twentieth Century Club at 595 Delaware Avenue was the site of Mabel's formal debutante Coming-Out Ball. Afterwards, as expected of young women of her class, she entertained herself seeking the affections of young men. To test her womanly powers with her country club friends, Mabel flirted with the fun-loving, irresponsible but rich Karl Evans, who was engaged to one of her friends. Mabel was just looking to enjoy herself and see if she could keep Karl away from her friend Elsie, but Karl fell for Mabel and tricked her into marrying him, followed by a large formal society wedding at Buffalo's Trinity Church. A year and a half later, they had a son, Mabel's father died and Karl was accidently killed in a hunting accident. Mabel became a young widow, with a one-year-old son, one day before her 25th birthday. After the disclosure of Mabel's affair with prominent Buffalo doctor, John Parmenter, shortly after her husband's death, Sara Ganson shipped Mabel and her son off to Europe.

In 1904, while en route to Paris, Mabel met architect Edwin Dodge. They married in 1905. After a winter in the Riviera, they settled in Florence, Italy. There she established herself as a salon hostess and influential socialite in Villa Curonia, a 15th century villa that had been owned by the Medici Family. She courted the Florentine expatriate society, with her salon hosting Pen Browning, the son of Robert Browning and Elizabeth Barrett Browning; Lady Muriel Paget, who was considered the de facto head of English society in Florence; and Lord and Lady Acton, leaders of the local international set. Mable cast herself as a Renaissance woman. In 1911, she met Gertrude Stein and her brother, American art connoisseur Leo Stein. Leo gave her an appreciation of modern art and Gertrude gave her an understanding of how language works and how to write. They encouraged Mabel to pursue a career in writing, resulting in Mabel leaving Florence, the Renaissance, and her husband behind by moving to NYC. However, before leaving, Mabel had a troubled liaison with her chauffeur that led to two suicide attempts, the first by eating figs containing shards of glass and the second with laudanum.

Upon arriving in NYC in late 1912, she assumed the role of a patron of the arts by assisting in staging and promoting the Armory Show of new European Art in 1913, which drew 100,000 people. She separated from her husband and launched the most successful salon in American history at her 23 Fifth Avenue apartment in Greenwich Village. At one of her Wednesday evening salons, you would find artists, philosophers, writers, reformers, socialists, psychiatrists, performers, and radicals of all stripes. Regular participants included Lincoln Steffens, Max Eastman, Emma Goldman and Margaret Sanger. At this time, she began writing a syndicated newspaper column for the Hearst organization, popularizing Freudian psychology and supporting various organizations, the Women's Peace Party, the

Figure 81 Intimate Memories 1st edition cover

Heterodoxy Club, the Women's Birth Control League, and the Twilight Sleep Association. She was heralded as the "New Woman," and experimented with free love, including an affair with radical journalist John Reed. After helping dancer Isadora Duncan and her sister Elizabeth open a school on land she gave them, she married her third husband, Russian-born artist Maurice Sterne in 1916.

Sterne introduced Mabel to the Southwest and New Mexico, which still retained its Spanish and Indian heritage. She moved to Taos, divorced her third husband, and married Tony Luhan, a full-blooded Pueblo Indian. Her Taos home Los Gallos hosted famous writers and artists; D.H. Lawrence, Georgia O'Keeffe, Ansel Adams, Robinson Jeffers, John Collier and others. It was in Taos during the 1930s that Mabel published her four volume memoirs, *Intimate Memories: Background, European Experiences, Movers & Shakers and Edge of Taos Desert*, along with four other books.

Mabel, who championed Indian affairs in New Mexico, died in Taos, after a serious illness, on August 13, 1962. Her home in Taos was designated a National Historic Landmark and is now a hotel and conference center.

MINNIE GILLETTE

Legislator, Saved Old Post Office as ECC City Campus

Minnie Gillette was the first African-American Woman elected to the Erie County Legislature and was a leader in converting the former main post office on Ellicott Street into the Erie Community College City Campus. Her life of distinguished service, a life committed to improving conditions for thousands of people in Buffalo, was a gift of sustained leadership in everything she did.

Figure 82 Minnie Gillette campaigning for office
Photo Buffalo Stories

Born in Apelia Alabama in 1930, Minnie Gillette was raised in Buffalo. After completing her education in the Buffalo Public Schools, Gillette worked at Columbus Hospital as a dietary supervisor and obtained a BA in Nutrition from Buffalo State College.

Before running for political office, she was active in organizations including the Community Action Organization, Western New York Health, and served as a director of the Model Cities program. Due to her visible and proactive involvement in the Ellicott District community, Minnie Gillette had the backing of the Democratic, Republican and Conservative parties when she was elected to the Erie County Legislature in 1977.

After she became a member of the legislature, she teamed with Legislator Joan K. Bozer to spearhead the conversion of the former post office into the Erie Community College City Campus. Another accomplishment was her leadership helping to establish the "Ram Van", a traveling lending library. Her well-earned reputation was based on overlooking the party lines and serving the interests of her constituents. She cared for the poor, the homeless, and the needy, and fought to help minority contractors receive a fair share of the county contracts.

*Figure 83 Former post office converted to ECC City Campus coordinated by Gillette
Photo credit Rick Falkowski*

When Legislators Gillette and Bozer started working on the conversion of the old post office, people in WNY did not always appreciate older buildings, including the inherent embedded energy in these buildings, their built-to-last construction, and products created from the earth rather than plastic. The Urban Renewal attitude made people believe knocking down anything old to build something new was better. In 1969 Erie County Democratic Chairman Peter Crotty called the building, "a mongrel structure of no authentic period, dungeon like in its aspect, repellent to the visitor and lacking in the convenience suitable for habitation." Yet Gillette and Bozer persevered! Their sustained efforts saved a monumental landmark building and created the downtown community college campus within this architectural treasure in the City of Buffalo.

In 1979 Gillette was honored as The Buffalo News Outstanding Citizen and in 1980 she received the University at Buffalo's Outstanding Women of Western New York Government Award.

After serving two terms in the Legislature, Minnie Gillette returned to work in the Ellicott Community. She served on the Board of Managers of the William-Emslie YMCA and helped establish a senior citizens center at the location. With her recognized leadership skills, Gillette served as chairwoman of the Seventh (Ellicott) District Planning Board and on the Advisory Board at the Equal Opportunity Center on Washington Street.

She was appointed the first director of the county's Victim/Witness Assistance Program and was also appointed as an elections inspector. Being a past president of the Association of Retarded Children, in 1986 Governor Cuomo appointed her to the Board of Visitors at the West Seneca Developmental Center.

She was past Worthy Matron of Paramount Chapter 57 of Eastern Star, and served on the Advisory Board of the Jesse E. Nash Health Center. Gillette was an early member of the Black Leadership Forum, organized Block Clubs, and helped register voters throughout her civic career. She was a member of the Erie County Chapter of the Christian Leadership Conference and the Buffalo Chapter of the NAACP.

During this time, in addition to all these activities, she continued to work at the food pantry in the Town Gardens housing development. As the coordinator of food distribution to the hungry, Gillette received a Martin Luther King award in 1990 at the annual Martin Luther King Awards Dinner sponsored by the Erie County Chapter of the Southern Christian Leadership Conference.

At the time of her death Gillette was president of the New York State Community Action Agency.

Figure 84 Millie Gillette on Freedom Wall mural

Minnie Gillette died at the age of 62 on January 7, 1992, survived by her three children Hasinah Ramadhan, Loretta Gillette and Calvin Gillette. Diagnosed with cancer a year before her death, she persevered with her amazingly powerful spirit by working on community projects until a couple weeks before she died. Gillette is honored with her portrait as one of the 28 people featured on the Freedom Wall at Michigan and East Ferry. Minnie Gillette Drive was named in her honor in the Ellicott Neighborhood as another public tribute to her legacy.

ELLA PORTIA CONGER GOODYEAR

Buffalo Socialite & Matriarch of the Charles Goodyear family

Ella Portia Conger was born in Collins Center NY in 1853. Her father Anson Griffith Conger was a banker and member of the legislature. She attended Miss Nardin's Academy and the Female Academy (now Buffalo Seminary). After graduating in 1873 she studied voice in New York City, Brooklyn and Washington but returned to Collins Center to work in her father's banking office.

While back in Collins Center she sang in the church choir but missed the activity of the city. She moved to Buffalo and made her debut as a soprano in a quartet at St. Paul's Cathedral. Ellen retained an active interest in music during her entire life, but after her marriage she only sang at informal events. She directed her energy of performance into her marriage, children and becoming a centerpiece of society.

Figure 85 Ella Goodyear

On March 23, 1876 she married lawyer Charles Waterhouse Goodyear Sr. As a wedding gift Ella's father gave the couple the money to build a grandiose mansion at 723 Delaware Avenue, across the street from Westminster Church. Charles served as Erie County District Attorney, and when Grover Cleveland was elected Governor of New York, Charles succeeded him in the law firm he founded and Cleveland, Bissel and Sicard became Bissel, Sicard and Goodyear.

In 1887 he gave up the practice of law to join his brother Frank in the lumber business, forming F.H. & C.W. Goodyear. Charles was an executive of the Buffalo & Susquehanna Railroad, Buffalo & Susquehanna Iron Company, Great Southern Lumber Company and New Orleans Great Northern Railroad. He was also a trustee of the Buffalo Normal School, organizing director of the Pan-American Exposition, Trustee of the Buffalo Historical Society, on the board of The Buffalo Fine Arts Academy, director of Marine Bank and president of the Buffalo Club.

After Charles assumed management of his brother's lumber company, he spent most of his time in Pennsylvania, actively managing the business from the logging of timber to the final processing of lumber. Ella and the Goodyear children spent summers in a frame house overlooking a sawmill in Austin PA. The children rode ponies on the dirt roads and fished in the mountain streams. Ella often said the summers in PA were the happiest times of her life. During the school year, the children were raised in their home at 723 Delaware Avenue in Buffalo.

Ella gave birth to three sons and a daughter

Figure 86 Children of Ella & Charles Goodyear

Charles and Ella had four children, Anson Conger born in 1877, Esther Permelia born in 1881, Charles Jr. born in 1883 and Bradley born in 1885.

Anson Conger Goodyear Sr. married Mary Martha Forman, daughter of George V. Forman, founder of VanderGrift, Forman & Company (which became part of Standard Oil) and Fidelity Trust & Guaranty Company (which merged with Manufacturers & Traders Trust Company to become M&T Bank). Anson, known as Conger, was one of the founders and first president (succeeded by Nelson Rockefeller) of the Museum of Modern Art (MOMA) in NYC. He influenced Seymour Knox to purchase modern art, resulting in the Knox donation that renamed the Buffalo art gallery as the Albright-Knox Art Gallery. Goodyear's estate donated his extensive art collection to the Albright-Knox Art Gallery upon his death.

Esther Permelia Goodyear married Arnold Brooks Watson in the Goodyear Mansion at 888 Delaware Avenue. They had three daughters, Ella, Esther and Ann, that married into the Spaulding, Crane and Bickford families.

Charles Waterhouse Goodyear Jr. married Grace W. Rumsey, daughter of Lawrence Dana Rumsey and Jeannie Cary Rumsey. Charles managed the Goodyear family businesses.

Bradley Goodyear Sr. married Jeanette Bissell, daughter of Arthur Douglas Bissell. He was a member of the 106th Field Artillery, serving in the Mexican Border campaign and in WWI. Bradley fought in the Battle of Verdun and was promoted to a Major, commanding officer of his regiment. A successful lawyer, after WWI he formed a Law Firm with William "Wild Bill" Donovan.

When their children got older, the Goodyears did a lot of traveling and became socially prominent. Charles remained close with Grover Cleveland. After Cleveland married Francis Folsom, Charles and Ella were the first guests they invited to The White House. Later they were overnight guests several times. They also regularly traveled to New York City and annually visited Europe. When the children reached the age when their parents felt that they would be interested in seeing the Old World, they accompanied them to England, continental Europe and the Mediterranean. The Goodyears often spent their summers on Cape Cod at a spacious home in the Wianno Colony in Osterville MA, overlooking the Nantucket Sound.

In 1903, Charles and Ella commissioned architect E.B. Green to build a mansion at 888 Delaware Avenue. The cost of construction for this eventual 64,538 square foot complex was about $500,000, equivalent to over $16 million current dollars. Frank Goodyear's home at 762 Delaware Avenue was a short distance from the Goodyear's new mansion. Before Frank's death in 1907 and the passing of Charles in 1911, it was not unusual for over 25 children and grandchildren to gather for Sunday or holiday dinners.

Ella recovered from a successful cancer operation in 1905 and converted from the Presbyterian to Christian Science religion. After Charles died in 1911, Ella remained at the home for another 29 years and held Christian

Figure 87 Ella in the dress she wore when guest of President Cleveland at the White House

Science classes at 888 Delaware Avenue, often attended by over 100 people. In 1913 she published the book *The Journey of Jesus*, printed in three editions, hosted lavish dinners and in 1919 King Albert, Queen Elizabeth and Price Leopold of Belgium stayed at her home. Ella was referred to as Madam Goodyear in Buffalo social circles. She retained fifteen servants, who she treated like family. When she died at the age of 87 in 1940, six of her servants had a total of 195 years of faithful service to Ella.

Figure 89 Goodyear mansion at 888 Delaware Avenue

The mansion at 888 Delaware Avenue was sold shortly after Ella's death to the Hospital Service Corporation and Western New York Medical Plan, better known as Blue Cross Corporation. It was their offices for ten years and in 1950 the mansion was sold to the Catholic Diocese of Buffalo, who converted it to the all-girl Bishop McMahon High School. In 1988 it was sold to Childrens Hospital, housing the Robert B. Adam Educational Center, until it was sold to become the Oracle Charter School in 2005. It is currently being converted to apartments and a boutique hotel.

Figure 88 Ella in her gardens at 888 Delaware Avenue

ANNA KATHERINE GREEN

Wrote first U.S. Detective Novel

Figure 90 Anna Katherine Green

Anna Katherine Green is considered the mother of the detective novel, author of the first American best-selling novel and she was married to acclaimed furniture designer Charles Rohlfs

She was born in Brooklyn in 1846, the daughter of prominent attorney James Wilson Green and Catherine Ann Whitney Green. The Green family can be traced back to The Plymouth Colony, with William Green being married to Elizabeth Warren, who was descended from the Pilgrim fathers and three barons that signed the Magna Carta. Catherine Ann Whitney Green died when Anna was three years old. Her father then married Grace Hollister of Buffalo and the family moved to Buffalo. She received her B.A. from Ripley Female College in Poultney Vermont in 1866.

Ambitious and educated, Green dreamt of becoming a poet writing romantic verse. Although she managed correspondence with poet Ralph Waldo Emerson, and publication for a few of her pieces, she failed to gain the recognition she aspired to. Not finding success with her poetry, she began secretly working on her first novel, *The Leavenworth Case.* Green published her groundbreaking novel in the soon-to-be genre of detective fiction in 1878. Her debut novel was a quick success and immediately garnered the praise of famous English mystery writer Wilkie Collins. However, it was much more than this one novel that earned Green a place in literary history books. The book was considered the first American detective novel and the first written by a woman. Anna gained knowledge of legal and police matters from her father, who was an attorney. Yale University so highly regarded the novel for its insight into legal matters that the school used the book in law classes to show the perils of relying upon circumstantial evidence.

Green made many contributions to the emerging detective genre throughout her writing career. Most notably, she expanded the concept from a singular detective novel, to a series which follows the same central detective through a variety of situations and circumstances. Green brought detective fiction to a more "cultured" reading public. She frankly and proudly wrote for a popular audience, but her books were published in hardbound editions by respected houses. No longer was the American mystery relegated to dime-novel status; prime ministers, presidents, and honored writers were avowed fans.

Leavenworth Case was the most successful book of Green's career, becoming a bestseller, with over three quarters of a million copies sold. It was made into a play and two movies. In both America and England, she was considered one of the best writers of legally accurate detective fiction. Her fans included Presidents Theodore Roosevelt and Woodrow Wilson, Agatha Christie, along with Sir Arthur Conan Doyle who read the book ten years before he created the Sherlock Holmes character. Doyle made a trip to Buffalo to meet Green when he came to America.

Green is credited with shaping detective fiction into its classic form, and developing the series detective. Her main character was detective Ebenezer Gryce of the New York Metropolitan Police Force, but in three novels he is assisted by the nosy society spinster Amelia Butterworth, the prototype for Miss Marple, Miss Silver and other creations. She also invented the 'girl detective': in the character of Violet Strange, a debutante with a secret life as a sleuth. Many of her plot devices are still used in the whodunit genre. Her ingenious touches made her books inventive and interesting.

Even though Violet is a feminist heroine for her time, Green's status in that regard is more dubious. She opposed women's suffrage, expressing particular abhorrence for the violent demonstrations by suffragettes.

In 1884 Green married actor Charles Rohlfs in Brooklyn. Her father agreed to the marriage only after Rohlfs promised to give up his acting career, which he did with the exception of returning to the stage for a production of Leavenworth Case. Green and Rohlfs moved to Buffalo in 1887, which was Anna's childhood home and where Charles was offered a job. Rohlfs had studied the design and crafting of iron stoves at the Cooper Union institute for the Advancement of Science & Art in NYC. He received a number of patents for stove designs and was hired by stove manufacturers Sherman S. Jewett & Company. The Rohlfs resided at 26 Highland Avenue, and after deciding to permanently stay in Buffalo, built a Craftsman style home at 156 Park Street in the Allentown district.

Figure 91 The Leavenworth book cover

However, Green was a pioneering writer, who continued in her work after marrying in her late 30s and having three children. She and her husband also enjoyed a remarkably happy, egalitarian, and supportive marriage for the time, involving themselves in each other's careers. He even designed a chair for her with an extra-wide right arm for her notebook, which a famous photo shows her sitting in. He listed her as "co-designer" on his work and reviewed her new writing every night. She supported women's right to work and to have more power and independence, but her views became more complicated beyond that. She also opposed class distinctions, marrying a man who was her equal in intelligence and interests, rather than one of her social standings. He was younger than her, too.

Charles Rohlfs began designing and building Arts & Crafts style furniture, in the manner of the Roycrofters, with his work preceding that of Gustav Stickley by ten years. Rohlfs opened his furniture company in Buffalo in 1898. Marshall Field's Department Store in Chicago featured an exhibition of his work in 1900. He participated in the Arts & Crafts Exhibition at the National Arts Club in New York in December 1900, with Stickley and Rohlfs both participating in presenting their work at the Pan-American Exposition in 1901 where Rohlfs assisted as an organizer of the Pan-Am. In 1902 Rohlfs was the only American to participate at the International Exposition of Decorative Art in Turin. This exposure resulted in Rohlfs being invited to become a member of the Royal Society of Arts in London. He also received a commission to provide a set of chairs for Buckingham Palace. His furniture now sells in the four to five-figure range, with some pieces selling for over $100,000.

Green raised three children and during her 45-year career she published 35 novels, 23 short stories and a volume of poetry. She died at the age of 88 on April 11, 1935 in Buffalo. The new queen of detective novels, Agatha Christie, later revealed that she began writing mysteries after having been influenced by the work of Anna Katherine Green.

Figure 92 Green-Rohlfs home on Park Street in Buffalo

SARA HINSON

Buffalo Teacher responsible for Flag Day

The design for the American flag was approved by the Continental Congress on June 14, 1777. The individual responsible for the original design or that made the first flag is thought to be Betsy Ross and it is Buffalo schoolteacher Sara Hinson who is credited as one of the founders of Flag Day.

Figure 93 Sara Hinson

Hinson was born on February 25, 1841, educated in the Buffalo school system and completed her education at private finishing schools. Sara began her teaching career at Buffalo Public Schools #13 and #4, transferring in 1864 to School 31 on Emslie Street, now the Harriot Ross Tubman School at 212 Stanton Street. Hinson remained at this school for 50 years, 30 years as a fourth-grade teacher and 20 years as the school principal.

She felt students were not properly honoring the U.S. flag and on June 14, 1891 she began the tradition of a formal ceremony of saluting and honoring the flag. Other teachers and schools joined the tradition and over the years it began to catch on across the country. President Woodrow Wilson agreed to set aside June 14th as a day of national observance of Flag Day and President Harry Truman signed the legislation making it a national holiday in 1949.

Other teachers also lay claim to beginning the practice of Flag Day. Wisconsin teacher Bernard J. Cigrand states he recognized the observance of Flag Day in 1885. He was a prolific writer, founder of the National Flag Day Organization and traveled across the country campaigning to make Flag Day a national holiday. However, his 1885 claim cannot be documented. Another early Flag Day proponent was George Bloch, who claimed he started the practice in NYC in 1891. Francis Bellamy wrote the Pledge of Allegiance in 1892 and promoted Flag Day in the schools. No one can prove they were first so Flag Day is considered a joint effort of various teachers, with those involved being listed here and others included as founders.

It has been historically claimed that Besty Ross helped design and stitched the first American flag. She was born Elizabeth Griscom in Gloucester City NJ in 1752, served as an apprentice upholster and married John Ross, a member of a prominent Philadelphia family that included one of the signers of the Declaration of Independence. John and Betsy operated an upholstery business and attended Christ Church, with George Washington and 15 other signers of the Declaration of Independence. Her husband was killed during the Revolutionary War in 1775. She sewed flags for the Pennsylvania Navy and supplied the Continental Army with goods such as tents during the war. Ross died in 1836, at the age of 84, but no proof could be found that Ross created the first flag. It was documented that NJ naval flag designer Francis Hopkinson billed the Continental Congress in 1780 for designing the Great Seal and the flag of the USA. He requested a cask of wine for his services but apparently the government never paid up. It was also determined that Philadelphia upholsterer Mary Young Pickersgill was paid to sew a flag during the War of 1812, and it was her flag that flew over Baltimore's Fort McHenry when Francis Scott Key wrote the Star-Spangled Banner.

The grandson of Betsy Ross, William J. Canby spread the story about Ross in an 1870 speech about the history of the American flag to the Historical Society of Pennsylvania. He stated that George Washington came to the shop of the grieving widow, asked Ross to create a flag for the new nation and it was Ross who suggested the five-pointed stars instead of the suggested six-pointed stars.

Use and respect for the U.S. flag exploded after the Civil War and the attack on Fort Sumter. His story was printed in Harper's Weekly and was embraced by the public. The 1893 Charles H. Weisgerber painting *Birth of Our Nation's Flag*, depicting Ross and her daughter sewing the flag under the watchful eyes of George Washington, further enhanced the Ross legend.

Regardless if Ross created the first flag, in the era of debate over expanding women's rights, it offered a vision of a female founder who contributed to the country without losing her femininity. A bridge in Philadelphia over the Delaware River has been named after Ross, she has appeared on postage stamps and the work of this seamstress is nostalgically part of the fabric of American history.

After Sara Hinson resigned as principal of School 31, she was appointed by Mayor Louis Fuhrmann as the first woman to serve on the Board of School Examiners, the predecessor to the Buffalo School Board, serving on the board from 1910 to 1916. She was also the chairwoman of the Teacher's Association Fellowship Committee. In this capacity she would visit the homes of teachers when they were ill. This was during the time when teachers were not allowed to marry, so they often did not have family members to help care for them.

Hinson died on March 20, 1926 at the age of 85. Her grave at Forest Lawn is marked by a flagpole with the American flag flying above her final resting place. The gravestone is engraved "Sara M. Hinson – dedicated teacher who with others gave us Flag Day."

Figure 94 Sara Hinson gravestone

MAUD GORDON HOLMES

Trailblazing Female Manufacturing Executive, Maud Gordon Holmes
Arboretum

Maud was born and received her education in Rochester NY. She moved to Buffalo in 1893 and in 1911 married Edward Britain Holmes, of the E & B Holmes Machinery Company.

E & B Holmes was formed in 1840 by brothers Edward and Britain Holmes as a lumber yard and planing mill in Lancaster NY. In 1852 they moved the company near the waterfront in Buffalo, locating at 59 Chicago Street near Mackinaw.

Edward Britain Holmes was born on February 3, 1872, the son of Edward Holmes. He attended Buffalo public schools and Cornell University, joining the family company upon graduation from college. When his uncle Britain Holmes died in 1905, followed by his father in 1906, Edward Britain Holmes became president of the company.

Figure 95 Maud Gordon Holmes

Edward and Maud resided in the Lakeview area of Hamburg, moving into the city during the winter. Their first Buffalo home was at 56 Linwood Avenue and in 1912 they had a Craftsman home built by contractor Washington B. French, designed by architect Stephen R. Berry at 44 Lincoln Parkway. They later lived at 577 West Ferry, were Edward died of pneumonia at the age of 62 in 1934.

After working with her husband at the company, upon his death Maud assumed his position as president of E. & B. Holmes Machinery Company. This was a time of male dominated leadership in manufacturing & industrial businesses, making Maud one of very few female manufacturing executives.

Maud was not a figurehead president. She was at her desk in the plant at 59 Chicago Street every day leading and transforming the company. She was a very shrewd, resourceful and intelligent woman. When the demand for wood barrels diminished after the utilization of metal and plastic storage technologies, Maud reallocated the expertise of the company from the diminishing cooperage industry to manufacturing a variety of woodworking and specialty machinery. The company held many patents for this machinery.

She successfully ran the company, and since Maud and Edward had no children, she decided to sell it in 1950 to long-time company employees Fred,

Henry, and Martin Elskamp. That ended over 100 years of Holmes family ownership. Subsequently purchased in 1971 by company treasurer Andrew S. Krafchak and his wife Elinor, until the Holmes Company's downsizing and relocation in 2022, it was reputedly the oldest business operating in the same location and under the same name in Buffalo. The complex of buildings was deteriorating and most had to be demolished, except for the former Pattern Building of the Cooperage complex. That building at 55 Chicago Street is now the taproom of the Resurgence Brewing Company. New construction has replaced much of the original Holmes complex.

In addition to running the manufacturing business, Maud was active in gardening. She was a member of the Derby Garden Club and founder of the Garden Center Institute of Buffalo, winning numerous awards for her gardens and her service. Holmes was director of the Garden Center Institute for 27 years and she stimulated interest in horticulture that resulted in many beautification projects in WNY. An example of their contributions was undertaking the Mirror Lake Japanese Garden project in Delaware Park.

An arboretum is a place where trees, shrubs and herbaceous plants are cultivated for scientific and educational purposes. Due to the influence of the Garden Center Institute, an arboretum was established on the campus of Buffalo State College at 1300 Elmwood Avenue in 1962. The following year it was renamed The Maud Gordon Holmes Arboretum at SUNY Buffalo State in her honor. A banquet chaired by the college president Dr. Paul G. Bulger was held in Holmes honor, with her generous donation advancing the arboretum's mission. Funds continue to be raised by the Friends of the Maud Gordon Holmes Arboretum for projects.

Dr. Edna M. Lindemann was a long-term friend of Maud Gordon Holmes and was instrumental in developing the arboretum and for it being named after her friend. In 1966, fueled by Dr. Lindermann's vision and perseverance, the Charles Burchfield Center in Rockwall Hall at Buffalo State College was dedicated. Her work with college president Dr. Bulger to establish the Charles Burchfield Center resulted in Lindermann being named curator of the center and its director in 1974. She was responsible for the creation of the Maud Gordon Holmes Arboretum and Charles Burchfield Center.

Maud Gordon Holmes died in 1964. She was one of the first female presidents of a manufacturing company and her contributions to gardening live on at the Maud Gordon Holmes Arboretum.

Figure 96 Dr. Lindemann with Charles Burchfield
Photo courtesy Suny Buffalo State Archives

KATHERINE PRATT HORTON

Socialite who donated home as DAR Buffalo Chapter Headquarters

Figure 97 Katherine Pratt Horton

K atherine Pratt Horton can trace her ancestry back to family members that accompanied William the Conqueror at the Battle of Hastings in 1066. The first Pratt to settle in America was John Pratt, one of the original settlers of Hartford Connecticut in 1639. Her great grandfather, Captain Samuel Pratt enlisted in the Continental Army on July 10, 1775, shortly after the outbreak of the American Revolution and served two enlistments.

In 1804 Captain Pratt relocated his family to Buffalo, arriving in the first two-wheel coach brought to the city. He built a log home on the Terrace and opened his store on the north side of Exchange Street where he traded with both whites and Indians. They selected Inner Lot #1 at the corner of Main and Exchange Streets as their homestead. This lot was on the high bank of the Terrace and extended to Little Buffalo Creek, which was subsequently buried. Upon the lot they built the first two- and one-half story frame house in Buffalo. Pratt's store was built next to the house on the south side of Exchange. The home was called The Mansion and it later became the site of the Mansion House, early Buffalo's premier hotel and meeting place. Captain Pratt died in 1812 and is one of twenty-five Revolutionary War veterans buried at Forest Lawn Cemetery.

Katherine was born in 1848, the eldest child of Pascal Paoli Pratt and Phebe Lorenz. Pascal worked with his brother Samuel Fletcher Pratt at Pratt & Company which began as a small retail store and became one of the largest wholesale hardware businesses with accounts in several states and extending beyond the Mississippi River. In 1848 Pascal, his brother Samuel, and William Letchworth formed Pratt & Letchworth, a manufacturer of malleable steel and iron castings that employed almost 2,000 people at their Black Rock plant. A supporter of Buffalo influencing businesses to relocate to the area, in 1856 with Bronson Case Rumsey, he formed Manufacturers & Traders Bank to make loans and provide banking services for new Buffalo factories and warehouses.

In 1869 Katherine married successful businessman John Miller Horton. They lived in France for ten years and traveled extensively. Upon returning to Buffalo, being the eldest daughter of Pascal Paoli Pratt, she shared her father's ambitions for the welfare of Buffalo and continued his work, becoming one of the most prominent benefactors in the social life and civic welfare of the city of Buffalo. She was considered the "Grand Dame" of Buffalo Society for the next 50 years.

She organized the Buffalo Chapter of the Daughters of the American Revolution in 1892. The Buffalo Chapter became the largest in New York State, second largest in the country and Buffalo hosted the organization's 1898 New York State convention. As Buffalo Chapter regent, Horton was a prominent figure at the national congress of the DAR in Washington. As vice-president of the Niagara Frontier Landmarks Association, Horton assisted in erecting tablets and monuments at important historic sites in the Niagara Frontier.

When the Pan-American Exposition was held in Buffalo in 1901, Horton was named a member of the Board of Women Governors and the chairman of the Ceremonies and Entertainment Committee. She is included in the last formal photograph of President McKinley and was with him when he was shot at the Temple of Music at the Pan-Am.

Figure 98 Katherine Pratt Horton
Photo courtesy DAR Buffalo Suny Buffalo

Figure 99 Horton in President McKinley's last formal
portrait at Pan-Am
Photo PD

Horton continued to represent Buffalo at other national events. She was the NYS commissioner at the Charleston Exposition in 1902 and National Conference of the DAR in Washington in 1903. Horton served on the Board of Lady Managers at the St. Louis Exposition in 1904, was Buffalo representative at the Panama-Pacific Exposition in 1915, presented flowers to the King and Queen of Belgium when they visited Buffalo after WWI and was chairman of the Women's Committee for the Tercentenary Celebration of the Landing of the Pilgrims in 1920. She also spoke at the Peace Conferences at Stockholm and Geneva, and to European parliaments.

In 1904 she organized the Niagara Frontier Buffalo Chapter, National Society United States Daughters of 1812 and in 1905 she founded the Buffalo Federation of Women's Clubs. Horton was a member of so many organizations that a complete listing would fill an entire page of this book.

Figure 100 DAR Buffalo Clubhouse
Photo credit Rick Falkowski

John Horton died in 1902 and Katherine died in 1931 at the age of 83. Since they did not have any children, she left the bulk of her estate to her sister Annie P. Chittenden and Frank B. Steele of the DAR in Washington. Horton bequeathed her 477 Delaware Avenue home and all of its furnishings to be the Daughters of the American Revolution Buffalo headquarters. She included $20,000 in her will to maintain the property. The townhouse retains the appearance of a turn of the century home, remains the Buffalo DAR headquarters and was renamed the Katherine Pratt Horton Buffalo Chapter, National Society Daughters of the American Revolution.

MARY JEMISON

White Women of the Genesee – Seneca Negotiator and Translator

W hile on the ship Mary and William, sailing from Ireland to Philadelphia in 1743, Mary Jemison was born to Thomas and Jane Erwin Jemison. Mary orally recalled the events of her life, recorded by James Seaver and published in 1824 as *A Narrative of the Life and Times of Mary Jemison*. In it she describes her capture by Indians at the age of 12, her adoption by a Seneca family and her life with the Native Americans.

The Jemison family settled in Philadelphia for a brief period until moving to the western frontier settlements of Pennsylvania, at that time the vicinity of Marsh Creek State Park. The family squatted on land under the authority of the Iroquois Confederacy about ten miles west of present-day Gettysburg. At the start of the French & Indian War (1754-1763) the area of their farm was near the hostilities.

Figure 101 Mary Jemison 1892
Photo PD

In the summer of 1755, the Jemison farm was attacked by four Frenchmen and six Shawnee Indians. Everyone in the household and people visiting were taken prisoner, except for Mary's two oldest brothers who were working in a barn away from the house. They later escaped to their grandfather's home in Virginia. After plundering the home of its goods and provisions, the attackers marched their captives through the woods to avoid detection by area militia. Mary and a little boy that was at the Jemison house were separated from the group and taken to a different camp. The next day they found all other Jemison family members and their houseguests had been killed and scalped.

Figure 102 1920 Photo of the statue of Mary Jemison in PA

Mary was taken to Fort Duquesne (now Pittsburgh) and given to two Seneca women, who lost their brother in wars against the American Colonists /English. They accepted Mary as compensation for their loss, taking her to their village where she was adopted by the two Seneca and considered their sister. She was given the name of Dehgewanus, translated as pretty girl, a handsome girl, or a pleasant, good thing. That is the name by which she was called by the Seneca for the rest of her life.

She married Sheninjee, a member of the Delaware tribe. They were married for three years, and Mary bore a son Thomas Jemison, who was born four and a half years after she was captured. During most of this time Mary was living in western Pennsylvania and in Ohio. She was persuaded by her husband to move to the home of the two sisters who adopted her in his native homeland, a large Seneca settlement named Genishau on the Genesee River in what was called Little Beard's Town. When in Genishau (the Gardeau Reservation) a Dutch agent tried to take her to Fort Niagara to collect a bounty for returning prisoners who were taken during the war, but Mary evaded him and hid to remain with the Seneca. Three years after her first husbands' death, in 1765 she married a Seneca named Hiakatoo, with whom she had six children.

During the American Revolution the Seneca sided with the British and George Washington sent an army of 5,000 troops under General Sullivan to destroy the Seneca's will and ability to fight by burning down their towns and farmlands. They specifically targeted Little Beard's Town and Mary with her children fled south for safety.

After the Revolution, for almost twenty years quiet and peaceful times prevailed in Western and Central New York, until a different army, made up of land speculators and pioneers, invaded the area. In 1797 a council was held near the present-day town of Geneseo. All the Seneca leaders and the women who would advise them convened at the summit. Mary was one of the translators at the council, along with Jasper Parish and Horatio Jones. The negotiations were long and difficult, with few pleased with the resulting treaty. In return for twelve reservations and payments, most of the Seneca homeland was turned over for sale to settlers.

Jemison was able to get some lands set aside for her family on the reservation where they resided. She owned one of the largest cattle herds in the region and the tribal grant made her one of the largest landowners. Her title to the land was confirmed by New York State in 1817, the same year Jemison was naturalized.

However, the times were difficult for the Jemisons. Three of Dehgewanus' sons were murdered between 1811 and 1817. People respected the Old White Woman of the Genesee and came to her for advice and support. In 1823 they encouraged a doctor and writer to interview her at Whaley's Tavern, resulting in her oral autobiography. Also in 1823, the Seneca gave up Gardeau Reservation, reserving two square miles for Dehgewanus' farm where she lived until 1831.

In 1831 Jemison sold the remainder of the land she was granted on the Gardeau Reservations and purchased a farm on the Buffalo Creek Reservation where the Seneca had settled five years earlier. A revered member of the Seneca Nation, she passed her days in peace and quietness, embracing the Christian religion. She died on Buffalo Creek Reservation at the age of 90 on September 19, 1833.

Jemison's remains were buried in the Indian Burial Ground at Buffum Street and Fields Avenue off Seneca Street and near Indian Church Road. In the Buffalo Creek Treaty of 1842, the reservation and cemetery were eliminated. Settlers wanted to remove the remains, especially those of Red Jacket and Mary Jemison but John D. Larkin, the owner of the Larkin Company and husband of Hannah Frances Hubbard who taught at the Indian Mission

Figure 103 Mary Jemison statue by Henry Kirke Bush-Brown in Letchworth State Park

House, purchased the cemetery, and donated it to the city of Buffalo to be utilized as a park. Red Jacket was reburied in Forest Lawn Cemetery. The descendants of Mary Jemison approached businessman William Pryor Letchworth, who arranged for her to be reburied in 1874 on his Glen Iris Estate, later part of Letchworth State Park, not far from her Gardeau Flats home.

Her heirs changed the spelling of their name from Jemison to Jimerson. When the Seneca were relocated during the building of the Kinzua Dam, they founded Jimersontown adjacent to the city of Salamanca. It is now one of the two capitals of the Seneca Nation.

BEVERLY JOHNSON

First Black Model on cover of Vogue Magazine

Figure 104 Beverly Johnson

Model, actress and businesswomen Beverly Johnson was the first Black woman on the cover of American Vogue magazine in August 1974. She later appeared in films, television and videos, along with becoming a successful owner of her own fashion and beauty products companies.

Johnson was born in Buffalo on October 13, 1952. Her father was a laborer at a steel plant and electrician, while her mother Gloria was a nurse and surgical technician. Beverly and her younger sister grew up in the Johnson home on Northland Avenue and went to St. Luke AME Zion Church. She attended School 74 (now Hamlin Park Academy) and graduated from Bennett High School. Academics were important in the Johnson family. The first time Beverly walked across a stage in front of a crowd of people was not as a model, it was at a Bennett High School Honor Roll presentation.

During high school Beverly worked at the Buffalo YMCA and taught swimming. She claims that when she returns to Buffalo more people know her for teaching them to swim, than recognize her as a model. Beverly won a number of swimming championships and nearly made the U.S. national team in the 100-yard freestyle for the 1968 Summer Olympics in Mexico City.

Johnson received a full scholarship to Northeastern University in Boston Massachusetts where she studied criminal justice and intended to become a lawyer. With the advice and encouragement of fellow students, after her freshman year she started working as a model. In 1971 she moved to NYC. After being rejected by several agencies, she went to Glamour magazine where she was hired for a cover shoot. The issue with Beverly on the cover set sales records but the 135 pound 5'9" Johnson was told she had to lose weight. By not eating her weight went down as low as 103 pounds, which resulted in her becoming anorexic and bulimic.

Glamour magazine featured Johnson on five subsequent covers over the next two years. She became an in-demand magazine model, highlighted when she was selected as the first Black female model to appear on the cover of Vogue in August 1974, another record selling issue. In 1975 she was on the cover for the French edition of Elle. During her career Johnson has appeared on over 500 magazine covers, including leading magazines like Cosmopolitan and Essence. Beverly was signed to be represented by Eileen Ford of Ford Models and later by Wilhelmina Models. She was featured in print advertising, television commercials and became a runway model for Halston, Calvin Klein and other designers. Johnson was definitely one of the top fashion models in the world.

Figure 105 Beverly in 1969 Beacon - Bennett High School yearbook

With her modeling career at its height Johnson decided to move into acting, studying with well-known acting teacher Lee Strasberg. She began acting in the 1970s but began receiving more parts in the 1990s. Movie credits include *The Meteor Man, How to Be a Player, Crossroads and Good Deeds*. She was in television movies and on television shows like *Emergency, Law & Order, Martin, Lois & Clark, 3rd Rock from the Sun* and *She's Got the Look*. Beverly also found time to appear in music videos by Michael Jackson and Bobby Brown.

Early in her career Beverly realized there was a lack of hair products, skin products and make up for Black women. She published several self-care books and assisted in creating product lines. Johnson launched lines of eyewear/glasses, wigs, hair and skin care to compliment all skin colors and with Target premiered the Beverly Johnson Luxurious Brand of hair and skin care products. In 2022 she received the Model Pioneer Award at the Women's Entrepreneurship Day Summit at the United Nations.

However, during her career she experienced racism. After a photo shoot at a five-star hotel they drained the pool because Beverly was in the water. While driving her white Mercedes in West Hollywood, the police stopped her to ask whose car she was driving. Tennis champion, Arthur Ashe, explained racial discrimination that he experienced, and thereafter Johnson always spoke up for oppressed people.

In 1971 Johnson married real estate agent Billy Potter, who she divorced in 1974. She married businessman and music producer Danny Sims. Their daughter Anansa was born on December 17, 1978 in NYC, but they divorced in 1979. At the age of 13 Anansa was signed to Wilhelmina Model Agency, following in her mother's footsteps.

Beverly Johnson has experienced a successful career in modeling, acting and starting her own businesses, but she has not forgotten her hometown. She still makes trips to Buffalo to visit friends and relatives. Plus, Beverly remains a major Buffalo Bills fan.

DORIS JONES

One of the first women in Buffalo television

Figure 106 Doris Jones in her first Channel 4
TV commercial in late 1940s
Photo courtesy Doris Jones

Doris was a pioneer in Buffalo television. She started out as a model on Channel 4 while still in high school, was the first woman on Channel 7 in 1959 and was the first weathercaster and full-time female staff announcer on Channel 2 in 1965. Doris also did commercials for all area stations and owned the Ski Rack.

She was born on October 27, 1932 in South Buffalo and her parents moved to Winspear Avenue near the UB South Campus before she started elementary school at Buffalo Public School 80. The principal at the elementary school recommended she enter speaking contests. When it was time to attend secondary school, she considered going to Mount St. Joseph's High School but decided to attend Amherst High School. Since she lived a block over the city line, she had to pay a tuition to attend the suburban school. The first-year tuition was $25, which increased to $125 for her sophomore year.

At Amherst High School she was a cheerleader and the principal suggested Doris had the potential to be a model. She became a member of the Teen Board and became a model for AM&A's and Hengerer's, doing events at the stores, the Tea Room, Statler Hotel and at special events. Modeling did not include speaking, so Doris wanted to expand her potential and took speech lessons at Studio Arena Theater. While still in high school, she took two buses across the city to attend Studio Arena classes at night after school. Her modeling career on television also began while she was still in high school.

Since her father passed away between Doris' freshmen and sophomore years of high school, she had to work for a year to save money to attend college. She got a job with the Telephone Company in the morning until noon and had the afternoons off to work as a model. At 7:00 at night she returned and worked until 10:00. After work the telephone company drove home all the female workers.

After graduating from high school in 1950 and working for a year, she attended Michigan State University. While home from college she went to see a friend who was modeling at Hengerer's. She told Doris that Berger's was looking for models. Doris was offered a job and decided not to return to Michigan State. Modeling at Berger's extended to television and at one time Jones was appearing in a variety of 15 different commercials per week. She explained that in the 1950s, television commercials were not expensive and every small store had TV spots.

Figure 107 Doris with her children at 90th birthday party in 2022
Photo courtesy Doris Jones

Doris gained a reputation as a fashion model and TV demonstrator. In 1957 she had a radio show on WHLD where she provided fashion and household hints, along with playing good music. In 1958 she was told WKBW-TV Channel 7 was auditioning women for a television show. At the audition they filmed her sitting on a stool in the studio and asked her to talk about what she would do on a TV show if a position was offered. She talked for over 40 minutes and when she was done the producer offered her the job, telling her everything she talked about doing would be included in the show.

Channel 7 signed on the air in 1958 and Jones was the fem-cee of *For the Ladies*, a 30-minute TV program that premiered in 1959. The show included fashion news, singing, dancing and interviews. A highlight was an interview with baseball great Jackie Robinson. The station had sports announcer, Stan Baron, assist her but Robinson was impressed with Doris' interview, writing about her in his New York Post newspaper column.

Figure 108 Doris with Stan Barron & Frank Robinson on Channel 7 in 1959

In 1953 Doris married Don Sherris, a buyer for Hengerer's. They had four children - Arieh (Scott) Sherris (a professor at Texas A&M), Dr. David Sherris (a facial plastic surgeon), Dr. Kirk D. Sherris (a podiatrist foot surgeon) and Tracy Sherris Makin (a Williamsville school teacher). In 1961 they opened The Ski Rack on Main Street in Williamsville. In addition to the suburban store, they operated an outlet at Glenwood Acres. They ran the stores with Al and Helen Weber. When Doris returned to television in 1965, Don continued to operate the store with the Webers, who continued to own the Ski Rack stores.

Figure 109 Weathercaster Doris Jones on Channel 2 in 1967

Photo courtesy Doris Jones

In 1965 Doris was hired as the weather "gal" at Channel 2. Union rules dictated that she become a full-time staff announcer, making her the first woman in that role in Buffalo. At WGR-TV she also anchored the local news broadcasts on the Today Show, emceed a Fantasy Island Kids Show, gave ski and boating reports and hosted local TV's first call in game show called Pay Cards. To personalize the weather set, Doris brought in new flowers every day. In addition, she flew in a helicopter for ski and other reports, claiming no men wanted to go up in the helicopter.

To become the weather announcer Doris received two weeks of meteorological training at the Buffalo Airport, quite a difference from the current four-year degree in meteorology. The forecast was received from the national weather ticker tape and there were no scripts or teleprompters. The weather details were smiley face clouds and other weather symbols that Doris pasted on a board (no green screens for digital images). She recalled a holiday when she thought it was a Sunday but realized it was a Monday workday. Doris was at the beach, in her bathing suit, and tried to call in sick. Her boss told her to hurry up and get into the studio. They quickly drove from Grand Island to Barton Street. Doris changed her clothes and did not have the opportunity to get the ticker tape weather forecast. She got on the set just in time and made up the forecast. After finishing the weather, her boss thanked her for getting to work and told her that was a great forecast. He did not know she made up the weather.

Figure 110 Irv Weinstein inducts Jones into Broadcasting HOF in 1999

Photo courtesy Doris Jones

She was on the air at Channel 2 from 1965 to 1971. In 1969 she married her second husband Frank Reppenhagen and had two more children - Frank Reppenhagen (aka Repp) and Jennifer Kate Reppenhagen (who passed away at an early age). In 2022 she celebrated her 90th birthday at a party her children gave her at the Saturn Club, with a performance by the band Grosh.

Doris Jones was inducted into the Buffalo Broadcasting Hall of Fame in 1999, introduced by her early WBKW station mate – Irv Weinstein.

MARY SEATON KLEINHANS

Music Patron who donated estate to build modern music hall

E dward Kleinhans was managing a store in Louisville Kentucky during the 1890s, when he met accomplished vocalist and pianist Mary Seaton Barret. She was born in Jefferson, Montgomery County, Kentucky on September 13, 1876 to Clarence and Carrie Seaton. After their marriage, Edward and Mary Seaton Kleinhans relocated to Buffalo.

Edward began working in the clothing store business in Grand Rapids Michigan at the age of 16 in 1880. He moved to Louisville Kentucky to work with his brother Horace, who had established one of the largest men's clothing stores in the south. After learning the business from his brother, Edward accepted a position as a manager of a store in Chicago and eventually convinced his brother of the retail opportunities in the north. Together they opened a store in Buffalo at 259 Main Street in 1893.

Figure 111 Mary Seaton Kleinhans

Their store became known for their upscale merchandise and quickly outgrew their first location. They became one of the first tenants of the Brisbane Building when it opened in 1896. Kleinhans occupied the basement and half of the first and second floors. Another tenant on the first floor was S.H. Knox, owned by Buffalo's Seymour Knox, who later merged his stores with his cousin to form F.W. Woolworth.

When Mary Seaton Kleinhans moved to Buffalo in 1901, the Pan-American Exposition was taking place in the city. With Mary's musical background, she relished the variety of entertainment being offered at the Pan-Am in her newly adopted city. With the prominence of Edward's store, he and Mary became leading citizens of Buffalo and patrons of the arts, often attending concerts at the Elmwood Music Hall.

The Elmwood Music Hall was designed as the 74th New York National Guard Armory in 1886 by female architect Louise Blanchard Bethune. New York State began building larger armories and in 1899 the 74th Regiment moved to the commodious Connecticut Street Armory. Just 13 years after it was built, the armory became vacant.

Buffalo did not have a convention hall and the city negotiated with New York State to obtain the former armory. Buffalo's Music Hall on Main and Edward had been sold as a commercial theater for use by music impresarios Louis W. Gay, Mai Davis Smith, Marian de Forest and Zorah B. Berry who did not have a venue for their concerts. In 1900 the city received ownership of the armory building and after $8,000 for improvements the building that originally cost $54,000 was converted to the new City Convention Center. With additional lighting, emergency exits, a stage and folding chairs, it seated 2,700 people and another 350 people in the balcony.

In addition to hosting sporting events, the City Convention Center hosted concerts by the Pittsburgh Orchestra, New York Philharmonic, Philadelphia Symphony, Cincinnati Symphony and Boston Symphony. Performers appearing the hall included well-known musical artists Pablo Casals, Sergey Prokofiev and conductors Victor Herbert, Camilli Saint Saens, along with Buffalo area future Metropolitan Opera stars Nina Morgana, Rose Bampton and Helen Oelheim. J.N. Adams purchased the organ from the Temple of Music at the Pan-American Exposition and had it installed at the hall where they continued the Pan-Am tradition of free Sunday organ concerts.

The hall was not well heated and did not have comfortable seating, but the acoustics delighted soloists whose voices carried perfectly without effort. However, the screeching of trolley cars around the curve at Elmwood and Virginia sometimes overpowered the music.

When the 65th New York State National Guard moved to the new Masten Armory in 1907, they gave the Broadway Armory at 201 Broadway to the city of Buffalo. After various improvements, it reopened in 1913 as the Broadway Auditorium and was also called the new Convention Center. It remained a concert and primarily a sports arena until Memorial Auditorium opened in 1940. It then became the Broadway Garage or Broadway Barn and was used for the department of public works storage, specifically for snowplows and salt storage. To avoid confusion between the Broadway and Elmwood Convention Centers, the building at Elmwood and Virginia was renamed the Elmwood Music Hall.

The Kleinhans were regular attendees of concerts at the Elmwood Music Hall. Their shared love of music took them to great music halls and performances worldwide. When they came back to Buffalo, at concerts you experienced cold drafts while sitting on folding chairs in a repurposed army drill shed. They personally experienced the problems with the building and wanted the people of Buffalo to have the best possible musical experience, in a world class music hall. Mary Seaton and Edward also realized the building would eventually have to be replaced and the last concert at the Elmwood Music Hall was Nelson Eddy on February 25. 1938.

Mary Seaton and Edward Kleinhans resided at the Hotel Lenox, Westbrook Apartments, 900 Delaware Avenue and 44 Middlesex Road. Edward died on February 2, 1934 and Mary followed less than three months later on April 29, 1934.

Figure 112 Kleinhans Music Hall under construction

They had no children and Edward's will stipulated that the proceeds of his estate be used for the building of a music hall as a memorial to his wife and mother. Mary's will disclosed that she desired the terms of her husband's will to be carried out.

The Kleinhans' estate was left to the Buffalo Foundation and it asked them to build a "suitable music hall for the people of Buffalo," This gave the Foundation the authority to proceed in planning, designing and constructing the new music hall. They leveraged $750,000 from the Kleinhans estate to obtain an additional $583,000 from the "New Deal" federal agency Public Works Administration. The PWA would only grant the funding if a new nonprofit corporation Kleinhans Music Hall Inc. was formed. That corporation was to be governed by a board of directors, the majority of whom must be city of Buffalo officials. George Rand and attorney Edward Letchworth led the committee to find a location for the building.

Several different locations and architects were considered for the music hall. Construction of the building in Downtown Buffalo was considered too expensive and a waterfront location was thought to be too cold. The East Side and West Side offered locations. Chauncey Hamlin obtained permission to build a museum of science in Humboldt Park (now Martin Luther King Park) and hired architect E.B. Green to design a music hall as an attachment to the science museum. Some people suggested building it in the former location of the Elmwood Music Hall at Elmwood and Virginia. A location was proposed near the Rose Garden in Delaware Park. A public poll favored the East Side location. However, the site of the Truman Avery mansion on The Circle, at Richmond and North Street, was offered to the city by family heir Lavinia Mitchell for $50,000. The Circle was originally designed by Frederick Law Olmsted and Calvert Vaux as part of their Buffalo Parks plan, and it was across from First Presbyterian Church. Its historic significance sealed approval of the Circle location and the circle was subsequently renamed Symphony Circle in 1958.

To oversee the planning phase, the Buffalo Foundation formed a Music Hall Committee headed by Edward Letchworth, with Franklyn Kidd, Sara Kerr and Esther Link being members. They hired the architectural firm of Franklyn and

William Kidd, but the committee wanted a modern design for the building and the Kidds specialized in more traditional designs. It was decided they needed a consulting architect.

Letchworth and Kidd met with international style architects Eliel and Eero Saarinen. They did not accept the offer to be consulting architects but agreed to be hired as design architects. Since the Committee could not afford to pay two design architects, Letchworth drafted a letter to decline their offer. Committee member Esther L. Link wrote a letter to all directors arguing that Saarinen should be hired as design architect with the Kidds because Saarinen would design a beautiful monument for Buffalo worthy of national renown. She added that the Committee should not worry about costs as her family would donate $10,000 to pay for Saarinen's work. Esther's letter changed the minds of the Directors as they offered Eliel and Eero $5,000 to submit a design that the Committee would pay. Now there would be two models for the new hall, one traditional and one contemporary.

When Esther L. Link (founder of Pitt Petri gift stores with her sister and brother-in-law, Elisabeth and Pitt Petri) was named director of the Kleinhans Music Hall project, she thought the Kidd design was a disaster and encouraged approval of architects Eliel and Eero Saarinen's design. After both models were presented, a vote was taken and members affiliated with the Kleinhans project were all in favor of the Saarinen contemporary design, while members from the City of Buffalo were in favor of the Kidd traditional design. Link and Letchworth continued to lobby for the modern design and eventually one member of the city of Buffalo group abstained. Saarinen's design of the curvilinear and sweeping lines, resembling the shape of a violin or cello, mirrored in the reflecting pools, won the day.

Kleinhans Music Hall opened on October 12, 1940 and today remains the home of the Buffalo Philharmonic Orchestra. The large auditorium is considered one of the best acoustically designed concert halls in the U.S. The smaller, more intimate concert hall is named the Mary Seaton Room. The building became a pilgrimage for architects and acoustical engineers from around the world.

If it were not for the generosity of the estate of Mary Seaton Kleinhans and the design direction of Esther L. Link (Emig), Buffalo would not be graced with Kleinhans Music Hall, designated a national historic landmark in 1989.

Figure 113 Kleinhans Music Hall

GRACE MILLARD KNOX

Knox Mansion, UB Benefactor, Philanthropist

Figure 114 Grace Millard Knox
Photo credit UB

Grace Millard Knox was the matriarch of the Knox family in Buffalo, NY. After the death of her husband Seymour Knox, one of the founders of F.W. Woolworth Corp., she directed and completed the design and construction of their new mansion at 806 Delaware Avenue (number 800 today).

Grace was born in Port Chester, NY in Westchester County on April 14, 1862 to Charles Abram Millard and Sarah Amelia Avery Millard. Her mother was a member of the Groton Avery Clan, an American Colonies family dating from the 17th century. Her ancestor, Captain James Avery, was one of the founders of Groton, Connecticut. The Millard family lived in Detroit and in 1890 Grace came to Buffalo for a visit with a group of friends from Detroit. One of her friends knew Seymour Knox, who entertained the group while they were in Buffalo.

"Especially attracted to Grace Millard, he saw her frequently during her stay here and it wasn't long after the visit that they were married in Detroit and returned here to make their home." --- Buffalo Evening News, August 31, 1936.

Seymour Horace Knox (1864-1915) was known as a "Five and Ten Pioneer". He was a first cousin and business partner of F.W. Woolworth. In 1884, they started a joint venture, opening a Woolworth and Knox Five and Ten Cent Store in Reading, PA. In 1888, Seymour opened his first Buffalo store. Within a year, he was able to buy out his cousin's interest. He established S.H. Knox & Company in 1889. By 1912, he operated 98 stores in the U.S. and 13 in Canada. In 1911, Woolworth had suggested that the rivals merge to form the largest store chain in the world. Knox's health was failing and the merger would allow him to cash out his interests. When F.W. Woolworth & Co. was listed on Wall Street in January 1912, the offer was oversubscribed. The Knox stores were valued at $12 million ($380 million today).

Seymour Knox used some of his wealth to fund the Knox Memorial Central School Building in Russell, NY, his birthplace. It was inaugurated July 30, 1913 and retained its name until a district merger in 1986. Their yearbook was called "The Seymour". He also invested in several high-profile initiatives to develop enterprise and civic pride in Buffalo. To this day he is celebrated as one of Buffalo's great pioneers and benefactors. When he died in May 1915 at age 54, all 700 stores in the U.S. and Canada chose to close their doors for the funeral. Frank Woolworth gave the eulogy, calling his cousin, partner, and long-time friend, "a prince among men."

After selling their shares of S.H. Knox in 1912 to Woolworth, Seymour and Grace began planning a move down the avenue and creating a grander home appropriate to their prominence in the community. Unfortunately, Mr. Knox died in May 1915 before all the plans were completed.

The Knox family homes were designed by significant architects. They lived at 414 Porter Avenue (designed by Milton Beebe), 467 Linwood Avenue (designed by Edgar E. Joralemon), and built a home at 1045 Delaware Avenue (1035 today) where they lived until 1918. Grace was not particularly happy with their home at 1045 Delaware as she thought it was too dark.

Grace announced in 1915 that she was going to move forward with building the $1 million home. Grace hired New York City architect C. P. H. Gilbert to design a new residence to replace an older Italianate house that stood on the property. The resulting structure was an extravagant stone mansion, 48,000 square feet, built over the course of three years and completed in 1918. The house was designed in the French Renaissance style with a symmetrical façade and a U-shaped floor plan. Cass Gilbert was a prominent architect of many homes on NYC's Fifth Avenue and grand mansions in Newport, Rhode Island. This magnificent home had 25 rooms, not including kitchens, pantries, bathrooms, maintenance quarters and cloakrooms. The house was built next door to the Clement mansion, now home to the Buffalo Philharmonic Orchestra and the Red Cross Headquarters. Her son Seymour H. Knox II, and daughters Marjorie and Dorothy lived with Grace in the mansion. It was ironic that two of the largest mansions on Millionaires Row were lived in by widows of affluent husbands who did not live long enough to enjoy the homes their wealth and success had created.

Figure 115 Knox Mansion at 800 Delaware Avenue
Photo credit Rick Falkowski

At the same time the Knoxes were planning their new home, the Buffalo Catholic Diocese was planning for a new cathedral, adjacent to Blessed Sacrament Church, to be built at the northeast corner of West Utica and Delaware. Over twenty years, the Diocese purchased residential properties at this corner from the Newman, Ralph, Hamlin, Burdict families, and lastly the Knox family. In 1911, the existing 4,000-ton Blessed Sacrament Church was moved back 200 feet to allow more room for the cathedral. St. Joseph's New Cathedral was then constructed between 1912 and 1915.

The Knox family continued to own 1035 Delaware until 1922. They had rented the house until selling it to the Diocese for use as the official residence of the Bishop and later as a residence for the priests.

When Seymour II married in 1924, Grace built him a home at 57 Oakland Place, directly behind the Delaware home. Elaborate gardens were shared between the houses. The Delaware Avenue home was so large that during the winter it required one to two tons of coal a day to heat it.

In 1916, Grace Millard Knox provided the first gift to establish an endowment fund at the University of Buffalo (UB). The gift, made in memory of her husband, was named the Seymour H. Knox Fund. The original gift of $250,000 (equivalent to $7 million today) established UB's first College of Arts and Sciences in Townsend Hall on Niagara Street in downtown Buffalo. Mrs. Knox wrote to the University at that time: "We can think of no finer purposes in creating a memorial in memory of Mr. Knox than be permitted to assist in the upbuilding and development of an institution of learning such as the City of Buffalo should possess." This inaugurated generations of the Knox family supporting UB.

On June 6, 1919, the Junior League of Buffalo was formed at the Knox mansion during their first meeting of the League. The meeting was scheduled by Grace and took place in the living room of the mansion. As a tribute to her leadership and hospitality, the mansion was the 2021 Junior League Decorators Show House. It was the 21st Biennial Decorators Show House. The previous 20 events organized by the volunteers at the Junior League have raised $4.4 million through 2019 to benefit non-profits in western New York.

In addition to the 800 Delaware home, the Knox family had a country estate in East Aurora as well as a winter home in Aiken, S.C. In East Aurora, Seymour Knox established the farmland as a place for raising and training polo horses. He named the property "Ess Kay Farms" after the initials of his first and last names. Today the 633-acre property is known as Knox Farm State Park.

Several homes were built on the farm property by the next generation of Knoxes.

In 1915, the Knox's daughter Dorothy married Frank Goodyear Jr. In 1916, they built the main house at "the farm". The two story 14,000 square foot Colonial Revival style home was designed by architects Frank Bell Meade and James Montgomery Hamilton in a simple classic design which exudes restrained elegance.

The first-floor rooms offer unparalleled grace and charm. It was a beautiful setting for the 2013 Junior League Show House.

Dorothy sold this house to her younger brother, Seymour II, in 1929 when the Goodyears decided to build a grander home at what is now Crag Burn Country Club on North Davis Road in East Aurora.

In 1927, Marjorie Knox Campbell built "Orchard House", an elegant brick country estate with a hunting lodge, stable, caretakers' cottage, swimming pool, tennis court and extensive gardens designed by renowned landscape designer Ellen Biddle Shipman. Shipman also designed gardens at many homes and estates in western New York and across the country.

Figure 116 Grace in the gardens behind 800 Delaware

Grace Millard Knox died at the age of 74 on August 30, 1934. Her youngest daughter Marjorie and her family continued living at 800 Delaware until 1969. They always called it "806" when sharing fond memories. It became "800" under new owners. The Montefiore Club, a private men's club was first. In 1978, the property was purchased by Computer Task Group (CTG) to serve as their headquarters. In 2020, the building was sold to Cellino Law for $2.475 million, and is headquarters for the firm.

As stated in the Obituaries of Mrs. Knox in 1936 in the Buffalo News and the Courier Express, "Travel was balm for Mrs. Knox after the death of her husband and she was heard to remark recently, "If I were 45 today, there would not be a place in the world that I wouldn't see." She has motored all over Europe, traveled in the Orient and over this continent. She has a particular fondness for Pasadena, Cal. Her charities were extensive but she preferred to keep them quiet."

In 1939, the Knox family donated funds to the Buffalo Fine Arts Academy (also known at that time as the Albright Art Gallery) to establish a room of contemporary art in memory of Grace Millard Knox. The Gallery used these funds to purchase works by Picasso, Matisse, Mir, Mondrian, Beckmann, and Braque. Seymour Knox II, also known as "Shorty", is well remembered for his leadership, generosity, and active engagement with the Gallery and the art world. He credited his interest in art to his parents Grace Millard and Seymour Knox I, who were both active in the Buffalo Fine Arts Academy and their names became included in the Albright Knox Art Gallery.

BELVA LOCKWOOD

Pioneering Female Attorney and U.S. Presidential Candidate

elva Lockwood (1830–1917) was a pioneer in the women's rights movement, an advocate for peace, the first woman admitted to the U.S. Supreme Court when she persuaded Congress to open the federal courts to women lawyers in 1879, and the first woman to argue a case before the Supreme Court. Lockwood ran for president in 1884 and 1888 on the ticket of the National Equal Rights Party and was the first woman to appear on official ballots.

Born Belva Ann Bennett on October 24, 1830 in Royalton, New York, she was the daughter of farmers Lewis J. Bennett and Hannah Greene Bennett. Life was hard, and Belva only attended school when she was not needed for farm work. At age 14, she was offered a teaching

Figure 117 Belva Lockwood

position at the local elementary school in Lockport, ending her formal education. This was her first taste of independence and also of sex discrimination. Belva was paid less than half the salary paid to her male counterparts. She protested this inequity as "… an indignity not to be borne

In 1848, when she was 18, Belva married Uriah McNall, a local farmer and mill owner. A daughter, Lura was born in 1850. Her marriage ended when McNall died of tuberculosis in 1853. Widowed at 22, and with a meager estate deeply in debt, Belva saw a gloomy future with no means to support herself or her toddler. Refusing the traditional dependency of a widow, she sold the farm and mill, paid off debts, and enrolled in Gasport Academy – over the objections and harsh criticisms of father who thought it unseemly, for a woman to seek an education.

About two years later, Belva left her daughter with her parents and departed for Lima, NY to enroll in Genesee Wesleyan Seminary, a school open to both men and women. While there, she heard her male classmates preparing to enroll at Genesee College (which became Syracuse University). Most women did not seek higher education, and it was especially unusual for a widow to do so. Despite the misgivings of the president of the college, she graduated with honors from Genesee College June 27, 1857 with a bachelor's degree.

Belva reunited with her daughter and became the headmistress of Lockport Union School. It was a responsible position, but Lockwood found that whether she was teaching or working as an administrator, she was still paid half of what her male counterparts were making. Belva stayed in Lockport until 1861, then became principal of the Gainesville Female Seminary; soon after, she was head of a girls' seminary in Owego, NY for three years. Her educational philosophy gradually changed after she met women's rights activist Susan B. Anthony. Encouraged by Anthony, Belva made changes at her schools. She expanded the curriculum, adding courses typical at schools for young men, such as public speaking, botany and gymnastics.

Shortly after the end of the Civil War, Belva sent her 16-year-old daughter to be educated at her alma mater, Genesee College. Belva then moved to Washington, DC in search of opportunity, especially to realize her goal to become a lawyer. While exploring the study of law she earned her living as a rental agent, newspaper correspondent, sales representative and lecturer.

In 1868, Belva married a much older man who was a Civil War veteran, Baptist minister and practicing dentist. Reverend Ezekiel Lockwood and Belva had a daughter Jessie, who died before her second birthday. Reverend Lockwood had progressive ideas about women's roles in society and encouraged his wife to study law.

In 1869 Belva and Ezekiel were invited to attend a lecture at the newly established Columbia Law School. This new school was looking for students. Ready to pay the fees, Belva presented herself for matriculation. On October 7, 1869, she received a terse note from the President of the school advising her that her admission would not be expedient, as she would likely be a distraction to the young men.

The following year, the new National University Law School opened in the district. Unlike Columbia, it invited a number of women to attend classes. In early 1871, Belva, with her grown-daughter Lura and 13 other women, enrolled. Male students objected to the inclusion of women as students, announcing they would not attend classes with any woman. The school then offered the women the option of completing their studies in a completely segregated program. Most of the women caved in to the rancor and vilification directed at them and left the school immediately. A few, including Lura, stayed for one year. Only Belva and one other woman, Lydia Hall, completed the course.

To recognize their achievement and confirm their completion of the program, Belva and Lydia expected to receive their diplomas. Yet again, the men complained, stating their refusal to even appear on the same stage with women. Not only did it appear Belva would not be on the stage to graduate, but she would not even receive her diploma. All successful candidates of a graduating law class would be presented as a group for admission to the D.C. bar. Without a diploma, Lockwood could not gain admittance to the bar. To have a successful full-scale law practice, she had to be admitted to the D.C. Supreme Court bar. In September

1873 Lockwood wrote a letter to President Ulysses S. Grant, appealing to him for justice, stating she had passed all her courses and deserved to be awarded a diploma. A week after sending the letter, Lockwood received her diploma at age 43.

Lockwood was finally admitted to the District of Columbia bar in 1873, becoming one of the first female lawyers in the United States. Several judges stated that they had no confidence in her, a reaction she repeatedly had to overcome. When she tried to gain admission to the bar in Maryland, a judge told her that "God Himself" had determined that women were not equal to men and never could be. When she tried to respond, he had her removed from the courtroom.

Judges used her marital status to deny her access to the courts. Although Lockwood's husband supported her, under the law she was regarded as subordinate to her husband. In many states, a married woman could not individually own or inherit property, nor did she have the right to make contracts or to keep money she earned unless her husband permitted it.

Lockwood opened a small law office in her home, working with Ezekiel, who had given up dentistry and was earning fees as a court-appointed guardian, overseeing the finances of minors and the mentally ill. He did not make a great deal of money, but he helped the family get by and opened doors for his wife. In the small world of Washington, his name became known, and so did hers as she learned judicial and administrative procedure through copying and filing clients' documents. Ezekiel introduced his wife to officials, and by 1873 she was earning fees as a court-appointed guardian. Lockwood began to build a practice and won cases. Even her detractors began to regard her as competent.

Lockwood became active in the fight for equal rights for women. She lobbied for an 1872 bill that would give federal employees the same salaries, no matter their gender; the measure passed. She testified before Congress in support of legislation to give married women and widows more protection under the law. She was active in several women's suffrage organizations, fighting for women's voting rights. Half of her courtroom work involved divorce actions. As a woman attorney, she attracted female clients and represented wives as complainants against defendant husbands. From 1875 to 1885 Belva represented at least 69 criminal defendants who were charged with virtually every category of crime from mail fraud and forgery to burglary and murder.

Belva was the 'rainmaker' for the family firm, attracting clients through her travels and lectures, writing the briefs and conducting the trials for the occasional high-profile case. Lockwood's daughter Lura and her niece Clara Bennett began to play important roles as Lockwood's legal assistants. The day-to-day law practice of mostly pension and land claims was handled by them. Lockwood found herself the primary breadwinner as her husband's health began to fail. Ezekiel Lockwood died in late April 1877. Five days after his death, she was back at her desk.

In 1876, the justices of the US Supreme Court had refused to admit Lockwood to its bar, stating, "none but men are permitted to practice before [us] as attorneys and counselors." Lockwood drafted an anti-discrimination bill to have the same access to the bar as male colleagues. From 1874 to 1879, she lobbied Congress to pass it. On March 3, 1879, Congress finally passed the law, which was signed by President Rutherford B. Hayes. It allowed all qualified women attorneys to practice in any federal court. Lockwood became the first woman member of the U.S. Supreme Court bar, sworn in amidst "a bating of breath and craning of necks." In 1880, she argued a case, *Kaiser v. Stickney,* before the high court, the first woman lawyer to do so.

In 1894 Belva Lockwood lost her beloved daughter Lura, who had been her mother's assistant in her legal practice and her constant companion. Lura had married a pharmacist and left behind a son who Belva continued to raise. After Lura's early death at age 44, Belva's law practice disintegrated.

In 1906, in a multiparty case, she continued to represent the Eastern Cherokee regarding money owed to them by the US government. In one of her most famous cases, she made a successful argument before the US Supreme Court and won a $5 million settlement for the Cherokee people, one of the largest made to that date to a Native American tribe for land ceded to the government.

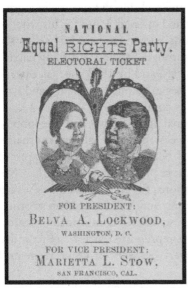

Figure 118 Belva Lockwood Presidential Campaign poster

Belva Lockwood was the first woman to run a full-fledged campaign for President of the United States. She ran as a third-party candidate in 1884 and 1888, telling voters she would improve the rights of women and minorities. Her platform included a broad range of policy issues: foreign affairs, tariffs, equal political rights, civil service reform, judicial appointments, Native Americans, protection of public lands, temperance, pensions and the federalization of family law. Without a broad base of support, she was not a serious contender. She could not vote, she told reporters, but nothing in the Constitution prevented men from voting for her. In an 1884 article, the Atlanta Constitution warned male readers of the dangers of "petticoat rule". She received fewer than 5,000 votes.

On January 12, 1885, Lockwood petitioned the US Congress to have her votes counted. With no rules or controls of the ballot box at that time, the ballot counters had refused to count her ballots. She told newspapers and magazines that she had evidence of voter fraud. She asserted that supporters had seen their ballots ripped up and that she had "received one-half the electoral vote of Oregon, and a large vote in Pennsylvania, but the votes in the latter state were not counted, simply dumped into the waste basket as false votes." Nothing was done.

Still, Lockwood was very pleased with her efforts. Her campaign had generated enormous publicity, opportunities to travel, large audiences who paid to hear her speak, and almost five thousand votes. She even made a small profit. Success prompted her to try again in 1888 but this campaign produced more disapproval and less satisfaction.

In 1909, Syracuse University awarded Belva Lockwood an Honorary Doctor of Laws in recognition of her achievements.

On May 19, 1917 Belva Lockwood died at the age of 86, almost a pauper. She is buried in Congressional Cemetery in Washington, DC where a simple gravestone bears witness to her extraordinary life.

Figure 119 Law School Graduate Belva Lockwood

Belva Lockwood's spirit has been remembered and preserved in the years after her death. Several villages and ships, including a Liberty Ship, were named after her. Stamps were issued, and coins minted, in her honor. In 1986, she was inducted into the Women's Hall of Fame at Seneca Falls.

MARY ELIZABETH JOHNSON LORD

Founder Buffalo SPCA

Mary Elizabeth Johnson Lord established the second SPCA in the country in 1867, was the daughter of the first mayor of Buffalo and was married to Dr. John C. Lord, pastor for 38 years of the Central Presbyterian Church.

Mary was born on January 6, 1812 to Sally M. Johnson and Ebenezer Johnson. Her parents met in Silver Springs NY where Ebenezer studied medicine with celebrated medical educator Dr. Joseph White. Sally and Ebenezer were married in Silver Springs in 1811 and Sally relocated to Buffalo where Ebenezer had moved in 1809.

When Dr. Johnson arrived in Buffalo, he opened a drug store and medical practice. During the War of 1812 he accepted an appointment as assistant surgeon to the New York State Volunteers, treating soldiers at the military hospital in Williamsville.

Figure 120 Mary Elizabeth Lord
Photo courtesy SPCA Serving Erie County

After the War of 1812 Johnson returned to Buffalo, opened a drug store and partnered with Samuel Wilkeson in numerous business ventures. They invested in real estate, opened a grain mill, participated in wholesale trade and opened a bank. Their most important project was the building of Buffalo Harbor, for which Johnson is known as one of the builders of Buffalo.

Johnson became one of the wealthiest citizens of Buffalo. In 1832 Buffalo was chartered as a city and voting by the Common Council elected Johnson the first mayor of the city of Buffalo. In 1832 he also built Johnson Cottage. It was a 25-acre estate on Delaware Avenue between Chippewa and Tracy Streets, at that time considered the rural outskirts of a small city. The estate included the most elaborate home in WNY, an artificial lake with a flock of swans, deer park and an orchard. The lake later became part of the private estate Rumsey Park.

The mansion at Johnson Cottage became the Female Academy in 1851, the most prestigious school for females in Buffalo. The school changed its name to

Buffalo Seminary in 1889 and moved to its present location on Bidwell Parkway in 1908.

In 1828, the 16-year-old Mary Elizabeth Johnson married John Chase Lord, who had been just accepted to the Bar as an attorney. The couple eloped because her father did not approve of the marriage, with only Lord's parents at the wedding. Mayor Johnson and Lord later became the best of friends.

Lord decided to enter the ministry and enrolled at Auburn Seminary in 1830. He was ordained a minister in 1833 and when the Buffalo Presbytery voted to add a second church, they appointed Lord as the first minister of Central Presbyterian Church. Lord remained pastor for 38 years, until he retired in 1873.

The American Society for the Prevention of Cruelty to Animals (ASPCA) was formed in 1866 by Henry Bergh. Later that year the secretary of the ASPCA wrote to former U.S. president Millard Fillmore inquiring about starting a branch in Buffalo. Fillmore found an enthusiastic promoter for the Buffalo Project in Mary Elizebeth Johnson Lord. Due to her efforts in 1867 the SPCA Serving Erie County has the honor of being the 2nd animal welfare organization formed in North America. The Erie County SPCA helped establish similar societies in Rochester (now Lollypop Farm) in 1873 and what is now the Niagara SPCA in 1883.

Although people were serviced by large animals, with dogs and cats starting to become household pets, there were no laws in the mid-1800s to protect the animals. The first organization established to protect animals was the Royal SPCA, formed in 1824 in England. It was not until 1866 that the concept was introduced to the U.S. The first chapter was in NYC, next was Buffalo in 1867 and followed by Philadelphia, Boston and San Francisco. Since horses pulled all the residential carriages and commercial wagons, along with powering all the farm work, horses were the prime recipients of the SPCA's attention. The most common home pets at this time were small birds and goldfish. After cars and trucks were able to take the work burden off these horses, the SPCA moved forward with greater emphasis on dogs and cats, as well as veterinary medicine for low-income pet owners.

Mary Elizebeth utilized her community and political contacts to get many community leaders involved with the SPCA. Board members included two presidents of the U.S. – Millard Fillmore and Grover Cleveland. They were joined by Buffalo mayors Orlando Allen, C.J. Wells and William Fargo, who was mayor during the Civil War and also founded American Express and Wells Fargo. Also recruited was Henry Martin the first president

Figure 121 Turn of the century SPCA dog catchers
Photo courtesy SPCA serving Erie County

of M&T Bank, George Washington Tifft of the Tifft Nature Preserve, and later members of the Knox, Albright, Wendt, Wurlitzer, Rochester, de Forest and Spaulding families signed on to help animals in need.

In 1895 the SPCA took over operation of the City of Buffalo Animal Shelter. The first building constructed for the SPCA Serving Erie County opened in January 1916 at 121 W. Tupper Street. The population of Buffalo and Erie County continued to increase, as well as the number of dogs and cats. Most cats lived outside but that changed when commercial cat litter was invented in 1947. The agency required more space to accommodate the animals and in 1962 a new location was built at 205 Ensminger Road in Tonawanda. They added farm and wildlife divisions, a shelter infirmary, and educational offerings like summer camp, increasing the facility to 26,000 square feet.

When the SPCA was operating at the Ensminger Road location, Barbara Carr was the executive director from 1993 to 2016. Her objective was to reduce the number of animals being euthanized and become a NO KILL animal shelter and rescue. During her 23 years leading the SPCA she accomplished that goal and succeeded in making the area SPCA nationally known for their education and animal service work. Spay and neuter services were expanded starting in the 1980s and by 2000 the pet population was under control, allowing the SPCA to do more for the most vulnerable animals coming to them. Her leadership garnered the support to move to 300 Harlem Road in West Seneca in 2017 which doubled the space of the Tonawanda facility to 52,000 square feet.

Figure 122 Executive Director Barbara Carr at SPCA Fundraiser
Photo courtesy SPCA serving Erie County

The Lords lived at 794 Potomac Avenue, with their lot extending to Inwood Place. Previous to this house they lived on Potomac near the corner of Delaware Avenue. Mary Elizabeth had substantial land holdings on the east side of Delaware Avenue, that she sold to Buffalo City Cemetery, now part of Forest Lawn. She also assisted in founding an orphan asylum in the city of Buffalo. Mary Elizabeth Johnson Lord died on May 26, 1885.

Due to the efforts of Mary Elizabeth Johnson Lord and former U.S. President Millard Fillmore, the SPCA Serving Erie County in 2023 has 114 employees and 1,200 volunteers. Most importantly, the animals now have laws protecting their welfare and they are receiving humane care.

MARIA LOVE

Founder of the first Day Care Center in the U.S. and the Maria Love Fund

Maria Love was a woman of wealth and privilege who sought to make a difference.

Maria Love was the pioneer of two projects to uplift the impoverished conditions of women and their families: founder of the Fitch Crèche (1881), first daycare center in the US, and the Church District Plan (1896) a city-wide interdenominational program designed to provide neighborhood-based community services for the poor. Maria Love originated the plan, which sectored the entire city and placed an identified district in the care of a cooperating church. In the first decade, the plan involved the cooperative efforts of 122 interfaith

Figure 123 Maria Love

congregations in Buffalo, and the plan was copied in other cities across the country. A prominent Buffalonian in the 19th century and early part of the 20th century, Maria M. Love never married or had children. She devoted her entire life to helping others. She was a staunch Episcopalian and a member of the Daughters of the American Revolution. She was one of the most prominent adherents to the "Social Gospel," a movement among late 19th century Protestants who were fervently humanitarian and interested in the solution to urban problems, especially poverty.

Maria Maltby Love always held a deep concern for the health and welfare of others. Born on a farm in Clarence, NY in 1840, she attended Buffalo PS 10 and Central High School. Maria (pronounced as though spelled Mariah) lived in a time wrought with change, both good and bad, for her beloved Buffalo, NY. Maria's father, Judge Thomas C. Love, was a prominent social humanitarian, political statesman, and the first Surrogate Judge of Erie County with the responsibility of safeguarding the interests of children placed in the care of the court. Her mother was known for her acts of kindness and charity. As prominent members of the community, they enlightened young Maria to the plight of others who were less fortunate. Maria, along with her three siblings, lived a close-knit family life with a firsthand view of humanitarian efforts to find solutions to society's problems. Her parents provided Maria and her siblings a legacy of sympathy for those suffering from poverty and servitude, as well as patriotism, independence of spirit, determination for a cause, and traits of benevolence and personal kindness.

Her father, Judge Thomas C. Love was wounded and captured at the Battle of Fort Erie during the War of 1812. Judge Love was the attorney who defended the Thayer Brothers, who were convicted of the murder of Johnny Love (no relation) in Boston, New York. They were executed in a public hanging in Niagara Square on June 17, 1825, near the current location of the front doors to City Hall. The Buffalo population of Buffalo was only about 2,000 people but over 20,000 to 30,000 witnessed the hanging.

Maria Love's brother, George Maltby Love, was awarded the Congressional Medal of Honor for assuming command after General Daniel Bidwell was killed at the Battle of Cedar Creek during the Civil War and for capturing the South Carolina flag.

After her father's death in 1853, Maria moved with her younger sister Elizabeth from the Love home at Mohawk and Franklin to the "Cary Castle" at 184 Delaware. Her older sister, Julia, had married Dr. Walter Cary, the son of Trumbull Cary and Margaret Brisbane. Trumbull Cary, a land speculator and formerly an agent for the Holland Land Company, was an incorporator and first president of Bank of Genesee in Batavia in 1829. The bank operated out of his home the first year. Cary served as president of the bank for over twenty years, and was a director of the bank until his death in 1869. In 1835, Cary along with George Lay purchased all the Holland Land Company property in Chautauqua County for $919,175. The land was disputed over who actually held the title, which led to questions about the Land Company's ownership. Cary and Lay were represented by William Seward and were found to be the rightful owners

Dr. Walter Cary was very wealthy and politically connected, evidenced by the fact that three presidents dined at the Cary Mansion in Buffalo. He remained a close friend of William Henry Seward, his father's attorney. Seward was Governor of New York from 1839 to 1842, the US Senator from New York from 1849 to 1861. He is best remembered for negotiating the purchase of Alaska from Russia when he served as Secretary of State for Presidents Lincoln and Johnson from 1861 to 1869.

Maria traveled extensively with Dr Walter Cary and her sister, Julia, crossing the Atlantic 14 times and visiting South America, the Middle East and the Far East. She believed that travel was the best means of education. During a visit to France, she became aware of the plight of working women and a dream was born.

Maria Love was well aware of the challenges many people faced, particularly women. Her empathy was turned to activism when she learned what was being done to help people in Paris where community crèches were established. The crèche was what we now call daycare centers.

"She was very surprised to learn that women would go off to work and sometimes leave children home alone because they didn't have any child care," explained Nancy Stevens, executive director of the Maria Love Convalescent Fund.

THE MARIA LOVE
CONVALESCENT
FUND
EST. 1903

After seeing the crèche system in France, she brought the idea back to Buffalo.

Figure 124 Maria Love Foundation promotion

Upon returning to Buffalo, she convinced Benjamin Fitch, a native Buffalonian and wealthy New York City philanthropist, to donate his former dry goods store at 159 Swan Street to serve as a childcare for children, while their mothers worked. Its aim was to help widows and deserted wives. Food, education, and much more were all offered in the program. The center was called Fitch Crèche, and opened on January 6, 1881, with Maria Love directing its operations for 50 years.

Initially, the 25 members of the Fitch Crèche Advisory Board paid for the costs of respite care. With the volume of those needing help expanding quickly, the program became too expensive for individual philanthropy to support. The mothers were then charged for the service but told they could pay when their financial conditions permitted.

Maria also organized and paid for trips to the Fresh Air Camps and time at Cradle Beach during the summer, and for mothers to go as well. She worked with William Prior Letchworth to plan for children from Buffalo orphanages to have two week stays at his home at Glen Iris.

The Fitch Crèche, nationally recognized as the first day care center for the children of working women in the United States, would serve as a model to be emulated by other American cities. It was the first to implement a Froebel Kindergarten in the U.S. It was the second in the World!

New York City taking notice of the creation of the Fitch Creche. Illustration from Frank Leslie's Magazine 1881.

Figure 125 Fitche Creche the 1st U.S. Daycare

Harpers New Monthly wrote in 1885 - "Think of having to take care of 20,000 babies! This is what the Fitch Crèche has done since 1879. This public cradle is the most interesting charity in Buffalo, because it is the most unique. Founded on the model of the London Day Nursery to care for little children whose mothers earn their support as char-women, it has so far outstripped it's progenitor as to be called the model crèche of the world."

At the Crèche, an onsite nurserymaid training school for young women was the first in the nation. Crèche staff provided family service outreach through home visitation. A system of convalescent care boarding homes was created for ill women and children. The Crèche and its innovative programs gained widespread national attention at the Chicago World's Fair (1893) and the Pan-American Exposition (1901).

As the numbers of those in need grew, and the costs of the venture became too great for personal philanthropy, Maria Love established the Convalescent Fund. In 1903, Maria Love organized a group of thirty-one prominent Buffalo women to raise funds and implement a program of convalescent respite care for mothers and their children: establishing the initiation of over 120 years of service to families in Erie County. This was the beginning of the Maria M. Love Convalescent Fund as it is known today.

Figure 126 Maria Love dressed as Queen Elizabeth at Waverly Ball in the Rumsey Mansion

These ladies created the first Charity Ball, an annual event that continues to this day. The organization uses the proceeds from the Maria M. Love Charity Ball to assist individuals who are residents of Erie County and have medical conditions by providing up to $300 that can be used for something simple, but life-changing, like a pair of eyeglasses or to cover time off from work for treatments at Roswell Park. The Maria M. Love Convalescent Fund annually provides over $150,000 in grants to WNY residents that have medical requirements and funds to not-for-profit agencies that assist Erie County residents.

In addition to operating the first daycare center in the US, Maria Love was a benefactor of the Red Cross. She was an amateur actress and starred in productions by local thespians. She also sang in the choir at Central Presbyterian and Trinity Church. After her sister Julia died in 1917, Maria took her sister's place in society and as mistress of the Cary mansion at 184 Delaware Avenue. She retained her love of horses throughout life, was a member of riding clubs and kept a horse, carriage and sleigh until 1929. When Maria died in 1931 her estate was only valued at $120,000, much less than it had been before the stock market crash of 1929.

After her death on July 20, 1931, Cary Castle became a rooming house and later the Normandy, an upscale restaurant and steak house. The property was sold to the federal government in 1964 and the Government Services Administration Building was constructed on Delaware Avenue between Huron & Cary Streets. Trinity Episcopal Church where she was a member, honors her memory with a room named after Maria Love in the church administration building.

"Happiness in life is not so much the possession of wealth or education as it is understanding of the human soul." Maria Maltby Love.

CARMELITA MITCHELL MERRIWEATHER

Founder Buffalo Criterion and mother of Judge Barbara Sims

C armelita moved to Buffalo in 1923 with her husband Frank Merriweather. They opened a print shop and in 1925 began publishing the Buffalo Criterion. The paper became a platform for issues impacting the lives of African-Americans. Carmelita's four children each made contributions to WNY.

Merriweather was born in San Antonio, Texas and after getting married in 1914 she and her husband moved to Houston then relocated to New York City. After moving to Buffalo, Frank and Carmelita opened a print shop at 456 Jefferson Avenue, moving two years later to 40 William Street. It was at the William Street print shop that the Buffalo Criterion began publication in 1925, She worked with her husband with writing, advertising, proof reading and layout of the Buffalo Criterion and other print jobs. Carmelita become one of the few women involved in the printing and newspaper business.

*Figure 127 Carmelita Merriweather
Photo courtesy Buffalo Criterion*

The Buffalo Criterion is the oldest African-American weekly newspaper in upstate New York and was an official publication of the NAACP. It advocated for African-American representation in politics, on the school board and other civic and community boards. The Criterion was instrumental in assisting with the establishment of the Willert Park housing project, the first African-American house project in Buffalo, constructed in 1939; the second in NYS after Harlem.

Politically, she assisted her husband in organizing the first Republican clubs for Buffalo African-Americans, the Booker T. Washington Republican Club for Men and the Martha Washington Club for Women. Carmlita was active in various clubs and held a leadership position in the Lit-Mus Club. In addition, from her club activities she was involved in many community endeavors.

When Frank Merriweather Sr. died at 71 years old in 1959, his son Frank Merriweather Jr. assumed control of the newspaper. Carmelita continued working at the Buffalo Criterion and assisting her son with the business operations until

Figure 128 Carmelita & Frank Merriweather Sr. at their print shop in 1923
Photo courtesy Buffalo Criterion

she retired in 1977. Shortly after retiring from the newspaper, she died on February 16, 1978.

Frank Jr. was born on September 15, 1917 in Houston and moved to Buffalo with his parents in 1923. He attended School 32, Hutchinson Central High School, the Buffalo Collegiate Center and Alfred State College. In 1935 he began assisting his parents at the newspaper, and like his parents, he became involved in the fight for African-American rights initiatives. He was a Republican committeeman for the 5th Ward, Masten District and served on the Erie County Republican Executive Committee. In addition, Frank Jr. was on the Board of the Rapid Transit, Crisis Services and Hickory Street Center. The Frank E. Merriweather Jr. Library on Jefferson Avenue, designed by Buffalo architect, Robert Traynham Coles, was named in his honor.

Upon the death of Frank Merriweather Jr. on May 22, 1995, his wife Evelyn Patterson Merriweather became publisher of the Buffalo Criterion. Like her mother-in-law Carmelita, she worked with her husband assisting on all newspaper operations and even learned to operate the Linotype typesetting machine. She made the transition to computers and until three years before her death in 2021, at the age of 98 she was preparing articles on her home computer for publication. Evelyn's children were raised in the business and she passed responsibility of the business to her children, the third-generation owners of The Criterion.

Each of Carmelita's three daughters were successful in their own right. Thyra Merriweather Charles received a diploma from the Edward J. Meyer Memorial Hospital School of Nursing in 1941, a Bachelor of Science degree in Public Health Nursing from UB in 1949 and a Master's degree in Supervision and Administration of Public Health Nursing in 1950. She was the second African-American woman to graduate from a Buffalo Nursing school and the first to receive a master's degree in nursing. Thyra was the Associate Director for Public Health Nursing at Meyer Memorial Hospital (now ECMC) and Clinical Associate Professor of Community Health Nursing at UB from 1952-1970.

Julit Merriweather Curry received her Bachelor's Degree in Music from the University Extension Conservatory in Chicago and became an Associate of the American Guild of Organists at the age of 30 in 1955. When she was 15 years old, Julit became the organist at Lincoln Memorial Methodist Church, later directing the instrumental and choral music at several area churches, including St. Phillips Episcopal Church, Bethel AME Church, Tabernacle Baptist Church and Calvary Baptist Church. With her husband Robert Curry, an accomplished baritone, they performed at recitals throughout WNY.

Barbara Merriweather Sims was the only child of Frank Sr. and Carmelita that was born in Buffalo. She attended Hutchinson Central High School and studied to be a teacher at Buffalo State Teachers College. In 1952 she earned the highest score on the citywide teachers' examination and accepted a position as a primary reading teacher at School 75 on Monroe Street. While still teaching, Barbara applied for law school at UB, from which she graduated in 1955. After graduation she entered private practice with her husband William Sims in the firm of Sims & Sims. In 1964 she joined the Office of the District Attorney of Erie County, later becoming a City of Buffalo Parking Violations Bureau hearing officer and being accepted to teach in UB's Law School. In 1970, she was appointed assistant to the president of UB

Figure 129 Judge Barbara Sims

for minority and women's affairs, also serving as the college director of the Office of Equal Opportunity and the Equal Employment Officer. Sims was appointed associate judge of the City Court of Buffalo in 1977, was president of the Women's Lawyers Association, vice-president of the National Association of Black Women Attorneys, local counsel to the NAACP and during her career received over 50 awards. Sims was the first African-American woman to graduate from UB Law School, to serve as an assistance district attorney in Erie County and to serve as a Buffalo city judge. She died at the age of 94 on June 10, 2018.

The Buffalo Criterion continues the legacy of Frank and Carmelita Merriweather by supporting and advocating for the Black community of Buffalo and WNY.

ANN MONTGOMERY

Owner of The Little Harlem and successful Black Businesswoman

Figure 130 Ann Montgomery

Ann Montgomery was born in 1889 in Americus, Georgia. Her family moved to Los Angeles when she was an infant and she attended school in Los Angeles, as well as Texas, before she moved to Buffalo in 1910. Upon her arrival in Buffalo, she opened an ice cream parlor at 496 Michigan Avenue. The business briefly became a billiards hall in 1922, a supper club in 1929 and The Little Harlem hotel and nightclub in 1934.

Upon moving to Buffalo, she met Dan Montgomery, who owned Dan Montgomery's Hotel at 158 Exchange Street and was one of the wealthiest African-Americans in Buffalo. Dan opened the restaurant and hotel in 1907, near the location of the New York Central Depot on Exchange Street. At first the restaurant catered to mostly Black clientele from Buffalo and rail workers at the train depot. Due to Dan's hospitality, soon clientele of all races and backgrounds frequented the business. Since Dan was the first widely successful Black restaurateur in Buffalo, many of Buffalo's Black owned restaurants and taverns can trace their roots to Dan Montgomery's Hotel. William Clore learned the business working for Montgomery and struck out on his own, with his brother, opening the iconic Venedome Hotel and nightclub in the Jazz Triangle. Dan Montgomery was also one of the first contributors to the Michigan Avenue YMCA, a cornerstone of the African-American community in Buffalo.

In the public record, Dan was usually listed as living at 158 Exchange Street, while Ann was listed at 496 Michigan Avenue. Together they also operated the Montgomery Hotel at 342 Curtiss Street, near the Buffalo Central Railway Terminal. After their divorce in the late 1930s, Dan retained ownership of the two hotels, while Ann became the sole owner of The Little Harlem.

Ann was a pioneer in providing entertainment for Buffalo. After she separated from Dan in 1922, she opened the billiards hall at 496 Michigan Avenue. Since this was Prohibition, not all businesses were what they appeared to be. She became the "Queen of the Cabaret" and felt Buffalo was ready for something naughtier, something jazzier, something more like the mostly Black entertainment for mostly white audiences, like that offered by the Cotton Club in NYC.

Through Ann's management and personality, The Little Harlem became one of the storied nightspots in Buffalo. She made certain all clientele felt welcome at the club, not only Blacks and whites, but also gays and lesbians. If you wanted an authentic night on the town in Buffalo, you went to The Little Harlem. The entertainers included the likes of Ella Fitzgerald, Della Reese, Sammy Davis Jr., Lena Horne and appearances by heavyweight champion Joe Lewis. Entertainers who were performing at other

Figure 131 Bar & bartenders at The Little Harlem

venues in Buffalo came to The Little Harlem to be entertained. In the audience you could find Louis Armstrong, Bing Crosby, Billie Holiday and Dinah Washington. Sinatra, Martin and many others found their way through the doors.

Ann Montgomery had the knack of hiring soon-to-be-famous band leaders and MCs at The Little Harlem. LeRoy "Stuff" Smith was the band leader and MC at the club in 1930. He is credited with being the first jazz violinist as a member of the Duke Ellington Band and was one of the 57 jazz musicians in the famous Esquire Magazine "A Great Day in Harlem" photo. In 1931, Jimmie Lunceford was the band leader, and he went on to develop the two-beat style which launched the Swing Era. In 1933, Lil Armstrong, the wife of Louis Armstrong led The Little Harlem 12-piece band. During the mid-1930s, years before she became a Tony and Emmy Award winning vocalist and actress, the MC at the club was Pearl Bailey. Vocalist Jean Eldridge was discovered by Duke Ellington while she was performing at the night-club. The quality of the entertainment at The Little Harlem was compared to the Cotton Club in NYC and Grand Terrace in Chicago. It was one of the country's foremost jazz night-clubs.

Prohibition agents raided The Little Harlem several times. It is a surprise that these agents received assistance from the local police because many of them probably frequented the club. When the raid was taking place, the cops had to be vigilant to check if their captains, chief or area politicians and judges were in attendance. It has been rumored that during Prohibition an alarm went off if a raid was about to take place and all the shelves behind the bar rotated, exposing water, soda and carbonated waters, instead of wine, rum and whiskey. After an unsuccessful raid, when the agents left, the shelves rotated back and the party continued.

Ann was a respected businesswoman and took care of her employees. She held picnics for her workers at Como Lake Park and at her waterfront home on Lake Shore Road in Wanakah where her guests enjoyed motor boating, fishing and swimming at her private beach. When not at the club or her home, you could find Ann driving around town, with her companions, in her luxury Packard. Montgomery was a member of the Buffalo Chapter of the National Association for the Advancement of Colored People (NAACP), the Michigan Avenue YMCA, and the Hadji Court 62, Daughters of Isis. She supported and contributed to the Boys Club of America, Negro College Fund, Salvation Army, United Way of Buffalo and Erie County, Catholic Charities, Police Athletic League and other civic and community organizations. In addition, she assisted many young people by giving them jobs at the hotel and assisting with funding their education. Numerous doctors, lawyers, judges, journalists, tradesmen, elected officials, community leaders and businessmen got their start through the generosity and tutelage of Ann Montgomery.

Ann Montgomery married Paul Woodson in the early 1940s and he became the manager of The Little Harlem in 1942. Before moving to Buffalo, Paul was stationed at the Army Air Corps base in Tuskegee, Alabama. Paul was a descendent of President Thomas Jefferson and Sally Hemings. Ann's sister Mamie Ellis also moved to Buffalo from Los Angeles in the 1920s. She operated the Gallent Fox jazz club in Buffalo. Mamie died in 1956 and lived at Ann's home on Lake Shore Road in Wanakah.

Ann passed away on April 11, 1978, at the age of 87. She operated her business for almost 70 years. The careers of many international stars were launched at her club and The Little Harlem was known by entertainers across the country. Paul managed the business after her death, but everyone still called the nightclub, Ann Montgomery's Little Harlem.

Figure 132 Ann Montgomery's Little Harlem on Michigan Avenue in Buffalo

The establishments built by Ann and Dan Montgomery outlived their namesakes. Mildred Montgomery, who Dan married after divorcing Ann, continued to operate the restaurant after he died at age 68 in 1954. It closed because the entire block was lost to urban renewal when the ballpark was being built in 1987. Paul Woodson continued operating The Little Harlem until he retired and sold the business to Judge Wilbur Trammell. Unfortunately, it burned down in an accidental fire in February 1993.

NINA MORGANA

Metropolitan Opera Star premiered as a child at Pan-Am

The parents of Nina Morgana emigrated from Palermo Sicily and Nina was born in Buffalo at 292 The Terrace on November 15, 1891. She began singing on the streets of Buffalo when she was four years old and a nine-year-old Nina made her professional singing debut at the Pan-American Exposition.

The Pan-American Exposition was a World's Fair and featured music throughout the fairgrounds. Two symphony orchestras were hired to perform; the Pittsburgh Orchestra directed by Victor Herbert and the Pan-American Orchestra, directed by Buffalo Symphony conductor John Lund and consisting of members of the Buffalo, Boston and New York symphony orchestras. Twenty professional bands were hired featuring the John Philip Sousa and Frederick Neil Innes Bands. Many brass bands were featured including three popular Buffalo bands; the 65th Regiment Band, 74th Regiment Band and The Scinta's Band led by Serafino Scinta. These orchestras and bands performed at large ticketed concerts in the Temple of Music,

Nina Morgana (1901)
"Little Patti"

Figure 133 Nina Morgana at Pan-Am in 1901

which seated 2,200 people, and on five gazebo bandstands placed throughout the esplanade. The Temple of Music also employed 71 organists performing on the enormous Emmons Howard pipe organ that had 3,288 pipes and was one of the largest organs ever built.

In addition to these scheduled concerts by orchestras, bands and organists, there were musicians from around the world performing throughout the midway and in the cultural exhibits. At the Venice in America exhibit, on gondolas in the canals or walking through the grounds accompanied by a troop of Venetian Street musicians, Nina Morgana was one of the best known and loved cultural performers at the Pan-Am. They called her Baby Patti after singer Adelina Patti. At the Venice in America attraction, she appeared as the true queen of the fairies.

One of eight children, Nina went to Public School #2 and later Holy Angels. She excelled at school and was the star performer in all her school entertainments.

Before and after the Pan-Am she sang at Buffalo churches, area schools and Sunday concerts. In 1908 she auditioned for Enrico Caruso at the Iroquois Hotel. He was so impressed with her performance that he arranged for her to study with Teresa Arkel in Milan

She studied in Italy from 1909 to 1913, accompanied by her father Calogero, while her mother Cangetta remained in Buffalo with their other children. Before leaving Italy, she made her operatic debut at La Scala in Milan in 1913.

At a Liberty Bond rally in 1917, Enrico Caruso again heard her sing and engaged her as his assisting artist on his concert tours. She traveled with him worldwide from 1917 to 1919. Caruso recommended her to the Metropolitan Opera as a leading soprano. She made her Met debut as Gilda in Verdi's *Rigoletto*, remaining with the company until 1935. Some of her favorite roles and operas were Bellini's *La Sonnambula*, Donizetti's *Lucia di Lammermoor* and *L'Elisir d'Amore*, and Rossini's *Barber of Seville*. She sang with Titta Ruffo in Buenos Aries operas in 1926 and said one of her most cherished memories was vocal performances of Beethoven's Ninth Symphony with the New York Philharmonic, directed by Arturo Toscanini. Nina sporadically returned to Buffalo as a solo artist and with Caruso to perform at the Elmwood Music Hall.

Morgana retired from the Metropolitan Opera in 1935. She stated in 1969 that she did not retire from the opera and concert stage in 1935 but did not accept any more engagements. She wrote "I chose to end my career at my singing best."

While working with Caruso, Nina met her future husband, Bruno Zirato. He was Caruso's private secretary and business manager. In 1921, they were married in Buffalo and Caruso was the best man. Zirato later became the publicity Chief of the Colon Opera House in Buenos Aires and managing director of the New York Philharmonic. They had one son Brunino Zirato, an executive with television game show producers Goodson and Todman, and was the sister of prominent WNY ophthalmologist Dr. Dante Morgana.

When Nina died at the age of 94 in 1986, she was the only surviving person to have sung on the same stage as Enrico Caruso - a stunning career that started on the streets of the Buffalo waterfront and at the Pan-American Exposition.

Other well-known female opera singers were from Buffalo. Rose Bampton was born in Lakewood Ohio but grew up in Buffalo. Her operatic debut was with the Chautauqua Opera in 1929. She was with the Metropolitan Opera and performed internationally from 1932 to 1950.

Helen Olheim was born in Buffalo in 1904, grew up in the Riverside section of the city and graduated from Hutchinson Central High School. She sang at Holy Trinity and Calvary Evangelical Lutheran Church and moved to Rochester where she studied at the Eastman School of Music. After graduation she relocated to NYC where she was a member of the Metropolitan Opera from 1935 to 1944, American Opera Company and performed concerts worldwide with the Community Concert Series.

After retiring from public performance, she taught at Mount Holyoke College in Massachusetts until retiring in 1996. She and her husband Frederic Michel moved to Sarasota Florida in the early 1970s where Helen was involved with the Sarasota Opera Society and Ringling Brothers Museum, giving lectures about her life in music. Her husband died in the late 1960s and Helen died on June 26, 1992

Genia Las was born as Genia Jakubczak on March 20, 1926 to Buffalo East Side parents who owned a bakery on Sycamore Street and had a baked goods stall in the Broadway Market. She was encouraged by a music teacher at Villa Maria Academy to study voice with Charles Moratti. Performing under the name Panna (Miss) Genia, at the age of 14 she made her debut with the Buffalo Philharmonic. Considered a child prodigy, she was a soloist with the Paderewski Singing Society and made many Buffalo appearances in her teens. After studying for six years in NYC she was a mezzo soprano at Carnegie Hall and the Metropolitan Opera House, member of the New York City Opera and appeared with symphony orchestras in Toronto, Detroit, and Chicago. In 1957 she accepted a grant to study in Italy for a year and ended up staying in Europe for twenty years, appearing at all the major European opera houses and concert halls. Genia returned to Buffalo in 1976 reducing her performance schedule to an occasional concert, church work and teaching. She taught voice at Daemen College and for 23 years served as chairman of the Voice Department at the Community School of Music. Genia died at the age of 92 in 2018.

Figure 134 The canals at the Pan-Am depicting Venice Italy

CHARLOTTE MULLIGAN

The founder of the 20ᵗʰ Century Club and Social Advocate

C harlotte Mulligan, a philanthropist known especially for her innovative work with boys, a formidable woman of many accomplishments, a pioneering social worker and activist, was born on September 25, 1844 to the socially active family of Henry and Sally Mulligan. She was the only daughter in a family which included five brothers. Charlotte Mulligan was one of the earliest graduates of the Buffalo Female Academy, later known as Buffalo Seminary, in 1863. At age seven she was the first student to enter the school, and all accounts describe her as a sturdy and spirited girl. Her early life was shaped by great loss. At age 19, she lost her two older brothers during the Civil War.

Charlotte, like many unmarried women of the era, pursued a career as a teacher. At seventeen, while a senior at the Buffalo Female Academy, Charlotte was teaching

Figure 135 Charlotte Mulligan

Sunday School at the Wells Street Chapel of the First Presbyterian Church of Buffalo. This class was comprised of rowdy young students almost her age, but soon the energetic students were "tamed" thanks to the skills of Miss Mulligan. Instead of enjoying teas and dances, she obtained satisfaction instilling Christian values, giving instruction to the poor, and helping those who were not fortunate to come from her wealthy and privileged class.

Her great grandfather was General Israel Chapin, who served in the American Revolution and was the General Agent for Indian Affairs of the United States, that oversaw the signing of the Treaty of Canandaigua with the Six Nations. Chapin was respected by the Iroquois, and Seneca Chief Red Jacket was one of the speakers at his funeral in 1795.

When the Civil War started, being a patriotic and peacemaking family, her two older brothers James and Gregg enlisted in the army. Both of her brothers died during the war. Charlotte made a vow in 1863 that she would never marry and would devote herself to the care of young men devastated by the war, many of whom were wandering the streets, hungry and homeless.

Out of her background of education and working with troubled students, she founded an early settlement house and reform program in 1868 called the Guard of Honor. They met on Sundays at First Presbyterian Church and their Wells Street Chapel as a reform-based organization for working class men. The mission was to guide the moral, religious, and social lives of the underprivileged. Members of the Guard pledged to abstain from alcohol, refrain from using "profane or vulgar language" and not quarrel or fight. They also pledged to desist from gambling or associate with men, women, or boys of "questionable character". She taught writing, arithmetic, geography, reading, music, and manners. Charlotte worked quietly behind the scenes to improve the lot of the poor, the incarcerated, and the mentally ill. She understood the frustration of social strictures for those not born white, male, and privileged.

When the membership got too large for the Wells Street Chapel, Charlotte secured permission to meet in Goodell Hall at the Buffalo Seminary on Johnson Park. When it outgrew the Buffalo Seminary quarters, she bought a lot opposite the Washington Market. Louise Bethune, an architect and the first female member of the AIA, was hired to design a boardinghouse for the young men. In June 1884 the cornerstone was laid for the first Chapter House for the Guard of Honor at 620-622 Washington Street. There was considerable publicity that the $12,000 building was designed by Bethune and paid for by selling bricks for twenty-five cents each. The Guard of Honor as a private philanthropy has escaped the notice of historians of women's achievements, possibly because the name sounds like a monument of some kind. It existed as a reform house until at least the 1930s.

For Civil War veterans she instituted an honor system. Privileges were awarded if they furthered their education, obtained a job or participated in social activities like the musical band she created. Charlotte also purchased a cemetery plot at Forest Lawn Cemetery for the Guard of Honor where deceased members were interred, and a memorial placed to honor each of them.

Charlotte and other graduates of the Buffalo Female Academy, later known as Buffalo Seminary, formed the Graduates Association in 1876. Charlotte Mulligan believed women should be as well-informed and accomplished as men. Her vision was to establish a gathering place that provided the educated women of Buffalo with a wide range of literary, artistic, and musical pursuits after graduation. They raised the funds and built a lecture hall at 95 Johnson Park, on land which was originally deeded to Buffalo first mayor Ebenezer Johnson, and on whose property the Buffalo Female Academy was located. That building, which was built in 1884 for the Graduates, in 1895 became the home of the Women Teachers Association (WTA), the first teachers' organization in the U.S.to have a permanent home and Buffalo's first teacher's union. Essenwein & Johnson were hired in 1905 to make modifications to the building. In the new second floor lobby, they installed a stained-glass window donated to the WTA by Charlotte Mulligan. Most recently the building was the New Phoenix Theatre on the Park.

The Graduates Association also wanted to establish an independent women's club, including more than just individuals who graduated from the Buffalo Female Academy. While the Graduates Association continued for "Sem" alumnae until 1997, the new organization was named the Twentieth Century Club in 1894 to herald the arrival of a new century. The ladies purchased the former Delaware Avenue Baptist Church at 595 Delaware Avenue, and hired the eminent architectural firm of Green & Wicks to make the necessary accommodations to the building. Over the years, the firm returned several times to expand the building, help plan necessary re-building after a few fires, and remodel as required. The Club even survived a Supreme Court challenge in 1988 over its all-woman membership policy. Unlike so many grand homes and buildings in Buffalo, the Twentieth Century Club still boasts its original façade, mission, and tenant.

In addition to her social and club activities, Charlotte Mulligan was an educator, musician and vocalist, who performed and taught violin and voice at her studio on Johnson Park. She sang soprano and founded numerous organizations at a time when women could not vote. For twenty years she was music critic for the *Buffalo Courier*, being one of the first female newspaper writers in Buffalo. She also founded music groups called the Morning Musicales and the Afternoon Musicales as well as the Scribblers, a writing group. In addition to being the founder of the Twentieth Century Club in 1894, Mulligan was the club president during its first four years.

Figure 136 Twentieth Century Club
Photo credit Rick Falkowski

136

The grand opening of the new Twentieth Century Club took place on November 20, 1896. Several additions were designed by the architectural firm of E.B. Green and W.S. Wicks, with their creation of the elegant façade on Delaware Avenue being constructed in 1895. The members looked forward to hosting dignitaries who would be attending the Pan-American Exposition, when they held receptions for Vice President and Mrs. Theodore Roosevelt and their daughter Alice; Governor and Mrs. Benjamin Odell; Mr. and Mrs. Booker T. Washington and the Chinese Minister, Wu Ting Fang. Mrs. Roosevelt and Mrs. McKinley were extended membership privileges during their time in Buffalo for the Pan-Am. Unfortunately, Charlotte Mulligan died in 1900 and was unable to be part of these historic moments in the history of her club.

The women's club movement of the late 19th century began as cultural organizations to provide middle and upper-class women with an outlet for their intellectual energies. To this extent the avowed purpose of the Twentieth Century Club is to advance the interests of education, literature and art. Miss Mulligan set a tradition of holding musical events and lectures on Wednesdays. This continues until the present day with noted writers, speakers and international personalities presenting talks on a wide range of subjects. Mrs. Franklin D. Roosevelt and violinist Isaac Stern, along with many other notable speakers and musicians have been featured at the Wednesday luncheons.

Figure 137 Charlotte Mulligan

The Twentieth Century Club was the first club run by women, for women, in the U.S. and is the second oldest women's club in the country, only preceded by the Acorn Club in Philadelphia. The building was listed on the National Register of Historic Places in 2011. When you enter the building, a painting by Evelyn Rumsey of Charlotte Mulligan, the club's founder, greets you in the lobby.

In an age when women were politically disenfranchised and seldom stepped out of their prescribed social roles, Charlotte Mulligan was a mover and shaker while sporting a white carnation in her lapel. The motto on the Twentieth Century Club's crest could also serve as an epitaph for its founder, Charlotte Mulligan: *Facta Probant* (Let Deeds Tell).

BARBARA SEALS NEVERGOLD

Educator, Buffalo Board of Education President, Community leader

Figure 138 Barbara Seals Nevergold
Photo credit Blanc Photographie Inc

Barbara Seals Nevergold moved from Louisiana to Buffalo with her parents in 1947. Her father, Reverend Willie Brown Seals, mother Clara Ellis Seals, three brothers and one sister, initially lived in a four-room apartment at 266 Walnut Street. They also shared their home with her father's sister and her family. Four more sons were born to the Seals family after they relocated to Buffalo.

Her father, known as W.B., was a minister, musician, photographer, historian and factory worker. In addition to retiring after working at the Tonawanda Chevy Plant on River Road for almost 25 years, W.B. was the assistant pastor of St. John Baptist Church. As church pianist, he established "The Bells of St. John" choir in 1948. He also served as pastor of the Cold Spring Baptist Church, New Hope Baptist Church in Niagara Falls, New Hope Baptist Church of Buffalo, and preached or taught Bible study classes at various churches. Through his company, "Seals Ebony Studio", he assisted individuals and groups to document the history of African-American families and became a photographer recording Buffalo's African-American culture. His files and photos are considered a valuable collection that portrays the rich history of an African-American community as seen through the lens of an African-American photographic artist.

The Seals family instilled the importance of education in their children. After attending grammar and high school in Buffalo Public Schools, Barbara enrolled at Buffalo State College. She considered majoring in history, but decided to major in French language education. Barbara said in interviews, "There was a certain practicality to selecting French as a major. When I looked around at the jobs that were available, and that the district was hiring for, they were hiring more language teachers than they were history teachers."

Barbara received her M. Ed degrees in French Education and Counseling from the University at Buffalo, and a Ph.D. in Counseling Education from UB In addition, she studied French at Laval University in Quebec, Canada and the University of Dijon in Dijon, France.

138

Her career started as a French teacher in the Buffalo Public Schools. She later worked for the Buffalo Schools as a guidance counselor, as well as in the areas of health education, social work, and higher education administration, before being appointed an at-large member of the Buffalo Public Schools Board of Education in 2012. Two years later, Barbara was elected to a five-year term on the board, and served as President of the Board from 2014 – July 2019. In addition, she served as Treasurer and President of the NYS Conference of Big 5 School Districts, was a member of the Resolutions Committee of the New York State School Board Association, and was on the Executive Board of the Council of Great City Schools. She held adjunct instructional positions at Empire State College and the University at Buffalo, including retiring as Director of Student Support Services at the University of Buffalo's Educational Opportunity Center.

Figure 139 6-year-old Barbara Seals
Photo credit Rev. W.B. Seals
Seals Ebony Studio

The importance of community service was also taught to the Seals children by Rev. W.B. and Clara Ellis Seals. Barbara has been Executive Director of Niagara Frontier Association for Sickle Cell Diseases, VP for Children's Services at Friendship House of WNY, CEO of Planned Parenthood of Buffalo and Erie County, and Regional Director for Berkshire Farm Center.

Dr. Seals has served on several national and local boards including Graycliff Conservancy, Afro-American Historical Association of the Niagara Frontier, Buffalo Psychiatric Center's Board of Visitors, Studio Arena Theatre, Heritage Centers, Buffalo General Hospital, Planned Parenthood Federation of America, Kaleida Health Trustee Steering Committee, Gethsemane Manor Senior Citizen Home, St. John Christian Academy, Columbus Hospital, YWCA of Buffalo & Erie County, Buffalo Rotary Club, WNY Council for African Relief and Buffalo Alliance for Education. She has received numerous awards, notably the William Wells Brown Award in recognition of her efforts to preserve local African-American History, the Keeper of the Flame Award from the National Women's Hall of Fame, the NAACP Medgar Evers Award, and many others.

Before serving on the Buffalo Board of Education, in 1989 she co-founded the Concerned Parents and Citizens for Quality Education, Inc. with Dr. Brooks-Bertram. The CPCQE was credited with increasing public awareness of education issues and organizing parents to be effective advocates. She served on Buffalo Board of Education committees and task forces, demonstrating the importance of parental involvement in local school politics.

139

In 1999, with Dr. Brooks-Bertram, she initiated the "Uncrowned Queens Institute for Research & Education on Women, Inc." It began as a project of the Women's Pavilion Pan-Am Centennial in 2001. Their goals were to commemorate the history of African and African-American involvement in the Pan-American Exposition of 1901, and to recognize and celebrate the accomplishments and contributions of African-American women during the period of the Exposition and in the one hundred years after the fair. The Institute's founders have written four books and over a dozen journal articles related to the history of Blacks, including the 1901 Pan-American Exposition, the 1905 Niagara Movement, Black history in the state of Oklahoma, and the 1921 Tulsa Race Riot. The initial project launched the Institute to become a 501c3 non-profit corporation in 2003. In 2006 Nevergold and Bertram began working full time on the establishment of the "Uncrowned Queens Center for Excellence" at the University at Buffalo. The Uncrowned Community Builders continues today to honor the histories of African-American women and men, recording the lives and stories of people that may have been lost to time without their diligent research and publications.

Figure 140 Barbara in the 1970s
Photo credit Rev. W.B. Seals - Seals Ebony Studio

Dr. Barbara Seals Nevergold and her husband Paul R. Nevergold celebrated their 50th wedding anniversary in 2019, have two adult children Alanna and Kyle, and four grandchildren. She continues to serve the community and Uncrowned Community Builders is considered the premier online organization researching, documenting and preserving the regional histories of African-American women and men in WNY and across this nation.

Dr. Nevergold and Dr. Brooks-Bertram received a much-deserved honor in September 2023 when they were recognized with the "Exemplary Citizenship Citizen of the Year" award by the Theodore Roosevelt Inaugural Site.

JOYCE CAROL OATES

Award Winning Novelist with over 60 published books

Joyce Carol Oates is one of America's most prolific authors, who has written over 60 novels in addition to at least 30 short story collections, along with a number of plays, poems, novellas, book reviews and essays.

She was born on June 16, 1938 in Lockport NY. Her father Frederic was a sign painter for theaters and tool & die designer at Harrison Radiator in Lockport, who enjoyed playing the piano and was adventurous enough to become a pilot. Her mother Carolina was always busy working on the family farm, which was the home of her stepparents John and Lena Bush. Joyce and her younger brother Fred wandered, exploring the countryside and Tonawanda Creek. It was Carolina's work ethic that made Carol such a productive writer. Oates also writes psychological suspense novels under the pseudonyms Rosemond Smith and Lauren Kelly.

Figure 141 Joyce Carol Oates & her husband Raymond Smith in 1977

When she was six years old her paternal grandmother Blanch Woodside took her to the Lockport Public Library on East Avenue in Lockport and she was given her first library card. Her grandmother had a big influence on Oates as at the age of nine she gave her a copy of the book that opened the literary universe to her: *Alice's Adventures in Wonderland* and its companion "*Through the Looking Glass, and What Alice Found There.*". She also gave Joyce her first typewriter. As a youth she read profusely, recalling that "I read books. Avidly, ardently! As if my life depended upon it." At Syracuse University she even got a job working at the university library for 70 cents an hour.

Oates went to a one room schoolhouse, District School #7, Niagara County in Millersport on Tonawanda Creek Road through grade five. During her last year at the school, she won the Buffalo Evening News spelling bee and was given a copy of Webster's dictionary, which she said "fascinated me: a book comprised of words!" Her mother attended the same school a generation earlier.

The Oates home was on Transit Road about a quarter mile from the intersection with Millersport Highway. For sixth grade she was transferred to the John E. Pound School on High Street in Lockport, about six or seven miles north of the family home. This was before the days of school buses, so Oates had to take a Greyhound Bus down Transit Road to Lockport and walk from the Lockport bus terminal to school. During junior high school she attended North Park Junior High in the northeast section of town near Outwater Park. Many days after school she would go to Grandmother Woodside's house on Harvey Avenue and later Grand Street. She remembered walking across the Cottage Street and Pine Street canal bridges and exploring the towpaths. She often sat reading in the Greyhound Terminal and since she could not go home for lunch, she walked to Main Street in downtown Lockport to eat alone in a restaurant. Some days after school she went to movies at the Palace Theater making certain she got back to the bus terminal to catch the 6:15 bus marked Buffalo.

For high school Oates went to Williamsville Junior-Senior High School, now known as Williamsville South. Oates was the first member from her family to graduate from high school. She graduated with a BA summa cum laude as Valedictorian of the Class of 1960 at Syracuse University and received her M.A. from the University of Wisconsin – Madison. She was rejected by the University of Wisconsin Ph.D. program, but at age 61 they invited her back to the school and gave her an honorary doctorate of humane letters. It was in Madison that she met her husband Raymond Smith, to whom she was married for 47 years. She taught in Beaumont Texas for a year and from 1962 to 1968 she taught at the University of Detroit, while her husband taught English at Wayne State University. Influenced by the Vietnam War and the 1967 Detroit race riots, in 1968 Oates and her husband accepted positions across the border in Ontario at the University of Windsor. They moved to Princeton New Jersey in 1978 where she taught at Princeton University for 36 years, retiring in 2014. Since 2016 she has been a visiting professor at the University of California, Berkley

Figure 142 Joyce in 1949 at her parents Lockport farm

She began writing at age 14 and published her first short story in Mademoiselle in 1959. Her first collection of short stories titled *By the North Gate* was published in 1963 and a year later she completed her first novel *With Shuddering Fall.* She founded the literary magazine The Ontario Review in 1974 with her husband, leading to forming the independent publishing company Ontario Review Books.

Much of her fiction is set in upstate rural New York and explores family relationships, many of them plagued by violence, poverty and addiction. She always offers a probing look at the dark side of human nature. She admits to getting her story ideas from life experiences and perusing the news. In the early 1980s, she dabbled in the horror genre.

Life and family events had an effect on her writing, as she experienced dark events during her lifetime.

When Carol was a young child, she saw a body being pulled out of the Erie Canal in Lockport.

Her maternal grandfather was murdered in a local tavern. Her paternal grandfather abandoned his family. Her mother was raised by relatives that she considered her stepparents, John and Lena. John died at 53, his lungs riddled with steel filings from the foundry in Tonawanda where he worked. Lena never learned to speak or read English. The older students at the one room schoolhouse she attended bullied, sexually molested and harassed the younger students. Her younger sister Lynn Ann was born on the same date of her birth but 18 years later in 1956. She was severely autistic and violent, to the point that her parents reluctantly had Lynn Ann institutionalized at the age of 15. Joyce Carol has not seen her younger sister since the early 1970s. Her grandmother's father tried to murder her grandmother Blanch and her mother, but only succeeded in killing himself. A friend's father was a violent abuser who burned his family house down. Another friend's father was a physician who committed suicide

She attended Good Catholic Church (although not at the same time) in Pendleton, which was also the childhood church of domestic terrorist, mass murderer Timothy McVeigh, the Oklahoma City Bomber. These events contributed to Oates' story ideas and to shaping her writing style.

Some of her over 60 novels include *A Garden of Delights, Them, Black Water* inspired by Chappaquiddick incidents, *We Were the Mulvaneys* that became a bestseller when it was an Oprah's Book Club selection five years after it was written, *Blonde* a historical fiction about Marilyn Monroe. *Lost*

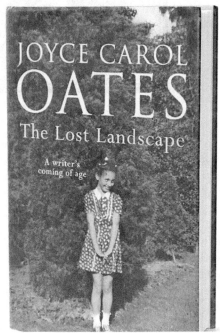

Figure 143 Cover of Oates book about growing up in WNY

Landscape: A Writer's Coming of Age published in 2015 is her memoir and explores her early years growing up in Lockport and Amherst during the 1940s and 1950s.

In October 2009 she was invited to inaugurate a lecture series at the Palace Theater in her hometown. It was 50 years since she left Lockport and this was the first time she had been formally invited back to speak. She expected a small turnout of 20 or 30 people, but over 800 people came to her presentation. The audience wanted information about her childhood, growing up in 1950s Lockport and its effect upon her writing. They wanted to know "If Without Millersport and Lockport – would there be Joyce Carol Oates?"

Figure 144 Oates receiving National Humanities Medal from President Obama in 2011

In 2010 Oates was awarded the National Humanities Medal by President Barack Obama. The medal honors those whose work has deepened the nation's understanding of and engagement with the humanities or helped preserve and expand access to important resources in the humanities. In addition to writing fiction, she is known for her literary criticism and essays where she has explored such diverse themes as boxing, serial killers, poetry and art. Five of her books have been Pulitzer Prize for Fiction finalists. Other literary awards include the U.S. National Book Award, the PEN/Malamud Award honoring excellence in the art of the short story, the O. Henry Prize for continued achievement in the short story, Prix Femina Étranger Award (for works translated into French) and the Kenyon Review Award for Literary Achievement.

MARGARET EVANS PRICE

First Fisher Price Toys based on her illustrations

Margaret Evans Price was married to Irving Price who formed Fisher Price Toys with Herman Fisher. The first toys released by Fisher Price were push pull toys based off illustrations of characters in her children's books. Margaret was also responsible for saving the 1826 home that Millard Fillmore built on Main Street in East Aurora, moving and restoring it as her art studio.

She was born on March 20, 1888 in Chicago Illinois to Elizabeth Sutherland and Evan Rees Evans. The family moved to Nova Scotia and in 1907 relocated to Boston Mass. She graduated from high school in Charleston Mass, studied at the Massachusetts Normal Art School and traveled abroad where she received further instruction in Paris, Ireland, Wales and Holland. At the Boston Academy of Fine Arts, she studied portraiture under Joseph DeCamp and design under Vesper George.

Figure 145 Margaret Evans Price

Her father was a member of the wealthy Evans family that held a monopoly in the building material industry in New York City. Brother Heathcliff Evans expanded his father's business to include a book binding business in Manhattan. Cousin Charles Evans Hughes Sr. was Governor of New York from 1907 – 1910 and Chief Justice of the U.S. Supreme Court from 1930 – 1941.

Her first illustrated story was sold to the *Boston Journal* in 1900, when she was 12 years old. After completing her training, she moved to New York City working as a freelance illustrator. Her works were published in magazines like *Rand McNally, Harper Brothers, Nature Magazine, Women's Home Companion, the Pictorial Review* and *Strecher Lithography*. During her career, in addition to works in adult books, children's books and magazines, she created murals, still life paintings and portraits, including illustrating hundreds of special occasion postcards.

In 1909 she married Irving Price, who was born in Worcester Mass and had a successful career with Woolworth's, being promoted to the executive ranks as a district manager. In his position with Woolworth's the family lived in various cities, including Cleveland Ohio and Rochester NY. They had three children Harriet, William and David.

The family moved to East Aurora in 1920 and Irving retired from Woolworth's in 1922 being elected mayor of the village in 1929. They lived at 259 Main Street in East Aurora. Margaret had an art studio in the Van Keuren Building at Main and Pine Street in East Aurora and they also maintained a home called Fernwall, at the South Hampton Parish in Bermuda.

In 1925 Margaret painted two murals for the Aurora Theater, which was owned by a group of businessmen including her husband and Elbert Hubbard II. After the unveiling of these murals, Margaret's artwork was exhibited at the Albright Art Gallery in Buffalo, several galleries in NYC, the Bermuda Art Association, the Boston Art Club, galleries in Buffalo and a number of galleries in East Aurora, including the Aurora Paint & Varnish Club and Meibohm Fine Arts.

Fisher Price Toys was formed in 1930 by Irving Price, Margaret Price, Herman Fisher and Helen Schelle. It was Elbert Hubbard II of the Roycroft Movement that persuaded Fisher to move to East Aurora to join Price and start the toy company. Irving was the main financial backer of Fisher Price Toys, providing the $100,000 investment to start the company. They premiered their toy line at the 1931 American International Toy Fair in NYC and Schelle's contacts placed Fisher Price toys at Macy's and hundreds of stores across the U.S. during their first year of operation. The Fisher Price creed was and has remained "Fisher

Figure 146 Dr. Doodle

Price toys should have intrinsic play value, ingenuity, strong construction, good value for the money and action." Their toys were immediately successful and today all Mattel preschool toys are marketed under the Fisher Price name.

In 1930 Irving purchased the former 1826 Millard Fillmore home on Main Street. They moved the home from its location next to the Aurora Theater to 24 Shearer Avenue in East Aurora where it was remodeled as Margaret's art studio. In 1975 the Aurora Historical Society acquired the home and restored it into circa 1826 Federal Period styling, complete with furniture owned by the Fillmore family in East Aurora,

Buffalo and the White House. It is one of ten National Historic Landmarks in Erie County.

The first toys produced by Fisher Price were called the Hopefuls, a group of 16 toys which included the Margaret Price designed Dr. Doodle and Granny Doodle. Fisher Price has created about 5,000 different toys since 1930. Some of the iconic Fisher Price products include Snoopy Sniffer in 1938, what may be their bestselling toy the Rock-a-Stack introduced in 1951, snap lock beads, corn popper and xylophone developed in 1957, Safety School Bus and Play Family in 1959, Chatter Telephone in 1961 and in 1979 the Fisher Price Phonograph. In 1985 the Play Family was renamed Little People, which is what everyone already called them and in 1997 the wooden peg style Little People were redesigned as plastic molded people and animals with detailed features. Over two billion Little People have been sold. And who did not have the Fisher Price Farm?

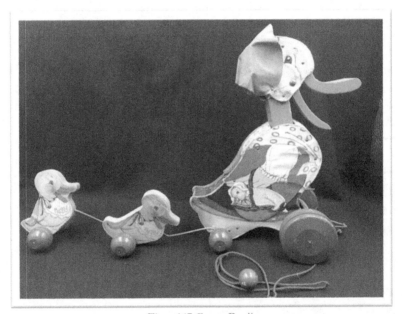

Figure 147 Granny Doodle

Margaret died after a long illness on November 20, 1975 in her East Aurora home. The dream of Irving Price, Herman Fisher, Helen Schelle and Margaret Evans Price lives on as the Fisher Price name continues to be associated with educational, creative and durable children's toys. They are the best-known preschool toy manufacturer in the world and their toys are sold in over 150 countries.

KEZIAH RANSOM

Mother of the first female and male child born in Buffalo

In 1797 Keziah Keyes Ransom accompanied her husband Asa Ransom when he moved to Buffalo. They built one of the first houses in Buffalo, only preceded by Cornelius Winney, William Johnston, Martin Middaugh/Ezekiel Lane and Black Joe Hodge.

Keziah was born in Sheffield, MA on July 29, 1771 and married Asa Ransom in Sheffield on October 12, 1794. They made their home in Geneva NY where Asa moved in 1788 and built a combination home and silversmith shop. He did a lot of trade with the Haudenosaunee who lived in the nearby town of Kanadasaga and he enjoyed working with the Indians. While living in Geneva, Keziah and Asa welcomed their first daughter when Portia was born on December 20, 1795.

The British finally transferred Fort Niagara to U.S. jurisdiction in 1796 and Asa decided to move further west. When Asa, Keziah and Portia arrived in Buffalo in 1797, they were the first family unit to move into the area. They built a log cabin at Main & Terrace Streets where the family lived and Asa operated his silversmith business. He specialized in making silver brooches, earrings and other ornaments that would be of interest to the Seneca Indians. The Seneca lived on the Buffalo Creek Reservation which was adjacent to Buffalo.

Figure 148 Ransom historic marker in Clarence

On February 27, 1798 the Ransom's second daughter Sophia was born. Sophia is considered the first white female child born in Erie County and the first in New York State west of the Genesee River, outside of children born in Fort Niagara.

In 1799 the Holland Land Company advertised lots ten miles apart, to any proper men who would build and keep open taverns upon them. The lots were to be sold at the company's lowest price, on long term and without interest. Asa and Keziah took up that offer with Joseph Ellicott of the Holland Land Company and purchased 150 acres in Clarence Hollow for $2.00 per acre.

The Ransoms built a log cabin, tavern and the first hotel in the area that became Erie County outside of the village of Buffalo. They later added a grist mill at the property near the current intersection of Main Street and Ransom Road. Joseph Ellicott set up the first Holland Land Company office and lived at Ransom's property before relocating the company offices in 1802 to Batavia. In November 1799 Henry Bolton Ransom was born, the first white male child born in Erie County.

Asa was appointed the Justice of the Peace for Erie County in 1801. He was active in many military, political and community activities, so Keziah often operated the tavern and hotel. Asa and Keziah had nine children that survived to adulthood: Portia Ransom Harvey (1795-1833), Sophia Ransom Merrill (1798-1850), Henry Bolton Ransom (1799-1872), Asa Ransom Jr. (1801-1891), Mary Ransom Turney (1803-1888), Franklin Ransom (1805-1873), Sarah Bigelow Ransom Whitaker (1806-1839), Catherine C. Ransom Stevens (1808-1890) and Susan Adelia Ransom Barnard (1811-1843). Since Asa Ransom was step-brother to the Hopkins family, Asa and Keziah were survived by numerous relatives in the WNY area.

Asa Ransom died in 1835 and Keziah survived him by two years, passing away in 1837 at the age of 65. The Ransom Hotel was referred to in 1799 as a large two-story log tavern on the west fork of Ransom Creek on Main Street in Clarence Hollow (then Pine Grove). From 1799 until 1837 there is mention of the property in legal notices, history books, maps and newspapers. After 1837 there is no mention of the Ransom property. It did not burn down and was not demolished. It is possible that it was purchased by the Masons and moved down the street to 10897 Main Steet. The home matches descriptions of the original Ransom Tavern and 10897 Main Street is never mentioned on any documents until after 1837. That means the original Ransom building is still standing at 10897 Main Street and may be the oldest existing building in WNY.

Keziah will be remembered as the first wife to move to WNY with her family, mother of the first white female born in Buffalo, mother of the first white male born in Erie County and proprietor of the first hotel built in WNY outside of the village of Buffalo.

Figure 149 Keziah Ransom gravestone

149

ANNA REINSTEIN

Doctor, Cheektowaga landowner, Socialist Labor Party

Anna Reinstein was the first female obstetrician-gynecologist in WNY, a Cheektowaga landowner and one of the leaders in the Socialist Labor Party (SLP). Her husband Boris left the U.S. in 1917 to assist Trotsky and Lenin with the Bolshevik Revolution. Anna remained in Buffalo but Boris stayed in Russia where he became Lenin's Secretary and Minister of Propaganda.

Anna Mogilova Reinstein was born on February 28, 1866, in Wloclawek, Poland, not far from Warsaw. Her family was of minor Russian nobility and resided near Kiev in the Ukraine. Two of her uncles were archbishops in the Russian Orthodox Church. When the Czar closed universities and there were no opportunities for Jewish students in Russia, Anna went to the University of Bern in Switzerland.

Figure 150 Anna Reinstein
Photo courtesy Julie Reinstein

At the university in Switzerland, Anna met Boris Reinstein and they were married in 1887. The University of Bern was one of two colleges in Europe that trained women to be practicing doctors, rather than just medical researchers. Her medical study at the university continued for five- and one-half years. Anna was one of the first 100 women to receive an M.D. degree from the university. Boris received a degree in pharmacy.

Boris was associated with the People's Will movement, a group of leftist idealists of various nationalities that accepted conspiratorial and violent methods and Anna joined this group. In 1890 she and Boris were arrested as Russian nihilists in Paris on allegations of a plot to assassinate Czar Alexander III. Boris was sentenced to a three-year prison term, but Anna was acquitted.

In 1891 Anna and her daughter left Europe and arrived by ship at Ellis Island in New York City with $100.00 in their possession. She asked to be directed to the closest concentration of Polish and Ukrainian immigrants. It was suggested that she go to Buffalo, so she purchased a one-way ticket to the city.

Upon arriving in Buffalo, she worked as a midwife until she passed the exams that enabled her to practice medicine. Due to the medical training she received in

Switzerland, she completed her U.S. medical studies in only two years during which time she also learned how to speak English. She opened an office at 511 Broadway, which also became the family home until they moved to Danforth Street in the Bellevue section of Cheektowaga in 1904. She was the first doctor to live in Cheektowaga. Anna spoke several languages, including Polish and Yiddish, and delivered babies throughout the East Side and early Cheektowaga neighborhoods. A story documented in a local history mural at the M&T Thruway Plaza branch, shows Anna using a railroad handcar to get to a Gypsy encampment where she performed a Cesarean section during a breech birth. She was paid two chickens for the successful delivery. At the turn of the century, Anna could be seen riding on her bicycle, medical bag in hand on the east side of Buffalo or in Cheektowaga, to make in home visits to her patients.

When her husband Boris was released from prison, he joined Anna in Buffalo. He obtained a second pharmacy degree from UB and opened two pharmacies. However, he devoted most of his time to working as a Socialist organizer, agitator and propagandist, writing articles and giving speeches across the country. He became associated with the NYC Socialist Labor Party. Boris unsuccessfully ran for political office in Buffalo and New York State, but in 1917 was approved as a delegate to a conference in Stockholm to the International Socialist Bureau. Instead of going to the Stockholm Conference he decided to return to Russia as the American representative of the Socialist Party. Coincidentally, Leon Trotsky was on the same ship to Europe and they became friends during the voyage. Boris survived the purge of Stalin and the Siege of Leningrad. When he died in 1947, he was considered one of the last surviving members of the founding members of the communist party and was buried with honors at Novodevichy Cemetery at the Kremlin Wall in Moscow.

Anna became active in the SLP (Socialist Labor Party of America) movement soon after she arrived in Buffalo. She expanded her political work among the Russian population and became an early organizer of the Polish socialist movement in Buffalo's 14th Ward. Through the SLP's Polish-language paper *Sila* (Strength), she shaped the paper's message and helped support it financially by organizing raffles, attending SLP meetings in NYC and writing letters for financial support from Polish socialists in London. During WWI, Anna remained active in the Socialist Labor Party and called for women's activism by organizing women's clubs. She personally organized the August Babel Club of Buffalo, as a money-making auxiliary of the party and for the purpose of agitating and propagating SLP principles in NYS and ultimately the country. Anna also held Sunday picnics at her Cheektowaga home, traveled to other communities to set up Babel Clubs and balanced her SLP activities with the demands of her growing medical practice, oversight of her rental properties and assisting her two grown children, who were launching their own medical practices. She continued her efforts and started traveling to out of town conventions and assisting with activities in other cities, while her children assisted in covering her ever- growing medical practice. After the end of WWI, Anna was Vice-Chairman of "Buffalo Relief for Russia" and worked with the "Soviet Russia Medical Relief Committee" and "Friends of Soviet Russia" to procure grain shipments to Russia during the famine of 1921-1922.

Anna's daughter, Nadina Reinstein was born in Zurich, Switzerland on January 5, 1888. She began the study of medicine at the University of Buffalo in 1906 and while studying abroad in Europe, she met and married Dr. Nahum Kavinoky in 1907. The couple returned to Buffalo where she completed her degree in 1910 and did post-graduate work at Charite Hospital Berlin in 1913. Since a Jewish surgeon could not practice at any hospital in Buffalo, they moved to California in 1919, with Nadina becoming interested in the standards of community health. She specialized in birth control, child spacing, feminine hygiene and for 25 years served as director of the Mother's Clinics in Los Angeles. Nadina was also an instructor of gynecology at several hospitals and lectured at University of California colleges. She died in 1985 at the age of 97.

Anna's son Victor Reinstein followed his mother by receiving an MD from the University of Buffalo and specialized in gynecology. He became interested in law after assisting his mother's attorney during her trials as a radical facing deportation. Victor also received a Law Degree and met his first wife Honorine Thiele at law school. Victor and Honorine had two children, Victor Jr. and Robert, but she died of TB in 1937. He subsequently married Julia Boyer and they had a daughter Julia.

After Anna moved to the Bellevue section of Cheektowaga in 1904, she began purchasing large tracts of land from the trolly company that ran a line to the former amusement park at Bellevue Park. She developed much of the property in the Bellevue section of Cheektowaga. Victor was ten years old when his mother moved to Bellevue and started purchasing land, and he again followed his mother into property ownership. Although he was a practicing doctor and attorney, he established most of his wealth by renting low-cost apartments and buying and selling land. At one point Victor was the largest landowner in Cheektowaga.

She received an award for her accomplishments as a physician and the assistance she provided in supporting females who were furthering their education. The Dr. Anna M. Reinstein Memorial Scholarship Fund was established in 1951, with a preference for female students in medicine, dentistry, law or pharmacy who live within a 50-mile radius of the city of Buffalo.

Anna Reinstein retired from practicing medicine in February 1948, after serving as a doctor for 57 years. She served four generations of families and always advocated for working people. The Reinstein family donated the funds necessary for building the Anna Reinstein Library on Harlem Road in Cheektowaga. That library houses the Reinstein Family Papers comprised of letters, photographs and printed material from 1805 to 1998.

JULIA BOYER REINSTEIN

Historian, Philanthropist, Women's Studies leader

Julia Boyer Reinstein was an educator who became involved with the Erie County Library System, started the Erie County Historical Federation and was the first historian for the town of Cheektowaga. After she married Victor Reinstein, they were benefactors to Cheektowaga, donating land for libraries and parks. Julia was also a proponent for women's rights and started the women's studies program at Elmira College.

She was born as Julia Agnes Boyer in Buffalo on November 3, 1906 but grew up in Warsaw NY. Her father Lee Boyer divorced her mother Julia Smith Boyer, a descendant of the early settlers of the Perry and Castile area, when Julia was one- and one-half years old. After the divorce, her mother returned to Castile and obtained a job as a schoolteacher. She married Charles Manson, owner of a general store in Silver Springs NY, but Julia Boyer remained in Warsaw, living with her great aunt and uncle, Julia Pickett Norris and Fred Norris, owners of the newspaper in Warsaw. She would visit her mother and stepfather on weekends, but per the terms of her parents' divorce, her father Lee Boyer was not to have contact with Julia until she was 18.

*Figure 151 Julia Reinstein painting
Photo Buffalo History Museum*

In 1924 Julia enrolled at Elmira College and two years later her father contacted her to build a father-daughter relationship. She graduated from Elmira College in 1928 and moved to Deadwood South Dakota where her father managed power plants throughout Missouri, Nebraska and South Dakota. Julia started a relationship with a fellow teacher named Dorothy, who also taught in the Deadwood school system. They developed a circle of friends in the lesbian community and her father was accepting of the relationship with Dorothy. After her father died in 1933, Julia obtained a teaching position in Castile where she was joined by Dorothy. They had separate apartments but spent weekends in a suite her parents built for them in their home, and summers in an apartment in NYC, both completing their master's degree at Columbia. Her master's degree was in History and curriculum construction.

Julia and Dorothy broke up in the early 1940s. Julia took a position teaching at Pine Hill High School before it became part of the Cheektowaga School System. Julia Boyer and Victor Reinstein met During WWII while volunteering as Civil Defense workers. Victor was the son of noted historical figure Anna Reinstein. Julia and Victor were married in Baltimore Maryland on September 28, 1942. Victor had two sons from his previous marriage, so Julia became the stepmother of Victor Jr. and David Reinstein. A daughter, Julia Ann Reinstein, was born to Julia and Victor. Julia stopped teaching after getting married, worked for UB and devoted her time to the development of libraries, history societies and later philanthropy.

Julia Reinstein began her interest in local history in 1951 when she learned that the State Legislature mandated that all towns name official historians. In 1953, she was appointed Cheektowaga's first historian, a position she held until 1992. She was the first president of the Municipal Historians of New York, co-founder of the Erie County Historical Federation with George G. Sipprell and helped create 28 historical societies in WNY. Julia was instrumental in establishing the Historical Building at the Erie County Fair Grounds, serving as its superintendent for 25 years. Julia also served on the Board of Managers of the Buffalo and Erie County Historical Society. She formed the Cheektowaga Historical Society in 1971, founded the Cheektowaga Historical Museum and was involved with the town's bicentennial celebration in 1976 and the sesquicentennial of Cheektowaga in 1989. Through her efforts, most of the town history was recorded and oral histories were recorded with numerous elderly residents.

Her interest in libraries dated back to 1937 when she participated in opening Cheektowaga's first reading room. She was the first appointee to the Cheektowaga Library Board in 1959 and served as chairman of the Cheektowaga Library Board. Victor donated the land and contributed $250,000 toward the library construction costs with the provision that the library be named after his wife. Julia paid $40,000 for the installation of the Losson Road Library's computerized card catalogue and information systems. On November 3, 1995, her 89th birthday, Julia Reinstein attended the dedication of the Julia Boyer Reinstein Library on Losson Road, one of the most advanced facilities in WNY. In addition, Julia was a member of the Cheektowaga Town Board, Cheektowaga Symphony Guild, was active in the Cheektowaga Chamber of Commerce, a member of the Conservation Forum of the Buffalo Museum of Science, and a trustee of Elmira College.

The Julia Boyer Reinstein Center is the small building in front of the Buffalo History Museum and next to the parking lot on Elmwood Avenue. It is the former Leonard Adams residence and music studio. The building was purchased by the museum in 1989 as a project of the "History Lives Here" capital campaign to serve as an office/meeting space. The building received the National Register of Historic Places honor, with restoration by contributions of Julia Boyer Reinstein and named the Julia Boyer Reinstein Center in 1992. A full-length portrait of Julia Boyer

Reinstein by Buffalo artist Mary Diebold Smith hangs on the landing of the split staircase.

For her accomplishments, she and Victor received the Service to Mankind Award of the Sertoma Club of Cheektowaga in 1969, she was awarded a commendation certificate by the American Association for State and Local History in 1971, was named Citizen of the Year by the Cheektowaga Cultural Society in 1971, received the Red Jacket Award from the Buffalo and Erie County Historical Society in 1974, and was named Citizen of the Year by the Cheektowaga Chamber of Commerce in 1989.

Figure 152 Julia & Victor Reinstein in 1978 Photo courtesy Julie Reinstein

In 1932, Victor Reinstein purchased 292-acres of forested wetlands and ponds, located off Como Park Blvd., in the populated Bellevue section of Cheektowaga. With his son Robert Reinstein and helpers, they planted 30,000 trees and constructed 19 ponds, marshes and swamps. The Park includes the stone summer home where the Reinstein family picnicked. After Victor's death in 1984, Julia was responsible for donating the nature reserve to New York State. Following the explicit instructions of her husband, Julia made certain that the NYS Department of Conservation complied to the preservation and education of wildlife and nature that Victor envisioned and started. In addition to the donation of Reinstein Woods Nature Preserve and Julia Reinstein Library, Victor Reinstein donated the land for Stiglmeier Park on Losson Road, Nokomis Park on Nokomis Drive, and the Anna Reinstein Library on Harlem Road named for his mother.

After the death of her husband, Julia resumed her life as a lesbian. She was the subject of an anthropological study of LGBTQ+ life to evaluate the difference between middle-class and upper-class lesbian lives. The study by UB's Elizabeth Lapovsky Kennedy was supplemental research to her book *Boots of Leather, Spillers of Gold*. Reinstein was a long-time voice for women's rights and started the women's studies program at Elmira College. To create the Women's Studies Program, she donated $25,000 a year for the 90/91, 91/92 and 91/93 school years. As a feminist and early lesbian activist, she donated the funding for the annual Women's and Gender Studies Symposium at Elmira College.

Julia Boyer Reinstein died on July 18, 1998, at the age of 91. It was fitting that her memorial was held at the library named in her honor on Losson Road. She is buried with her mother at Grace Cemetery in Castile and was known as "Cheektowaga's Great Lady."

MARGARET ST. JOHN

Only home left standing after Buffalo was burned during War of 1812

When the British and Mohawk Indians burned Buffalo, in retaliation for the American burning of Niagara on the Lake (Newark), the only home left standing was that of Margaret St. John.

The British attack began on December 30, 1813 and most residents escaped by taking Main Street to Williamsville, Harris Hill or Clarence. Others crossed Buffalo Creek for the safety of Hamburg and other settlements south of the village. Asaph Bemis, the husband of St. John's second oldest daughter Aurelia, gathered his wife and six of the younger St. John children into his wagon and tried to flee towards Williamsville but the road was blocked. He returned to the village and told his mother-in-law that he was taking the children to Hamburg and he would return to get Margaret and two of her older daughters, Maria and Sarah.

Figure 153 Margaret St. John

Margaret realized she was stranded in the Village of Buffalo and she pleaded with British General Phineas Raill to spare her home and the lives of her and her daughters. She explained to Raill that earlier during the war her son Cyrus died of distemper from the military camp in Buffalo and her husband and son Elijah drowned on June 6, 1813 in the Niagara River while ferrying supplies in their boat to resupply American troops occupying Fort Erie. The war had already taken her husband and two sons, so she did not want to additionally lose her home. Raill agreed to assign his interpreter to be stationed in front of the St. John home, so the Mohawk did not destroy it.

She was born in Wilton, Connecticut on July 15, 1768, the daughter of Presbyterian clergyman Cyrus Marsh. She married Gamaliel St. John and in 1788 they moved to Danbury, Connecticut where five of their children were born. The lure of opportunities in the west drew the St. John family to Westmoreland, NY where Gamaliel helped build seven miles of the road between the Cayuga and Owasco Lakes and where three more children were born to the family.

The family continued moving west and in 1807 the St. Johns moved to Williamsville, settling on a farm owned by Andrew Ellicott, the brother of Joseph Ellicott. Gamaliel inspected the lands in WNY and decided upon moving to the Village of Buffalo where in 1810 they purchased Lot #53 from Mrs. Chapman. The lot included the frame of a front building and a completed small back building. Gamaliel and his sons Elijah and Cyrus cut the logs and moved them to the Williamsville saw mill for cutting into lumber and made the shingles during the winter of 1809/10, along with cutting the blocks for the basement from Granger's quarry near Scajaquada Creek. The family's eleventh child was born in the back building while the front house, at 460 Main Street was being completed.

Margaret and her daughters watched the British and their Mohawk allies burn down the homes and businesses of Buffalo. Even with a guard posted in front of their home, Mrs. St. John and her daughters had to ward off threats during the burning of December 30 and 31. During the evening Sarah St. John would sneak out of the home to forage for food, catching chickens and pigs, along with gathering vegetables and collecting water from the well.

On January 1, 1814 the Mohawk returned to burn all buildings that were not destroyed. On this day they burned the tavern the St. John family built next to their home. That morning several Indians broke into the St. John home and the people who had taken refuge in the house fled in panic. Sarah was chased by an Indian who had a raised tomahawk in his hand. Out of fear, Sarah stopped, turned toward her assailant with raised hands and started laughing. The Indian was stunned. He shook Sarah's hand, painted her face and motioned her back to her house. A British officer stopped her and asked why her face was painted like an Indian. He told her to wash off the war paint, but she refused fearing the Indian may return and become upset if she removed the paint. Extraordinary courage for a 16-year-old girl.

The St. John home was the only residential building not burned during the British attack on Buffalo. The only other buildings left standing were the stone walls of the jail, David Rees' stone blacksmith shop and part of Captain Pratt's recently built barn where the timbers were still too green to be burned by the fires.

Sarah Lovejoy lived in the house across the street from the St. John family at 465 Main Street, later the location of the Tifft House and Hengerer's Department Store. Margaret encouraged Sarah to cooperate with the British and Mohawk, but she objected trying to stop them from taking items from her home. Sarah was killed by the Indians, the only civilian casualty during the burning of Buffalo and the 465 Main Street home was torched.

When the residents of Buffalo began to return to the city, several of them just put roofs over their cellars and lived underground to survive the winter. During the war Margaret lost her husband, two oldest sons, their tavern and most of their possessions, but she still provided food and shelter for the returning villagers. She was left to raise her family with her youngest son being only three and a half years old. The family persevered, regained their position in the village, were respected by all for the bravery shown during the burning of Buffalo and acknowledged for the assistance they provided to the people of the village.

Several of Margaret St. John's children and their descendants played significant roles in the development of Buffalo. Maria St. John married Abram J. Fisk and their daughter Calista Maria Fisk married prominent businessman Orson Phelps. Her monument, created in Rome by famous sculptor Nicola Canatamessa-Papotti, is one of the finest in Forest Lawn Cemetery. Sarah St. John was the second wife of Mayor Samuel Wilkeson, the builder of Buffalo harbor. She lived in the Wilkeson Mansion on Niagara Square, now the site of City Hall. Sarah's grandson by marriage, Tellico Johnson, was the developer of Orton and St. John's Place. Sarah was known for her charitable contributions assisting the poor and was given the honor of turning over the first shovelful of soil to commence the construction of the Erie Canal in Buffalo on August 9, 1823. Parnell St. John married Jonathan Sidway. After Jonathan's death in 1847 she remained at the Sidway mansion on Hudson Street and her bachelor brother Le Grand St. John moved in to help maintain the home and assist in raising her children. Le Grand was an engineer, inventor and artist. He received a NYS patent for a steam heater in 1851 and U.S. patent for an improved boat propeller in 1858. His drawings of the Burning of Buffalo during the War of 1812, to which he was an eyewitness, are in the collection of the Buffalo Historical Society, now the Buffalo History Museum.

After her children left home, Margaret St. John lived in a house on Seneca Street. She died in 1847 and the home at 460 Main Street that survived the burning of Buffalo was demolished in 1871.

The only dwelling not destroyed at the burning of Buffalo
36

Figure 154 St. John tavern & house from Le Grand St. John drawing

Figure 155 Drawing of St. John house

CHARLOTTE N. SHEDD

Co-Founder Hospice Buffalo

The hospice movement was developed in London during the 1960s. Cicely Saunders, an English doctor who founded the first modern Hospice in London, gave a series of lectures at Yale University. Charlotte and her husband attended these lectures and brought the concepts of Hospice and Palliative Care to Buffalo when they moved to WNY.

Born Charlotte Newsom on August 31, 1922 in Oklahoma City, she was raised in Wichita Falls Texas and Shreveport Louisianna. After graduating from Centenary College of Louisianna with a degree in music, she was studying for her master's degree in nursing at Yale University where she met her future husband Dr. Donlad P. Shedd, a head and neck surgeon. Both were students in educational programs sponsored by the U.S. Army during WWII.

Figure 156 Charlotte N. Shedd
Photo courtesy Hospice & Palliative Care Buffalo

They married and after graduation, Don being a military doctor, he was assigned to various postings across the country. He expected to be sent overseas but was stationed at a hospital in New Haven where he completed his training as a surgeon and accepted a position on the Faculty of Surgery at the Yale University School of Medicine. Because of their education, both Charlotte and Don believed that the medical enterprise was focused on the preservation of life and combating disease. However, after the battle was lost and the patient was considered terminal, there was little effort or understanding expended toward providing for the physical, psychological, social or spiritual needs of the patient.

At Yale in 1963, her husband heard the lectures by Cicely Saunders and asked that she provide literature to him about hospice. Don came home and told Charlotte that hospice care was possibly the solution to their dilemma about terminal care for patients. Dr. Saunders returned to Yale in 1966 and gave talks to the Yale School of Nursing. Florence S. Wald, the Dean of the nursing school was so impressed with the hospice concept that she took a six month leave of absence from Yales to study under Dr. Saunders at St. Christopher's Hospital in London where Saunders pioneered the idea of hospice. Upon returning to Yale, Wald opened the first hospice in the U.S. in New Haven. The Shedds were too occupied with their professional and family responsibilities so they were aware of the project but could not participate.

Dr. Donald P. Shedd accepted an appointment at the Roswell Park Cancer Institute in Buffalo in 1967. Charlotte accompanied her husband to Buffalo and began working from her dining-room table. While caring for her mother and four children, she began to establish a hospice program in WNY. She and her husband recruited like-minded community leaders and health care professionals. A former Army air evacuation nurse Irene Mahar was an early recruit, along with attorney Michael Swart, who served with Charlotte on the Visiting Nursing Association (VNA) board of directors. Don Shedd suggested they add representatives from the clergy to their small group. They added retired Lutheran pastor Ralph W. Loew, Catholic priest Father Eugene Ulrich and Rev. Dr. C. Charles Bachmann, the Director of Clinical Pastoral Counseling Education at what is now ECMC. Dr. Thomas S. Bumbalo, the hospital director, joined the board in 1979. The initial board of Buffalo Hospice was complete with Charlotte Shedd as the Chairperson, Irene Mahar the treasurer, Dr. Bumbalo the President, along with the three clergy. Board meetings were held at the homes of the Shedds, Lowes and Irene Mahar.

Charlotte Shedd traveled across the country to meetings of state and national hospice organizations, being a founder of some of these groups. She visited established hospice programs, provided guidance to fledging organizations and appeared at hearings in Washington D.C. and Albany when important legislation was pending. After getting the Courier Express to publish several articles about hospice, Shredd and Mahar scheduled talks by well-known hospice speakers and eventually signed up over 200 potential volunteers.

Figure 157 Dame Cicely Saunders - London founder of Hospice concept
Photo courtesy Hospice & Palliative Care of Buffalo

Through these efforts and talks she met Dr. Robert A. Milch, a surgeon with Buffalo Medical Group. In 1978 Milch was asked to chair an annual conference with the American Cancer Society and Roswell Park. He decided to offer something new at the conference and presented a session on hospice that involved doctors, nurses, social workers and chaplains. Milch shared in the receipts from the conference and more than 250 people attended. When he received $4,000 from the session, he gave the money to Shedd and it was reported he said, "Let's Start."

With additional funding from the Junior League, the Margaret L. Wendt Foundation and other organizations, they formed Hospice Buffalo, believed to be

160

the 11th Hospice formed in the U.S. The efforts of Shedd, Mahar and Milch trained 120 volunteers and they had the people power that enabled Hospice Buffalo to begin providing services to the community. They initiated Hospice home care on a volunteer basis.

The first office for Hospice Buffalo was a second-floor office at 2929 Main Street near All-High Stadium in Buffalo. A free-standing hospice unit was needed for inpatient care. Brothers of Mercy offered use of a domiciliary unit in Clarence but that opportunity fell through. They came to an agreement with Erie County Executive Ed Rutkowski to rent seven unused rooms in the Erie County Home & Infirmary in Alden for $1.00 a year. That became the first Hospice Buffalo in-patient unit, now located on Como Park Blvd. in Cheektowaga. The original volunteers became employees of Hospice Buffalo and in 1993 Dr. Milch became the full-time Medical Director.

Figure 158 Donald & Charlotte Shedd
Photo courtesy Hospice &
Palliative Care Buffalo

The organization has grown to include not only the campus in Cheektowaga, but also hospital-based facilities in many area hospitals, a Hospice-at-home program of visiting doctors and nurses so that patients can die in their home, and a program called Essential Care that provides for the needs of dying children and their families.

Shedd was an original member of the Hospice Buffalo Board of Directors. She retired in 1989 after serving as executive director of Hospice Buffalo for 11 years. Shedd was a co-founder of the New York State Hospice and Palliative Care Association and was an early member of the governing board of directors of the National Hospice & Palliative Care Organization. She continued her musical career, was director of the chorus and harpsichordist at Holy Trinity Lutheran Church in Buffalo where she became acquainted with Pastor Loew.

Charlotte and her husband had four children Carolyn, Ann, Laura and David. She received a Distinguished Alumna Award from the Yale School of Nursing in 1992 and was named a Buffalo News Citizen of the Year in 1980. Her husband Donald wrote the book *Early History of Hospice* Buffalo with Dr. Abel K. Fink, published in 2003 by The Center for Hospice & Palliative Care.

After Charlotte was diagnosed with Alzheimer's disease, her husband cared for her at home. When she reached the end stage of the disease, she was admitted to the Center for Hospice & Palliative Care in Cheektowaga which is part of her legacy to the Buffalo area. She died at the age of 84 on April 28, 2007 in the facility she co-founded; a facility that brought comfort and care to thousands of terminally ill patients and their families in the WNY area.

APRIL STEVENS

Grammy-winning WNY Vocalist

April Stevens was born Caroline Vincinette LoTempio on April 29, 1929 in Niagara Falls. Her brother Antonio Bart LoTempio was born in Niagara Falls on January 6, 1935. Their father Sam was a grocer, and their mother Anna was an aspiring entertainer who was held back from pursuing a musical career due to her husband's traditional values.

Anna LoTempio may not have become a performer but was instrumental in launching her children's entertainment careers. She coaxed a seven-year-old Antonio into telling bandleader Benny Goodman he made a $10.00 bet that he could sing with the band. Just after Peggy Lee finished singing, Antonio approached the stage at Shea's Buffalo, tugged at Benny Goodman's jacket and told him about the bet. Goodman fell for the story and explained to the audience this was not

Figure 159 April Stevens

planned and asked Antonio what he wanted to sing. He replied "Rosetta in the key of C with a tag at the end" and commenced to bring down the house. Goodman realized the audience enjoyed his song so much that he invited little Antonio to return to do the same bit for their remaining six shows at the theatre. This experience made Antonio interested in becoming a singer and actor. He even took clarinet lessons (later switching to tenor sax) to emulate Goodman. At the age of nine Antonio appeared in *George White's Scandals of 1945*.

In the 1940s the LoTempios moved to California so Antonio could further his acting and singing career. He was in the 1949 movie The Red Pony, played in high school dance bands, performed with Horace Heidt's Band and began working as a session musician. He decided to change his name to Nino Tempo.

Caroline began singing while she was still attending Belmont High School in Los Angeles. She was discovered at the famous Wallich's Music City record store at Sunset & Vine in Hollywood. Tony Sepe, the owner of Laurel Records asked her if she could sing and signed her to record a few songs for his independent label. Caroline felt a song she was asked to record was too suggestive. Not wanting to record the song under her actual name, like her older brother, she decided to change her name. She chose April for the month of her birth and Stevens because she thought it sounded American. April admitted to revising her birthday from 1929 to 1936 so she could compete with younger artists.

162

While still in high school she recorded several songs for Sepe's Laurel Records and was signed to Society Records. Her first record with Society was titled "Don't Do It", a song that was banned from airplay by the 1950s guardians of public morality. The record sold under the counter by word of mouth and became successful.

Henri Rene, head of Artists & Repertoire for RCA Victor Records heard Don't Do It and sensed an unusual quality in April's sensual alluring vocals. In 1951, as the lead vocalist with Henri Rene & his Orchestra, their song "I'm in Love Again" remained on the charts for 15 weeks and peaked at #6. It was especially popular with Korean War servicemen. She also had another Top Ten hit with "Gimme a Little Kiss, Will Ya Hah?" "And So to Sleep Again" also made it to the charts. Other recordings and international club engagements followed.

During the 1950s Nino Tempo expanded upon his acting career. He appeared in The Glenn Miller Story with James Stewart in 1954, in Operation Petticoat with Cary Grant in 1959 and performed with Steve Lawrence, Eydie Gorme and Rosemary Clooney.

In 1959 April Stevens recorded the Nino Tempo composed "Teach Me Tiger" another sensually suggestive song that was banned in many markets but still reached #86 on the Billboard Top 100. The song was recorded by other artists, including Marilyn Monroe. It became a camp classic in the U.S. and foreign countries. Even the Space Shuttle Challenger astronauts requested "Teach Me Tiger" as their wake-up song on April 6, 1983. April was invited to the craft's landing.

Although Nino Tempo was receiving success as an actor, the majority of his time was dedicated to working as a studio musician. He became a member of the Wrecking Crew, a collection of studio musicians that played on a large number of hit records in the 1960s. In addition, he worked closely with producer Phil Spector and collaborated with Sonny Bono.

Tempo played sax on a couple of Bobby Darin's hits. During a Bobby Darin recording session in 1963, Ahmet Ertegun of Atlantic Records heard Tempo playing some new songs he had written on piano for Darin. Ahmet was impressed with Nino's bluesy style and was familiar with April Stevens previous songs, especially liking "Teach Me Tiger." When he heard Nino was April's brother and they were planning to put a duo together, he offered them a recording contract on the Atlantic subsidiary ATCO Records.

Their first single on ATCO was a live recording of "Sweet and Lovely." Ertegun supervised the recording and they were backed by top studio musicians, including Glen Campbell on guitar, and background vocalists, including Darlene Love. This first single reached a respectable #77 on the charts. Their second single "Paradise" did not break the Top 100.

The last song recorded for their first album was "Deep Purple." It was recorded in two takes that took a total of 14 minutes. Stevens and Tempo wanted to release "Deep Purple" as a single but Ertegun did not like the song. Tempo wanted to record with Phil Spector so he told Ertegun if the song was not released, they wanted to be released from their recording contract. Ertegun relented and "Deep Purple" reached the top of the charts in the fall of 1963. This gave Stevens the dubious distinction of waiting the longest time (12 years) between her first national hit and her first #1 hit. That honor was later claimed by Tina Turner. "Deep Purple" was recorded note for note by Donnie and Marie Osmond in 1975 and again charted as a Top 20 hit.

During the recording of "Deep Purple", Nino was unsure of the lyrics, so April whispered them to him ahead of each line. The whispers could be heard, resulting in the exchange that is a hallmark of the record.

Figure 160 April & Nino receiving #1 Record Award from Billboard Magazine's Eliot Tiegel (right) with Atlantic/Atco president Ahmet Ertegun (left)

Deep Purple winning a Grammy for best Rock N Roll Recording in 1963 was an indication of the Grammy Committee's questionable grasp of what constituted rock music. April Stevens and Nino Tempo's recordings were basically easy listening material but had a slight pop rock feel to their arrangements. They were categorized as a rock and roll group. However, their music was more on the line of Tin Pan Alley popular music than the rock material that was being composed by a new group of songwriters centered in the Brill Building. The definition of rock music was solidified with the 1964 British Invasion, led by The Beatles.

Due to the British Invasion, the duo of April Stevens and Nino Tempo, known for their rework of Tin Pan Alley classics, were considered more of an Adult Contemporary, rather than a pop group. They had hit singles with "Whispering" (#11 Pop and #4 Adult Contemporary), "Stardust" (#32 Pop and #13 AC) and recorded an upbeat version of the Cole Porter standard "Begin the Beguine." This success resulted in television appearances on American Bandstand, The Lloyd Thaxton Show, Shindig, the Joey Bishop Show and Smothers Brothers Comedy Hour, one-nighters, college concerts, and clubs dates from Las Vegas and Reno/Tahoe to Europe and Australia.

In 1966 they recorded "All Strung Out", a Phil Spector influenced arrangement, referred to by critic Richie Unterberger as the greatest Phil Spector inspired production of all time. It peaked at #26 and in 1978 "All Strung Out" was a Top 40 hit for John Travolta. Ironically Tempo wrote the song for the Righteous Brothers who recorded what is considered the greatest Phil Spector production "You've Lost that Lovin Feeling."

During the early 1970s April and Nino signed with A&M Records, continuing to record standards and new material written by Tempo. They experienced some success, but later in the 1970s Stevens semi-retired while Tempo continued performing, concentrating on playing sax. He was a member of the Maynard Ferguson Band and did studio work with Linda Ronstadt, Dion, John Lennon, Cher and Kenny Rankin. He even had a disco hit with his instrumental "Sister James" co-written with producer Jeff Barry.

Through the 1990s Stevens and Tempo performed some dates solo and as a duo. In 1991 April released the cabaret style solo album "Carousel Dreams" and during the 1990s Tempo released three critically acclaimed jazz albums.

Figure 161 April Stevens & Nino Tempo

April Stevens and Nino Tempo were inducted into the Buffalo Music Hall of Fame in 1999, during a ceremony at The Tralfamadore Café. April attended but did not perform because Nino Tempo could not make arrangements to appear at the ceremony.

Figure 162 April at 1999 BMHOF Induction Ceremony

She died on April 17, 2023 in her Scottsdale Arizona home at the age of 93.

MARY BURNETT TALBERT

Civil Rights Advocate

Mary Burnett was born on September 17, 1866, in Oberlin Ohio to Caroline Nicholls Burnett and Cornelius Burnett. Oberlin was a town in Northeastern Ohio famous for its history in the abolitionist movement and in 1866 was filled with free people of color and runaway slaves who settled in the area. The community, unaware of the future civil rights icon in their presence, watched as Mary Burnett graduated from Oberlin High School at the age of 16, an uncommon case in Black America for her time.

Figure 163 Mary Talbert
Photo Iowa State University Archives

Following graduation, she enrolled at Oberlin College, the first college in the U.S. to admit African-Americans in 1835 and women in 1837. Mary excelled in her academic studies at Oberlin. A story often told is one of her trigonometry instructor reluctantly admitting her to the class. In the class, Mary earned a term score of 5 and an examination score of 5.5 out of 6. Not only did she excel in the academics of Oberlin, but she also embraced involvement in extracurricular activities. Mary became the Treasurer of Aeolian, one of two college societies for young women and she was also one of six representatives for Class Day Exercises. At the age of 19, she graduated with the equivalent of a Bachelor of Arts from Oberlin College. Mary Burnett was the only African-American in her graduating class of 1886.

Following her graduation, Mary obtained a position teaching science, history, math, and Latin in a high school and at Bethel University in Little Rock, Arkansas. Quickly navigating the Jim Crow South, Mary was elected Assistant Principal at Union High School in Little Rock in 1887. This was the highest position held by any woman or African-American in the state. Shortly after becoming an Assistant Principal, Mary met William H. Talbert, a leading advocate of African-American men in Buffalo.

Mary and William were married in 1891 and moved to Buffalo. She became a member of the historic Michigan Avenue Baptist Church, famous for its part in the Underground Railroad. While at the church Mary formed the Christian Culture

Congress, an organization that brought African-American leaders such as W.E.B DuBois and Mary Church Terrell, to Buffalo to speak to the congregation. In 1894, Mary became Buffalo's only African-American woman to join the Association of Collegiate Alumnae.

In Buffalo, Mary became a fervent member of the civil rights movement. Prior to the Pan-American Exposition, she protested the exclusion of African-Americans from the Planning Committee. During this protest, she called for the appointment of an African-American board member and for an exhibit on the lives of African-Americans. At a November 12, 1900 meeting, Talbert read an essay entitled "Why the American Negro Should Be Represented at the Pan-American Exposition." This resulted in the Negro Exhibit being added to the Exposition. Created by W.E.B DuBois, it featured hundreds of photographs documenting African-Americans at the homes of prominent individuals, on the grounds of African-American Universities, at businesses and churches. Literary works were exhibited, along with displays highlighting Black accomplishments, such as listings of patent holders and Black servicemen who received medals fighting for the country. The Negro Exhibit countered the "Old Plantation" Antebellum South and "Darkest Africa" exhibits, that negatively depicted African-Americans.

She helped found the Phyllis Wheatly Club of Colored Women, Buffalo's first affiliate of the National Association of Colored Women (NACW), an organization of which she become President in 1899. This club organized a settlement house in Buffalo and helped found chapters of subsequent organizations in other cities. Under her leadership, the organization called for Buffalo Police to focus on crimes committed in African-American neighborhoods. The organization was so demanding that Talbert was invited to join a citywide committee which monitored police enforcement in Buffalo. Talbert also established a junior YWCA and girls' clubs around the city, dedicated to delicate subjects like personal hygiene, and moral improvement. They regularly visited jails, established kindergartens, supported homes for aged adults and wayward girls. In 1901, Talbert lectured at the Biennial Conference of NACW.

Talbert and her husband secretly hosted a meeting around the dining table of their Michigan Avenue home in July 1905. The meeting included W.E.B DuBois, John Hope, and thirty others. This secret meeting is often referred to as the first meeting of the Niagara Movement. The following day, the group officially convened at the Erie Beach Hotel in Fort Erie, Ontario. The Niagara Movement was the precursor of the National Association of Advancement for Colored People (NAACP). In 1908 she became a charter member of the Empire State Federation of Colored Women, eventually becoming Parliamentarian and President of the organization. After the NAACP was founded in 1909, Mary became one of the first women members of the newly minted organization and was elected to the organizations Board of Directors.

Figure 164 Historic marker of Talbert home location next to Michigan Avenue Baptist Church
Photo credit Rick Falkowski

In 1916, Talbert became President of NACW (1916-1921) and the Vice President of the NAACP. In these positions, Talbert spearheaded a federal effort to pass national anti-lynching legislation which didn't became a federal law until 2020. During the United States involvement in WWI, Mary took a pause in her civil rights activism. In 1917, Talbert was one of a handful of Black Red Cross nurses to serve on the Western Front in Europe. While on the front, Talbert became secretary of the YMCA in France, offered classes to African-American soldiers, and served on the Women's Committee of National Defense. Following the war, she served on the Women's Committee on International Relations which selected women nominees for the predecessor of the United Nations, the League of Nations. Talbert also became the first African-American delegate to the International Council of Women. During a speech in Christiana Norway, she called for nations to be judged by their ability to uphold human rights and for laws and administration to be free of racial or gender bias. Additionally, following the war, she served as National Director for the NAACP Anti-Lynching Campaign and became chairwoman of its committee. In her advocacy for anti-lynching legislation, Talbert specifically called for the passage of the Dyer Anti-Lynching Bill introduced by Missouri Congressman Leonidas Dyer. Due to her efforts, she became the first woman to be awarded the NAACP's Spingarn Medal, its highest award offered. Not only was Talbert an advocate for civil rights, but she was also a historical preservation pioneer. As President of NACW she created a committee to consider the possibility of assisting the trustees of the Frederick Douglass Memorial and Historical Association. Talbert worked to raise money to pay off the mortgage on Frederick Douglass's old home and began maintenance and preservation efforts. By 1922, NACW completed the restoration of the home of this abolitionist pioneer.

Talbert was also a fierce advocate for women's suffrage. Talbert's organization, the Phyllis Wheatly Club of Colored Women, organized seminars on the power of the African-American female vote and organized other political clubs to get out the vote. In 1915, she spoke at the "Votes for Women: A symposium by Leading Thinkers of Colored Women" in Washington D.C.

Figure 165 Mary Talbert picture on Freedom Wall mural

On October 15, 1923, at the age of 57, Mary Morris Burnett Talbert passed away in her home in Buffalo and is buried at Forest Lawn Cemetery. For her accomplishments she was inducted into the Women's Hall of Fame in 2005, Talbert Hall at the UB North campus is named after her, and her portrait is one of 28 individuals included on the Freedom Wall at Michigan Avenue and East Ferry Streets. Talbert's contributions paved the way for the 1950s-60s Civil Rights Movement and she was considered by her peers as "the best-known colored woman in the United States."

ANNIE EDSON TAYLOR

First person to survive plunge over Niagara Falls

A nnie Edson Taylor was the first person to go over Niagara Falls, making the trip in a wooden barrel. She had hoped the daredevil stunt would bring her fame and fortune, but bad luck followed her throughout her life and she died in poverty and relative obscurity twenty years after surviving the plunge over the falls.

Born in the Finger Lakes region of New York on October 24, 1838, Annie was described as a young woman with a dreamy disposition, lively imagination and an insatiable thirst for adventure

Figure 166 Annie Taylor with her barrel & cat
Photo Niagara Falls Public Library

stories. With this personality it was no surprise when at an early age Annie moved out of the small town of Auburn to experience what the country had to offer.

At the age of 18, Annie married David Taylor, the older brother of one of her best friends. David died shortly after their wedding, resulting in Annie moving from city to city where additional various misfortunes continued. In Chattanooga Tennessee she survived a house fire. In South Carolina she lived through an earthquake. When riding in a stagecoach in rural Texas, robbers attacked the stagecoach. Annie refused to give them the money that was hidden in her dress.

After continued moves, Annie settled in Bay City near Saginaw Bay Michigan. She opened a successful charm school, teaching children of the local gentry everything from dancing the waltz to proper table manners. When her income dwindled due to the aging of her students, she started searching for other money-making activities. She wanted to do something that was not done before and got an idea after reading that the Pan-American Exposition would be taking place in Buffalo from May 1, 1901 to November 2, 1901.

Taylor decided to go over Niagara Falls in a barrel and do it in late October when the area would be filled with visitors for the scheduled closing of the Pan-Am on November 2. During the Expo 10,000 to 50,000 people daily visited the Niagara Falls Reservation State Park, taking the train excursions from the Pan-Am. It was reported that she did not look the part of a daredevil. Matronly, stout and greying, Annie lied about her age claiming to be 42 not 62.

She designed and built a cardboard and string protype of the barrel. It was manufactured by a company that made beer kegs, Taylor selected each piece of lumber, the barrel was built to her five-foot height, only three feet at its widest width, secured by ten metal hoops and weighted with a 200-pound anvil, to keep the barrel upright.

A couple days before she attempted the stunt, a test run was conducted with Annie's cat making the trip over the falls in the barrel. When the cat emerged unharmed, Annie felt confident she would survive the plunge. On the day of her attempt, crowds were drawn to see Annie either make history by surviving going over the falls or experiencing something terrible. Annie entered the water from the U.S. side upstream of the Horseshoe Falls. Her assistants William Holleran and Fred Truesdale rowed her out into the water, releasing the barrel so she would descend over the Canadian Horseshoe Falls. Extra air was pumped into the barrel, Annie was secured in a harness and they packed pillows around her to further cushion the fall. Crowds lined the shore to watch the barrel bob in the rapids.

The barrel paused at the brink before gravity plummeted it 160 feet into the gorge. Taylor felt the barrel spinning as it was being tossed below the falls. It hit a rock and was shot like an arrow back into the churn from the falls. Twenty minutes after the barrel entered the water, Taylor was pulled to shore and rescued.

With spectators watching from both the American and Canadian sides, Taylor was removed from the barrel. Startled, seasick, bruised with a cut on her head, she was led to the shore, still clutching waterlogged pillows. To celebrate the rescue of Taylor, the Maid of the Mist blew its horn and megaphones announced her success to crowds above the gorge. National press did not immediately report the daredevil stunt. The Boston Globe reported that Taylor accomplished a feat "never attempted except in the deliberate commission of suicide." It is believed that she went over the falls on October 24, 1901, Taylors 63rd birthday.

After recuperating from the ordeal at Dr. Pierces Invalid Hotel and Surgical Institute in Buffalo, Annie wanted to reap the financial

Figure 167 Rescue of Annie Taylor after going over Niagara Falls in a barrel
Photo Niagara Falls Public Library

rewards for her daredevil stunt. However, her manager stole the barrel and left town. He even hired a woman to portray a younger Taylor and successfully toured the theater halls. Annie spent most of her money on private detectives trying to locate the stolen barrel. She went on tour without the barrel, making speeches and posing for photographs. That was successful for a short period of time. However, Annie advertised she was in her early 40s but with her matronly appearance, theater crowds doubted she was actually Annie Edson Taylor.

In 1910 she returned to Niagara Falls in attempt to sell her memoirs and try other moneymaking schemes. In addition to selling postcards and other souvenirs from a stand in front of a store near the falls, she tried working as a clairvoyant and offering "electric and magnetic" medical treatments. She sold all the mementos of her stunt but died indigent, blind and almost penniless at the Niagara County Infirmary in Lockport in 1921, at the age of 82. Her friends paid for her plot in the Stunters Rest section of Oakwood Cemetery, reserved for daredevils who braved Niagara Falls and emerged either dead or alive.

Figure 168 Annie Taylor selling signed photos at survivor stand
Photo Niagara Falls Public Library

She appeared in a silent film reenactment of her 1901 stunt but there was one thing she said she would never again duplicate, "I would rather face a cannon than go over the falls again."

Almost a century after her death Taylor finally received some notoriety for being the first person to go over the falls and survive. In 2011 an Off-Broadway play *Queen of the Mist*, telling the story of Taylor's stunt, successfully premiered. When Nik Wallenda in 2012 decided to make his tightrope walk above the brink of the Horseshoe Falls, most of the newscasters told the story of the first and oldest person to go over the falls.

DOROTHY THOMPSON

First Journalist to warn the World about Adolph Hitler

D orothy Thompson was a journalist, radio broadcaster and suffragist who was born in Lancaster NY on July 9, 1893 to English born preacher Reverend Peter Thompson and his American wife Margaret Grierson Thompson.

Figure 169 Dorothy Thompson V for Victory in 1940
Photo National Archives

She grew up in the parsonage at 180 Union Street in Hamburg, across the street from the school and adjacent to the church. Dorothy recalled an early childhood of church suppers and sleigh rides, ice cream socials and benevolent orders, swimming and skating, canning and quilting, singing in the choir, going berry picking and roasting chestnuts. Her father often took her on visits to parishioners in the suburbs of Western New York. His sermons of the celebration of life, love and forgiveness, not of fire and brimstone, influenced her life.

When Dorothy was eight years old her mother died. Her father wanted a maternal figure to assist in raising his three young children, so he married the church organist Eliza Abbott. Dorothy did not get along with her stepmother claiming she felt her stepmother had an allergy to children. She claimed one

Christmas her stepmother gave her a baby's bottle in a wrapped package with the card reading "Merry Christmas to a cry-baby."

In 1908 her father sent Dorothy to live with his two sisters, Margaret Kenning and Henrietta Thompson in Chicago. She blossomed under her aunts' guidance and attended Lewis Institute Junior College. There she showed a passion for literature and discourse. To continue her education in 1910, she enrolled at Syracuse University where tuition was free for the children of Methodist ministers. Upon graduation with a bachelor's degree, she moved back to Buffalo in 1914 and got a job stuffing envelopes for the Woman Suffrage Party.

Thompson eventually took a leadership role in the Women's Suffrage Party campaigning in an eight-county region, speaking at rallies, writing press releases and organizing parties and parades. She later took positions in Cincinnati and New York City, but activism did not pay well, so Dorothy also worked in advertising and publicity to help support her younger siblings through college.

When the 19th Amendment granting the right to vote was ratified in 1920, Dorothy decided to move to Europe and obtain work as a journalist. During the 1920s she began working for International News Service as a freelance writer in Europe. This gave Dorothy the opportunity to travel throughout Europe. She enjoyed her varied assignments and was successful due to her persistence and luck in obtaining interviews. Dorothy was the last person to speak to Sinn Fein leader Terrence MacWiney before he died. King Karl I was the deposed former emperor of Hungary and rumors were circulating that he was seeking to reclaim the throne. Dorothy obtained an exclusive interview by sneaking into his castle disguised as a Red Cross nurse. It was the only interview that King Karl granted.

Due to her success as a journalist, Dorothy was offered a full-time position as Vienna correspondent for the Philadelphia Public Ledger. In this position, she developed a deep understanding of central European policies which was bolstered by her fluency in German and marriage to Hungarian writer, Josef Bard. In 1925 she was named the chief of the Central European Service for the Ledger. When the Ledger and New York Post started sharing foreign services in 1927, she was appointed head of the Berlin bureau. This resulted in Thompson becoming the first woman to head a foreign news bureau of any importance.

Thompson became interested in Hitler dating back to unsuccessfully requesting an interview when he was taking refuge in Bavaria after his failed 1923 Munich Beer Hall Putsch. In 1931 Hitler was looking for some positive press in the U.S. and since Thompson was now a popular journalist who was read by millions in America, he granted her an interview.

She prepared by reading Mein Kampf and was not impressed. When she entered Hitler's salon in Berlin's Kaiserhof Hotel she thought she would be meeting the future dictator of Germany but after less than a minute questioned that belief. Her assessment of his character was scathing, explaining, "He is formless, almost faceless, a man whose countenance is a caricature, a man whose framework seems cartilaginous, without bones. He is inconsequent and voluble, ill-poised, insecure. He is the very prototype of the Little Man…"

Her interview appeared in Cosmopolitan magazine in March 1932 and in her book, *I Saw Hitler*. Other news sources downplayed Hitler's violence against Jews as propaganda, but Thompson continued to write about his ruthless crackdown and persecution of Jews and others. She wrote a series of articles that warned the world of the dangers of the person she called the Little Man. There was no journalist who spoke louder than Dorothy in the fight against Nazism.

Hitler had the Gestapo keep tabs on Thompson's writing and activities. In August 1934 she was expelled from Germany for her numerous anti-German publications. This made her the first American journalist expelled from Germany by the Nazi regime.

Figure 170 Cover of Thompson's I Saw Hitler *book*

Back in the U.S. in 1936, she mounted a one-woman crusade against the Nazis. Three times a week she wrote a column named "On the Record" that ran in the New York Herald Tribune and more than 170 other newspapers, reaching more than nine million readers. That column continued for 22 years. Thompson also had a monthly column in the Ladies Home Journal, that ran for 24 years until her death in 1961, and even more people listened to her NBC radio broadcasts, making her the most syndicated woman journalist in the country. When Germany invaded Poland in 1939, she went on the air for fifteen consecutive days and nights.

One of her most publicized outrages against Hitler was during a February 20, 1939 rally at Madison Square Garden. Twenty-two thousand Nazi supporters, many wearing grey uniforms, crowded the stadium, decorated with swastikas and portraits of Adolph Hitler. Thompson was seated in the first row of the press gallery. As the speakers delivered their anti-American and anti-Semitic messages of hate, she laughed loudly, derisively and defiantly, disrupting the festivities. The audience started chanting "Throw her Out." When the Storm Troopers escorted her out of the Gardens, it was one of her finest moments.

When Kleinhans Music Hall opened in Buffalo they had a three-day celebration. The Buffalo Philharmonic performed an opening night concert on October 12, 1940. On October 14, 1940 an enthusiastic audience reacted to

Thompson's speech about supplying money, munitions and ships to England, to assist Europe in defeating the Nazis and safeguarding democracy. Afterwards she continued to tour the U.S. giving talks warning of the coming war, urging a strong military and advocating an American alliance with Europe to defeat Nazism.

In 1923 Dorothy married Hungarian writer Josef Bard who she divorced in 1927. She married Sinclair Lewis in 1928. Lewis won the Nobel Prize for Literature in 1930 for his five novels in the 1920s, *Main Street, Babbitt, Arrowsmith, Elmer Gantry* and *Dodsworth*. He initially declined the award because he was against prizes that recognized or honored one author over another. When he finally agreed to accept the award, he was the first American author to win the prize. Lewis was one of the most popular authors of the 1920s as his books captured many details of daily life while exposing the dullness, conformity and hypocrisy of average, middle class citizens of the U.S. Dorothy married her third husband, artist Maxim Kopf, in 1945 and died at the age of 67 in Lisbon, Portugal.

In 1939 Time magazine placed her on the magazine cover and called Thompson and First Lady Eleanor Roosevelt, "undoubtedly the most influential women in America." Thompson's tireless work opposing Hitler was one of the inspirations for *It Can't Happen Here*, a 1935 dystopian novel by her husband Sinclair Lewis which imagines the rise of a fascist demagogue in America. Katherine Hepburn depicted a character based on Thompson in the 1942 movie *Woman of the Year,* and a Broadway musical based on Thompson starred Lauren Bacall. Thompson gained a reputation. She was regarded as the "First Lady of American Journalism,"

Figure 171 Time Magazine cover in 1939

HARRIET TOWNSEND

Women's Union of Buffalo, Townsend Hall at UB

Harriet Townsend founded the Women's Union of Buffalo. They donated their downtown city building to UB which named it Townsend Hall. When the Niagara Square facility closed, the Townsend Hall name was transferred to a building on the UB Main Street – South Campus.

Born as Harriet Austin in Buffalo in 1839, Harriet was the daughter of prominent attorney Benjamin Hale Austin. She was raised in the Unitarian faith and graduated from Buffalo Seminary. Her father regularly engaged her in current events and the issues of the day.

In 1861 Harriet married George Townsend, a partner in Clark, Townsend

Figure 172 Harriet Townsend

and Company, grain merchants associated with the Niagara elevator. The Townsends did not have any children, allowing Harriet to work full time for women's advancement and women's rights. Among her friends were women's advocates Abby Morton Diaz, Susan B. Anthony, Frances Willard and Julia Ward Howe.

She was the founder of the Women's Literary Club of the Universalist Church in 1880. The Literary Club sponsored a talk in 1884 at the Fitch Creche on Swan Steet by Abby Morton Diaz, the founder of The Women's Educational and Industrial Union of Boston. Two weeks after that lecture the second Women's Union in the country was formed in Buffalo and Harriet Townsend was named president of the organization.

The Women's Educational and Industrial Union declared that their organization was intended to "provide a common meeting place for women with an atmosphere so cordial that none should be out of place, where the rich woman should forget her riches, the poor woman her poverty; to freely give the advantages women need – graces of heart, culture of the intellect, employment of the hand and brain, a more exalted opinion of home life, protection from the oppressor, access to good literature and to offer a welcome and sympathy to all who should cross its threshold." Membership was $1.00.

The Women's Union purchased the Becker House on Niagara Square in 1886 (now the site of the City Court Building) as their offices and classrooms. They raised the $12,000 downpayment on the $18,000 building in only six weeks. In 1894 they built a larger new building where they had the space to offer expanded services to the women of Buffalo. It became the meeting place for women of all classes and the headquarters for any women's groups visiting the Buffalo area.

Figure 173 Women's Educational & Industrial Union on Niagara Square in 1915
Photo PD

The organization was not an association of benevolent upper-class women reaching down to help the poor and persecuted women. It was a union of all classes and conditions of women. They gave scholarships to women so they could attend Bryant & Stratton and trained others for low wage jobs like cooks, domestics or seamstresses. Lectures, classes and vocational training were given for the moral and intellectual welfare of women, including how to navigate the bureaucracy of government. The Union advocated for vocational training, night school, free kindergarten, physical education and lobbied for Legal Aid, equal women's rights in divorce and even got a woman elected to the School Board.

As founder and president of the Women's Union, Harriet often received the praise and credit for its accomplishments. She always answered, "Oh no, it wasn't Mrs. Townsend who did that, it was the Union."

In addition to her leadership of the Women's Union and presidency of the Literary Club, Harriet Townsend published four books on Emerson, Dickens, Thoreau and "Reminiscences of Famous Women" as fundraisers for the Women's Union. She also presented numerous papers at state and national conferences and wrote articles for national magazines. Townsend was affiliated with the Association of the Achievement of Women, a national association promoting opportunities for women.

In 1915 the Women's Union closed as they felt their mission was over. Most of their programs were adopted by educational, government and civic organizations. The building was donated to the University at Buffalo and became the first home of the UB College of Arts and Sciences. Townsend Hall also became the UB night school in 1923.

At the formal presentation of Townsend Hall to the university in 1915, UB Chancellor Charles P. Norton honored Harriet Townsend by saying, "The Women's Union has founded the University; here is the woman who founded the Union." Harriet Townsend died of pneumonia in 1916 at the age of 77.

Figure 174 Renovated Townsend Hall at UB South campus

UB sold the building in 1954 and the Townsend Hall name was transferred to the UB South Campus. The night school program became the UB Millard Fillmore evening division and moved to the former nurse's dormitory for the Erie County Almshouse, designed by George Metzger in 1903 and renovated by E.B. Green. As part of the South Campus Master Plan, Townsend Hall was remodeled into the home of the Human Resources Department for the university.

HARRIET TUBMAN

Underground Railroad, Spy, Scout, Suffragette

H arriet was one of the main conductors on the Underground Railroad, leading many enslaved people through WNY to Canada. In addition, she served as a scout, spy, guerrilla soldier and nurse for the Union Army during the Civil War and afterwards a suffragette. Tubman is associated with WNY but she did not live in Niagara Falls or Buffalo. However, her influence on area residents made the area one of the most important stations to freedom.

She was born around 1820 on a plantation in Dorchester County Maryland as Araminta Ross to Harriet Green and Benjamin Ross. She had eight siblings and she was called Minty. Her mother, known as Rit, was a cook in the plantation's "Big House" and her father was a timber worker. When Minty was five years old she was rented out by the plantations owners as a nursemaid where she was whipped if the baby cried. She was then rented out to a planter to set muskrat traps and was later rented out as a field hand.

Figure 175 Harriet Tubman
Photo Niagara Falls Underground Railroad
Heritage Center

In 1840 her father was set free and Minty learned that in the last will of the owner of the plantation where she was enslaved, her mother and all her children were set free. The new owner of the plantation refused to recognize the will and kept Rit and her children in bondage.

Slaves were not legally allowed to marry but in 1844 Minty entered a marital union with John Tubman, a free Black man. She took John's last name, to honor her mother dubbed herself Harriet and became Harriet Tubman. The marriage to John was not good and Harriet continued her resistance to the abuses of slavery. Her brothers Ben and Henry were about to be sold and that provoked Harriet to plan an escape with her brothers.

On September 17, 1849 Harriet, Ben and Henry made their escape from the Maryland plantation. Her brothers decided to discontinue their flee and return to the plantation but Harriet persevered and continued 90 miles north to freedom in Pennsylvania. She obtained a job as a housekeeper in Philadelphia but decided she wanted to help others become free. In her first trip south, she led her niece and children to Philadelphia via the Underground Railroad. She tried to persuade her husband John to flee north but he remarried and chose to stay in Maryland.

The Underground Railroad was created in the late 18th century by Black and white abolitionists. The people guiding enslaved people to freedom were called conductors and those escaping were called passengers. It was most utilized in the spring and fall when the days were shorter and they could travel for longer periods at night. At first Tubman used the established routes but after building a friendship with other abolitionists like Frederick Douglass, Thomas Garrett and Martha Coffin Wright, she created her own Underground Railroad network and stations.

When the Fugitive Slave Act of 1850 was passed, escaped slaves could be captured in the North and returned to their owner's plantations. Many already in the north moved across the Canadian border. So, Tubman relocated her family to St. Catherines Ontario. She and her family passed through Buffalo to get to Canada.

With it being more dangerous to assist the enslaved leave the south, she carried a gun for protection and to encourage her passengers on the Underground Railroad that might be having second thoughts. She claimed she never had to use the gun and never lost any of her passengers. However, she did admit to drugging babies and young children to prevent slave catchers from hearing their cries. It was reported she emancipated 300 enslaved people but the number was probably much lower. It was documented that she personally led 70 people to freedom, including her elderly parents. Her efforts encouraged other conductors to guide people to freedom on the Underground Railroad, influencing the freedom of thousands. Regardless, Tubman was so successful that slaveowners posted a $40,000 reward for her capture or death.

Men sitting on cliff, Suspension Bridge in background, albumen silver print by William England, 1859. Courtesy of the Museum of Modern Art. Licensed by SCALA / Art Resource, NY.

Figure 176 Suspension Bridge crossing
Photo Niagara Falls Underground Railroad Heritage Center

Tubman led the enslaved to Niagara Falls where they could cross the International Suspension Bridge or be rowed across the Niagara River.

Figure 177 Cataract House
Photo Niagara Falls Underground Railroad Heritage Center

One of the most important locations in the Underground Railroad network was the Cataract House, located along the rapids above the falls. It was operated by the Whitney family and they hired African-American waiters for the dining room staff. Sixty percent of the waiters at the Cataract House listed their birthplaces as a southern state or unknown /unlisted, suggesting that many of these people had escaped from slavery. Led by head waiter, John Morrison, the waiters spoke to the enslaved traveling with southern guests, letting them know that if they entered Canada they obtained freedom from slavery. Often the waiters or John Morrison himself ferried people to freedom. Rachel Smith was from a Quaker family in Pennsylvania who often-sent freedom seekers to Morrison. She wrote that during her stay at The Cataract House on two nights, Morrison rowed a group of people across the river to Canada.

Due to the efforts of Tubman and WNY individuals that assisted the Underground Railroad, many former enslaved people settled in Niagara Falls Ontario, St. Catherines, Niagara-on-the-Lake and Fort Erie. They obtained freedom from slavery because since 1793, by setting foot on Canadian soil enslaved people set themselves legally free.

Figure 178 Freedom Wall at Michigan & E. Ferry in Buffalo
with Tubman as first painting
Photo credit Rick Falkowski

182

During the Civil War Harriet was recruited to assist fugitive enslaved people at Fort Monroe in Hampton Roads Virginia. It was the only installation in the Upper South to remain under union control and a refuge for escaped slaves. Harriet worked as a nurse, cook and laundress, using her herbal medicine knowledge to treat sick soldiers and fugitive enslaved people. From her Underground Railroad experience, she had knowledge of southern towns and transportation routes that she shared with Union military commanders. She would disguise herself as an elderly woman to wander the streets of Confederate areas to obtain information from enslaved people about troop positions and supply lines. Later she would help these informants find food, shelter and jobs in the North.

After the Civil War Tubman settled on land that she owned in Auburn NY. She married former Union soldier, Nelson Davis, who was born into slavery and was twenty years her younger. She cared for the elderly in her home and in 1874 adopted a daughter. In 1896 she purchased land near her home and established the Harriet Tubman Home for the Aged and indigent Colored People. Her husband died in 1888 but it took until 1895 until she received $8 a month widow's military pension. In 1899 she finally personally received a $20 monthly pension for her service.

In addition, Harriet joined the suffrage movement working with Elizabeth Cady Stanton and Susan B. Anthony. Although illiterate, she gave speeches throughout the northeast for women's suffrage and collaborated with white writer, Sarah Bradford on her autobiography. Tubman moved into her namesake rest home in 1911 and died from pneumonia on March 10, 1913. She was buried with full military honors at Fort Hill cemetery in Auburn NY.

Figure 179 Prototype of the Harriet Tubman $20.00 bill

Schools and museums bear her name and her life story has been revealed in books, movies and documentaries. You can find information about Harriet Tubman and other individuals involved with the Cataract Hotel or assisting the enslaved fleeing into Canada at the Niagara Falls Underground Railroad Heritage Center next to the Amtrak train depot in Niagara Falls. She will soon be replacing former President and slaveowner Andrew Jackson on the $20.00 bill, honoring Harriet Tubman's legacy.

FLORENCE WENDT

President of Buffalo Philharmonic Orchestra Society

Mrs. Edgar Wendt

Figure 180 Florence Wendt

Florence Wendt was usually referred to as Mrs. Edgar Wendt. She was well known in Buffalo society for her contribution for saving and creating the Buffalo Philharmonic Orchestra, but few people knew she had the first name of Florence.

Note: It was the accomplishments and lack of the acknowledgement for Florence Wendt and other women like her that initiated my highlighting the accomplishments of Buffalo women in my *Profiles: Historic and Influential People from Buffalo and WNY* books. After I began giving a presentation on Buffalo Women, people attending the talks asked if I had a book just on Women from Buffalo. They were disappointed when I explained the information was compiled in all of my books. Some people requested a book dedicated to the women in the presentation be released. So, you could also state that Florence Wendt was responsible in influencing the writing of this book.

Born in 1893 to Cora Blanche Blakeley and Harry Risley Brigham, Florence Eleanor Brigham married Edgar Wendt on May 27, 1914 at Grace Episcopal Church in Buffalo. Florence was born in Pennsylvania but moved to Buffalo with her parents.

Her husband, Edgar Wendt was born in Buffalo on November 6, 1888. His father Henry was one of the principals of Buffalo Forge Company and his mother was Edith M. Forsyth Wendt. After graduating with a degree in Mechanical Engineering from Cornell University in 1911, Edgar went to work for Buffalo Steam Pump in North Tonawanda, a subsidiary of Buffalo Forge. He transferred to the Squire Division to learn that business and became the sales manager. After WWI Edgar and his brother Henry Jr. entered the general management of Buffalo Forge. Edgar was a cousin to well-known Buffalo philanthropist Margaret Wendt.

Edgar's uncle, William Wendt became part owner of Buffalo Forge in 1878, bought out his partners in 1883, brought his brother Henry into the business and Henry became a partner in 1888. Henry Wendt, Edgar's father, purchased his brother's share of the company in 1916 for $1 million. The company manufactured

184

gear driven forges that were more efficient than the traditional blacksmith bellows. It became involved with air movement devices and in 1902 an engineer at Buffalo Forge named Willis Carrier, created the air conditioner. He received a patent for the air conditioner in 1906. Buffalo Forge formed Carrier Air Conditioning Company of America and manufactured air conditioners until Willis Carrier amicably formed Carrier Engineering in 1915 and moved that manufacturing to Syracuse.

Figure 181 Florence Wendt BPO Society President 1935 Campaign Fund

Upon the death of Henry Wendt on June 12, 1929, his sons, Henry Jr. who resided at 633 Lafayette Avenue and Edgar Wendt who lived at 731 Lafayette Avenue, took over management of the business. At its peak, over 1,500 people worked at Buffalo Forge. In 1929 Edgar became company president and Henry Jr. the chairman.
When Edgar F. Wendt retired in 1958, Henry Jr. became president of Buffalo Forge retiring in 1966.

Edgar and Florence moved into his father's former home at 120 Lincoln Parkway, after his death. It was in this 5,638 square foot mansion, built in 1923 and designed by architects Franklyn J, and William A. Kidd that Edgar and Florence raised their family and lived for the rest of their lives.

Their daughter, Susanne Brigham Wendt, was born on May 18, 1918 and married George B. Kellogg. Daughter Phyllis Eleanor Wendt was born on March 20, 1925 and married Frederick S. Pierce. Edgar died on August 2, 1968 while Florence lived until September 18, 1978.

During the summer the Wendt family enjoyed the 164-acre family estate Ridgewood, on the shore of Lake Erie in the town of Evans. This summer home was built by Henry Wendt and was enjoyed by the Wendt family. It was sold to Erie County and is currently operated by the Erie County Department of Parks, Recreation and Forestry. The mansion and outbuildings have deteriorated and have fallen victim to vandalism.

Figure 182 Wendt Beach the former Wendt family summer home

Florence Wendt was interested in music and supported many Buffalo cultural societies and institutions, especially philharmonic symphony orchestras. The Buffalo Philharmonic Orchestra was formed from previous orchestras and under Lajos Shuk, as a prelude to the future orchestra, performed classics, children's, family and Pops programs on 24 WABC national radio broadcasts. The BPO performed its first concert on November 7, 1935 and the BPO Society was incorporated in spring 1936. The president of the BPO Society, Florence Wendt, organized a fundraising campaign that kept the orchestra operational until federal Works Progress Administration (WPA) funding arrived.

In establishing the BPO, Wendt collaborated with Samuel Capen, Cameron Baird and Frederick Slee who were also responsible for creating the music department at UB. They worked with the federal program Emergency Relief Bureau (ERB) to obtain funding under the FDR public works program and bring conductor Lajos Shuk to Buffalo. For their accomplishments Capen, Baird and Slee are considered the founders of the BPO. Florence Wendt was the Chairman of the BPO Board of Directors from 1936 to 1939.

Figure 183 120 Lincoln Parkway Wendt mansion
Photo credit Ellen Mika Zelasko

In 1981 the Wendt family members decided to sell their shares and the company was acquired by Ampro-Pittsburgh. In 1993 the company was sold to Howden Group and the former plant at Broadway and Mortimer was demolished in 2006. The Wendt home at 120 Lincoln Parkway was sold by the estate of Steve Barns in 2021 for just under $2 million. The former 164-acre Ridgewood estate, now Wendt Beach, received Covid 19 Stimulus funding with $4 million appropriated for restoration of the former mansion and grounds.

MARGARET WENDT

Philanthropist who founded the Margaret L. Wendt Foundation

Margaret Wendt inherited her father's estate which benefited from his founding the very prosperous Buffalo Forge Company. She chose to use her wealth to establish the Margaret L. Wendt Foundation.

In 1885 Margaret was born in Buffalo to William Franz and Mary Gies Wendt. Her father was the founder of Buffalo Forge Company and with his brother Henry, built the business into the largest forge company in the U.S. The company was formed to manufacture blacksmith's forges, drilling machines, steam engines and steam pumps. Her family lived at 19 Irving Place until they built their mansion at 570 Richmond Avenue in 1895. Margaret lived at this home for the rest of her life.

She attended Buffalo public schools and graduated from Buffalo Seminary in 1903 when classes were held at the Twentieth Century Club and the Heathcote School. However, her father did not want her to pursue a college education. Her older sister, Gertrude, was considered too frail for

Figure 184 Margaret Wendt
Photo Margaret L. Wendt Foundation

school, died in childbirth in 1909. This resulted in Margaret's parents becoming over processive of Margaret. She continued living with her parents and never married.

In 1916, her father sold his share of Buffalo Forge to his brother. In 1917 William purchased a long-established farm on Chestnut Ridge Road in Lockport, establishing the W.F. Wendt Farm. He purchased the horse farm because Margaret loved horses. William left the Buffalo area, living in Los Angeles from 1918 to 1923 and Margaret applied her talents managing the farm. She tended to the business of the farm for many years and indulged her personal interests, building a large aviary of exotic birds and keeping peacocks on the grounds. An experienced rider, she could be found riding horses and seen out in her horse and buggy on Millersport Highway to the farm.

Figure 185 Wendt family on horse carriage
Photo Margaret L. Wendt Foundation

Margaret was close to two of her first cousins, Edith on her father's side and Harriet Geis Geiger on her mother's side. Harriet married J. Marion Geiger, a chief engineer for Niagara Mohawk. Their daughter Ruth was a source of memories about Margaret. Margaret and her mother made several ocean journeys to Europe, beginning before WWI. They also traveled the U.S. by automobile, often accompanied by her cousins.

When William Wendt died in 1923, he willed everything to his wife, Mary Gies and daughter, Margaret who handled management of the home at 570 Richmond and their farm in Lockport. After her mother died in 1940, Margaret sold the family farm to William Kenan's Randleigh Farms and continued to live at the 570 Richmond home with her housekeeper Mary and chauffer who lived in the carriage house above the garage. She purchased beachfront property in Thunder Bay Ontario and built a substantial structure in a colony of well-to-do summer homes. Starting in 1948 Margaret was often seen walking with one of her Irish Setters. She was known for her love of animals.

Figure 186 Margaret after graduating
from Buffalo Seminary in 1903
Photo Margaret L. Wendt Foundation

Margaret was a private person interested in helping people without receiving publicity for her contributions. She met Reverend Ralph Loew during one of her walks when Loew's daughter asked to pet her Irish Setter. After continuing to meet on walks, Margaret started attending Trinity Lutheran Church and became close to the reverend's family. She often spoke to her pastor Reverend Ralph Loew to discover various ways she could quietly meet community needs. Loew became one of the three founding trustees of the Margaret L. Wendt Foundation with investment broker Samuel D. Lunt and attorney William I. Morey.

The Margaret Wendt Foundation was created in 1956 when Margaret discussed starting the organization with Reverend Ralph Loew and established it with a $750,000 donation. It is dedicated to charitable and public service purposes in the WNY area. The foundation does not focus on any specific cause and any 501c3 corporation in WNY may apply. They seek projects with a potential impact on the well-being of the entire community. Trustees meet quarterly to review grant applications. Some of the organizations the Foundation has helped include restoration of Elbert Hubbard's Roycroft Inn, restoration of Frank Lloyd Wright's Darwin Martin House, Shea's Performing Arts Center, Graycliff and the 1833 Buffalo Lighthouse. It supports cultural institutions and organizations like the BPO, Museum of Science, Albright-Knox, Buffalo Zoo, Historical Society, Forest Lawn Cemetery and Buffalo Seminary, along with creating a permanent display of Mark Twain's Huckelberry Finn manuscript at the Buffalo and Erie County Public Library.

Margaret suffered a stroke in 1959, remaining in a coma for thirteen years, never regaining consciousness. Her financial adviser Samuel Lunt kept the Richmond Avenue house in order, her housekeeper maintained the home and her chauffeur kept the Chrysler tuned up in the driveway just in case Margaret recovered. Unfortunately, she never regained consciousness and died in 1972.

The bulk of her estate of $14,577,348 was left to the Foundation. After she provided $1.25 million to create lifetime trusts for a number of relatives and cash donations to charities, the balance went to the Foundation. This $11+ million bequest was worth over $120 million by 2002 and the Foundation invests or grants about $5.5 million a year into the local economy.

The Foundation remains low key in its contributions to education, the arts and social services. Margaret's goal was for her family fortune to be a major social and cultural force in the years that followed her death. In 1997 Wendt was one of the first 12 women named to the Western New York Women's Hall of Fame. Her vision was fulfilled as the Foundation annually accomplishes her goal, supporting charitable and public service purposes in WNY.

Figure 187 570 Richmond Avenue
Photo Margaret L. Wendt Foundation

CAROL WINCENC

Internationally-renowned Flute Master

C arol's father, violinist Joseph Wincenc, was a "violin prodigy and distinguished educator who was best known as the flamboyant founder and longtime conductor of three community orchestras". Her mother, Margaret Wincenc, was a pianist. She grew up in an active musical family, has performed on five continents over five decades and New York Magazine hailed her as "Queen of the Flute,"

Born on June 29, 1949 in Buffalo, she started taking violin lessons from her father at the age of four and flute lessons at the age of nine. Her father, Dr. Joseph Wincenc, was the Assistant Concertmaster for the BPO at their first Kleinhans Music Hall concert in 1940. He was the founder of the Amherst Symphony Orchestra in 1946, Orchard Park Symphony Orchestra in 1950 and the Clarence Outdoor Concerts in 1959. He was also responsible for starting

Figure 188 Carol Wincenc
Photo credit Cori Wells Braun courtesy BPO

the Buffalo State College Music Department and with the BPO served as associate conductor, concertmaster and first violinist.

As a teen Carol studied in Italy with Severino Gazzelloni at Accademia Musicale Chigiana in Siena in 1966-7 and at the Accademia di Santa Cecilia in Rome 1967-8. She was a pupil of Robert Willoughby at the Oberlin Ohio College of Music 1967-1969, studied with Harold Bennett at the Manhattan School of Music in New York 1971 and Arthur Lora at the Julliard School in New York 1972. Carol received her bachelor degree in music from The Manhattan School of Music in 1971 and two master degrees from Julliard in 1972. She also holds diplomas from the Santa Cecilia and Chigiana Academies.

Carol was the first flutist in the National Orchestral Association in New York in 1970-71, the Aspen Colorado Festival Chamber Orchestra in 1970-72 and the St. Paul Minnesota Chamber Orchestra 1972-77. After winning the Concert Artists Guild Award, she made her recital debut at Carnegie Recital Hall in 1972 and won first prize at the Naumburg Competition in 1978.

After winning the Naumburg Solo Flute Competition, Wincenc began appearing as a soloist with major world orchestras as a recitalist and as a chamber music player. In the U.S. she appeared with symphony orchestras and chamber music ensembles in St. Louis, Atlanta, Seattle, St. Paul, Chicago, San Francisco, Pittsburgh, Philadelphia, Los Angeles, Detroit, Buffalo,

Figure 189 Carol's father Dr. Joseph Wincenc

Aspen, Sarasota, Palm Beach, Dallas, Cleveland, New York City and other major cities. Overseas she has performed in Beijing, Tokyo, Warsaw, Prague, Venice, Nice, Greece, Stuttgart, Frankfort, Budapest, London and more. Wincenc has premiered numerous works by classical composers including Christopher Rouse, Henryk Gorecki, Lukas Foss, Jake Heggie, Paul Shoenfeld, Tod Machover, Yuko Uebayaskim, Thea Musgrave, Andrea Clearfield, Shi-Hui Chen and Joan Tower. She has also collaborated with many renowned pop and classical performers like Yo-Yo-Ma, Oliver Messaien, Rudolf Serkin, Joshua Bell, Christoph Eschenback, Loren Maazel, Michael Tilson Thomas, Peter Glass, Andre PrevinJessye Norman, Emanuel As, Judy Collins and Paul Simon.

In addition to performing, Wincenc has been active in the academic community and has taught at The Manhattan School of Music 1980-86, Indiana School of Music in Bloomington 1986-88, Rice University 1986-1993, Juilliard School of Music since 1988 and SUNY Stony Brook. She has mentored and graduated countless students who now hold principal flute positions with major symphony orchestras and as university professors.

As a recording artist, she was nominated for a Grammy Award for the 2005 Naxos recording of works by Yehudi Wyner with Richard Stoltzman and other renowned colleagues. Her recording of Christopher

Figure 190 Carol being presented with BMHOF Induction Award at Kleinhans Music Hall by Rick Falkowski

191

Rouse's Flute Concerto for Telarc with Christopher Eschenbach and the Houston Symphony won the highly coveted Diapason d'Or. She has also recorded for Nonesuch, London/Decca, Deutsche Grammophon, Telarc, Music Masters and Naxos where Gramophone Magazine selected her work with the Buffalo Philharmonic as "Pick of the Month."

In 1972 she joined the St. Paul Orchestra where she met her future husband, clarinetist Ronald Dennis. After five years in Minnesota, they moved back to New York City where Wincenc attended college. She has remained a resident of NYC for most of her life - at least that is her home base when not touring the world. Carol later married lyric baritone, Douglas Webster, and they had a son in 1993. Carol feels her son was born into music and touring. She was seven and a half months pregnant when she premiered a Gorecki Concerto in Amsterdam and he traveled with her to Europe four times before he was two years old. Nicola Wincenc is a psychedelic rock singer and guitarist who has performed and recorded individually and with his band the Caverns.

Wincenc was a 2011 Lifetime Achievement Award recipient from the National Flute Association, the National Society of Arts and Letters Gold Medal for Lifetime Achievement in Music and received Distinguished Alumni Awards from Manhattan School of Music and the Brevard Music Center. She was the first classical performer inducted into the Buffalo Music Hall of Fame in 1998.

Figure 191 Carol with her son Nicola Wincenc in 2019
from Carol Wincenc post

PENNY WOLFGANG

NYS Supreme Court Judge, Radio/TV Host

Wolfgang was a two-term member of the NYS Supreme Court and is also known to WNY audiences for her radio and television programs that have aired since the mid-1970s.

Henrietta Joan Moonelis was born on April 23, 1940 in New York City to Claire Klausar and Edgar Moonelis, a printer of legal forms. Her childhood nickname of Henny morphed into Penny, the first name by which she is known and now her legal name. Penny graduated from the High School of Performing Arts in NYC where she concentrated on the theater

Figure 192 Judge Penny Wolfgang
Photo courtesy John DiSciullo

department. She received a B.A. in 1961 from Fairleigh Dickinson University in New Jersey and attended law school at New York University - NYU.

During her senior year at NYU while at a political event, a friend introduced her to Michael G. Wolfgang, an attorney and Buffalo Assistant District Attorney from Niagara Falls. Michael was the state chairman of the Young Republicans. After she graduated with a J.D. from the NYU School of Law in 1964, they got married and Penny moved to Buffalo. Her first employment in WNY was with the law offices of Jaeckle Fleischman. Penny continued her theatrical career starring in *Pygmalion* at the Niagara Falls Little Theater in 1966. In the early 1970s she appeared with WKBW-TV anchor Irv Weinstein in *3 Men on a Horse* at the Jewish Center and starred in the Amherst Players' production of *Born Yesterday*.

After working at Jaeckle Fleischman, et al from 1964 to 1966, she was employed at Lipsitz Green, et al from 1966-1967 and served with Legal Aid of Buffalo beginning in 1967 (staying until 1978), subsequently becoming the director of the Prisoners Legal Assistance Project where she served as a public defender and attorney-in-charge of the Appeals Division.

The Bar Association approached Legal Aid about developing public announcements about criminal rights and landlord-tenant issues. Penny was asked to take on the role of arranging and appearing in the spots. She approached

Channel 7 and since TV stations had to do a certain amount of public service announcements to maintain their license, Wolfgang did a legal spot once a week on Dialing for Dollars. That led to her producing and moderating The Law and You on WKBW-TV for five years. WKBW radio asked her to create a radio program. During the 1980s she hosted legal segments on the WGRZ-TV program Big Picture with Rich Kellman. She also continued her WKBW radio show, expanding it to eventually include the Entercom stations WBEN, WGR, WKSE, 102.5, 107,7 and WWKB. Penny acted in Buffalo 66; the Vincent Gallo movie filmed in Buffalo in 1997. She played the role of Judge Penny Wolfgang and was required to join the Screen Actors Guild union, being paid for her appearance and receiving residuals from the film.

In 1978, after being with Legal Aid for over a decade and with her television and radio exposure, Wolfgang was well known in the community and decided to run for the office of Erie County judge. She had not been active in politics nor had any political affiliation, so her campaign was a grassroots effort of volunteers led by her husband Michael Wolfgang. There were two openings for six candidates but since she received little political backing, Michael and his crew canvassed the county garnering signatures for Penny's candidacy. On primary day she came in first on both the Democratic and Republican lines. Her parents traveled from NYC to assist in their daughter's election as Judge of Erie County.

Wolfgang completed her seven-year term on the County Court bench and in 1985 was elected to a 14-year term as a New York State Supreme Court judge. She was elected to a second 14-year term in 1999. When she reached the mandated retirement age for a judge at 70, extensions were granted and Wolfgang did not retire until 2016, shortly after her husband passed away.

Penny and her husband Michael had a daughter Robin born in 1968. Robin has run for public office and worked in Community Relations for several companies, now as VP of Community Relations at Trocaire College. Judge Wolfgang has passed her legal knowledge and experience on to subsequent generations by teaching trial techniques, family and criminal law and introductory law classes at the UB School of Law and as a member of the faculty at the Erie County Law Enforcement Training Academy.

Figure 194 Wolfgang with Russell Salvatore at Make-A-Wish event on Big Picture
Photo courtesy John DiSciullo

One of the bright spots of her career was experienced while campaigning for office.

She was joined at a campaign event by George Bush when he was running for the U.S. presidency. She knew Tim Russert from his early days in politics and media. After Russert became host of Meet the Press, they always kept in touch. When Russert was visiting Buffalo, Wolfgang got to turn the tables on Russert by interviewing him on her show.

For Penny Wolfgang, retirement does not mean not working. She continues her *On Target* radio show In the Community on the Audacy network of stations, the former Entercom stations. When Buddy Shula purchased WECK she started the radio show *In Our Community* on that station. In addition, she is on the Big Picture WBBZ-TV weekly television show. In 2023 State Supreme Court Justice Penny Wolfgang received the Service to Broadcasting Award from the Buffalo Broadcasters Association Hall of Fame.

Recognizable from decades as a judge and a radio/TV host, when someone hears the name Penny Wolfgang, their response usually is – The Judge.

Figure 195 Penny with her daughter Robin Wolfgang at Russell Salvatore's 90th Birthday Party
Photo courtesy John DiSciullo

195

CHRISTINE ZIEMBA

First Female Chief of Police in WNY

C hristine Ziemba decided she wanted to be a police officer while she was in high school, was the first female police officer in the Town of Cheektowaga, and when appointed chief of the Cheektowaga Police Department, she was one of four female chiefs in New York State and one of the women pioneers in police work for the country.

Figure 196 Christine Ziemba retirement speech
Photo courtesy Christine Ziemba

She was born in December 1954 in Buffalo to Eleanore and Jerome Ziemba. Jerome retired after 42 years as a microscope inspector at American Optical. They lived on the East Side of Buffalo on Goodyear Avenue between Genesee Street and East Ferry, a few blocks west of Bailey. Christine had two brothers and she attended St. Matthew's Parish School on Wyoming Street at East Ferry. At grammar school graduation she received a dictionary for being the Spelling Bee Champ and a Bible for being the Top Student.

Her first year of high school was at Archbishop Carroll on East Delevan Avenue in Buffalo. In 1969 the Ziemba family moved to Clover Place in Cheektowaga with Christine attending Maryvale High School. While in high school she started sending out letters to various agencies about career opportunities for women in Law Enforcement. Christine recalled, "I received a letter back from one gentleman stating that if he had a daughter, he'd encourage her to pick a different career, as the opportunities for women in Law Enforcement were so limited." She graduated in the top 5% of her class and when it came to career plans, she was not to be deterred.

Christine enrolled in the Police Science program at Erie Community College - ECC. When she walked into the Police Science room during orientation she was greeted with the comment, "Secretarial Science is down the hall." She did not walk down the hall to the Secretarial Science wing. She stayed in that classroom and graduated in 1974 with an Associate in Applied Science Degree – with Distinction – in Criminal Justice.

After graduating from ECC, she attended Buffalo State College, graduating with a Bachelor's Degree in Criminal Justice in August 1976. As a prelude to eventually being hired as a police officer, from 1974 to 1976 she worked as an Administrative Intern for the Cheektowaga Youth Bureau, assigned to the Police Department Juvenile Division, accepted a position as Campus Police Officer at UB and attended the Erie County Police Academy, graduating in 1976. She finished the Academy with an A average, had no problems meeting the physical fitness standards and did well in firearms training. Christine had discontinued in-person classes at Buff State to accept the Police Officer position at UB. She completed her college credits while doing Independent Study at the same time as the Police Academy, taking summer school classes and working the midnight shift at UB.

Figure 197 Christine Ziemba high school photo in 1972
Photo courtesy Christine Ziemba

All the hard work paid off; Christine Ziemba was hired as the first female police officer in Cheektowaga in September 1976. Being first is often difficult. She recalled, "While many officers were friendly, supportive and welcoming, others were not so, refusing to work with me as a car partner." To be accepted by her male counterparts she often put in extra effort on the job. She continued, "What really turned the tide is that I took on a number of dangerous assignments, serving as a decoy in rape investigations and working on narcotics cases. After that I started to be accepted more and more."

Being the first female on the force also presented some challenges. The Department's only familiarity with female uniforms was that of crossing guards. The hat differed from that of police officers and the suggested cross tie was a safety hazard, as compared to the clip-on tie worn by officers, that breaks away if someone grabs it. The tie was too long and since women's shirts button opposite to men's, the tie clasp was upside down. Outer wear was men's small sizes, that still needed to be altered to fit. Bullet proof vests were also an issue as Christine recalled, "they were not designed to allow for women's breasts." According to Ziemba, "as the number of women on patrol increased, uniform companies began to design and produce appropriately styled and sized clothing – pants that allowed for women's hips, shorter ties, appropriate tie clasps, vests that were more comfortable and rain coats that did not reach the ground."

Figure 198 Ziemba 8th grade graduation in 1968
Photo courtesy Christine Ziemba

When hired by the Cheektowaga Police Department, she was initially assigned as a Patrol Officer. In 1978 she was assigned as a Family Assistance Officer – Juvenile Division where duties included investigating child abuse and sexual assault cases and crimes committed by persons under the age of 16. The position included being the female member of the Sexual Assault Investigation Unit, along with designing and presenting school educational programs from Kindergarten through Grade 12.

Ziemba placed first on the Lieutenant civil service examination and was promoted to Lieutenant in the Patrol Division in 1985. This resulted in another first, as she was the first female lieutenant with any suburban police force in Erie County. In this position she supervised and guided shift officers, worked with Neighborhood Watch Groups and presented programs to area groups and schools.

Figure 199 1985 promotion to Police Lieutenant
Photo courtesy Christine Ziemba

In 1991 she was assigned as Lieutenant of the newly created Crime Resistance Unit. She was responsible for the D.A.R.E. Program, Neighborhood Watch, Citizen Police Academy, National Night Out, Do the Right Thing Recognition Program, Community Crime Prevention Presentations, Explorer Program and the high school and college intern programs. Ziemba also coordinated recruitment efforts, was successful in obtaining numerous grants, was the Sexual Harassment Officer for the Department and served on the Cheektowaga Task Force on Diversity.

She took the promotional civil service exams for Captain, Assistant Police Chief and Police Chief, placing first at each position level. In 2002 when an opening became available in Cheektowaga with the retirement of the existing chief, the Town Board interviewed three candidates and she was appointed the first Female Police Chief in WNY and only the fourth in NYS. Some of her accomplishments as chief included overseeing the installation of data terminals in all patrol vehicles, acquiring specialty SWAT specialty vehicles and Segways through grant funding, the extension of cross border enforcement with the Buffalo Police Department and dealing with an increasingly diverse population. In 1980 the population of Cheektowaga was 92,000 people with 98.6% white and less than 2% minority. In the 2005-2009 estimate, the population was 75,000 with 88.6% white and over 10% Black, Hispanic or Asian.

In addition to being the first female police officer, Lieutenant and Police Chief, she was the first female to join the fraternal organizations for those ranks. After being promoted to Lieutenant Ziemba joined the Erie County Captains and Lieutenants Association. Upon joining, she was offered the position of Secretary and later was elected President. Upon becoming Chief, she was welcomed into the Erie County Chiefs of Police Association and eventually elected as its President, becoming the first female President of both organizations.

Ziemba followed her dreams to become a police officer but her dedication to policework delayed marriage. She was married to William Kricfalusi three years before her retirement. They had started dating after she became Police Chief and without a law enforcement background, he had to become acquainted with the extensive and erratic work hours of a police chief. Christine and William do not have any children.

After 34 years of service, retirement day on February 26, 2011 included the ceremonial final salute when a retiring police officer leaves the building for the last time and receives a final ride home in a marked patrol car, escorted by all available units with flashing lights and roaring sirens. However, Mother Nature did not make it easy for Ziemba to retire. Due to a snowstorm, the escorted ride home had to be led by a Town of Cheektowaga Snowplow.

Figure 200 Ceremonial Final Salute when retiring in 2011
Photo courtesy Christine Ziemba

In 2002, according to the State Office of Criminal Justice Service, Christine Ziemba was one of four full time and one part time Police Chiefs in NYS. At that time, the National Association of Women Law Enforcement Executives identified only 194 female police chiefs or sheriffs in the country. As of July 2023, out of 3,895 police chiefs nationwide, only 8.3% are women. One of those trail blazers was Chief Christine Ziemba of the Cheektowaga Police Department.

THE SPIRIT OF BUFFALO WOMEN

Prominent Women who called WNY their Home

Rick Falkowski

HISTORY & MUSIC PRESENTATIONS

Available from Rick Falkowski

Early Buffalo Music & Entertainment
Rock N Roll Buffalo
Historic & Influential People from Buffalo & WNY
– the early 1800s
Late 1800s Industry, Business & Culture
Early 1900s Society & Culture
Early 1900s Industry & Manufacturing
German Americans from Buffalo & WNY
Philanthropists & Social Benefactors of WNY
Spirit of Buffalo Women

To inquire about scheduling a presentation
contact rickfalkowski@aol.com

BUFFALO HISTORY BOOKS

By Rick Falkowski

HISTORY
OF
BUFFALO MUSIC
&
ENTERTAINMENT

Rick Falkowski

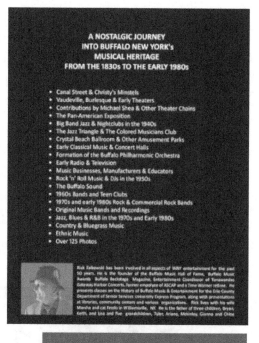

A NOSTALGIC JOURNEY
INTO BUFFALO NEW YORK's
MUSICAL HERITAGE
FROM THE 1830s TO THE EARLY 1980s

- Canal Street & Christy's Minstrels
- Vaudeville, Burlesque & Early Theaters
- Contributions by Michael Shea & Other Theater Chains
- The Pan-American Exposition
- Big Band Jazz & Nightclubs in the 1940s
- The Jazz Triangle & The Colored Musicians Club
- Crystal Beach Ballroom & Other Amusement Parks
- Early Classical Music & Concert Halls
- Formation of the Buffalo Philharmonic Orchestra
- Early Radio & Television
- Music Businesses, Manufacturers & Educators
- Rock 'n' Roll Music & DJs in the 1950s
- The Buffalo Sound
- 1960s Bands and Teen Clubs
- 1970s and early 1980s Rock & Commercial Rock Bands
- Original Music Bands and Recordings
- Jazz, Blues & R&B in the 1970s and Early 1980s
- Country & Bluegrass Music
- Ethnic Music
- Over 125 Photos

Rick Falkowski has been involved in all aspects of WNY entertainment for the past 50 years. He is the founder of the Buffalo Music Hall of Fame, Buffalo Music Awards, Buffalo Backstage Magazine, Entertainment Coordinator of Tonawanda Gateway Harbor Concerts, former employee of ASCAP and a Time Warner retiree. He presents classes on the History of Buffalo Music & Entertainment for the Erie County Department of Senior Services University Express Program, along with presentations at libraries, community centers and various organizations. Rick lives with his wife Marsha and cat Frodo in Williamsville, NY. He is the father of three children, Bryan, Keith, and Lisa and five grandchildren, Tyler, Ariana, Melinian, Gianna and Chloe.

Profiles Volume I:

Historic & Influential People
from Buffalo & WNY
the 1800's

Rick Falkowski

Profiles Volume I: Historic & Influential People from Buffalo & WNY - the 1800s chronicles 100 profiles of people from Buffalo and Western New York who helped shape local, regional, New York State and American history during the 1800s. It includes the accomplishments of area residents in politics, law, medicine, manufacturing, religion, music and other fields of business. In addition, the book describes events that affected the Buffalo area. From the War of 1812, building of the Buffalo Harbor, opening of the Erie Canal, financial crisis of 1857, development of Delaware Avenue mansions, building the railroads, beginning of manufacturing, creation of neighborhoods, Olmsted Parks and harnessing the power of the Niagara, meet the people that created and participated in the evolution of the WNY community.

People Profiled Includes

Adams, Albright, Allen, Barton, Becker, Bennett, Birdsall, Bird, Birge, Boother, Brown, Cary, Clinton, Cleavland, Conway, Coit, Cook, Cornell, Day, Elliott, Ely, Evans, Fargo, Farwell, Fletcher, Fillmore, Forman, Germain, Goodyear, Granger, Goodrich, Green, Grosvenor, Hamlin, Hanguse, Heacox, Hodge, Hooly, Howe, Hoyt, Jewett, Johnson, Johnston, Kamman, Kibler, Lang, Larkin, Lincoln, Letchworth, Lord, Love, Macridge, Marcy, Murray, Milburn, Morgan, Milligan, Newman, Noah, Olmst, Olmsted, Pratt, Parker, Peacock, Perry, Pierce, Plum, Pooley, Pratt, Rumsey, Rathbun, Red Jacket, Rice, Rumsey, Rochford, Scheidhaupt, Shelton, Shelby, Shepard, Sidway, Spaulding, Sprague, St. John, Stedman, Sterke, Stevenson, Tesla, Thompson, Tifft, Tweed, Tracy, Urban, Wilder, Wilson, Watson, White, Wilcox, Williams

and over 175 photos, drawings and maps

RICK FALKOWSKI presents classes on Buffalo History and Buffalo Music History for the Erie County Department of Senior Services University Express Program, along with giving presentations at libraries, community centers and various organizations. In addition, he is a regular contributor to Forever Young Magazine and is the author of the book History of Buffalo Music & Entertainment. NY lives in Williamsville, NY with his wife Marsha.

$22.95 USD

PROFILES VOLUME II:
Historic & Influential People
from Buffalo & WNY
the Early 1900s

RICK FALKOWSKI

Future books that will be published by Buffalo History Books

Profiles Volume III: Historic & Influential People
from Buffalo & WNY – the Late 1900s

Profiles Volume IV: Historic & Influential People
from Buffalo & WNY – the 2000s

Several Area History Books by other Authors
are also being considered for publication

Books available at book stores, gift shops, museums
and other locations across WNY
Available on-line at Amazon.com and store web sites

SOURCES

Sources for Joan Baez
Baez creates a buzz in visit to onetime Clarence home by Mark Sommer, Buffalo News 11/5/2011
Joan Baez: My life is a Crystal Teardrop, The Atlantic August 1968
Bio at joanbaez.com
Joan Baez publicity bio printed in An Evening with Joan Baez at BabevilleBuffalo.com
Positively Fourth Street: The lives and times of Joan Baez, Bob Dylan, Mimi Baez Farina and Richard Farina by David Hajdu, 2001
Families of Continental Flight 3407. 3407memorial.com

Sources for Lucille Ball
Mike Buckley created the abridged version of this profile from Volume III edition
Karol, Michael A. Lucy in Print. iUniverse, Inc. Lincoln, NE 2003
Love Lucy. Lucille Ball, G.P. Putnam's Sons, New York 1996
National Comedy Center – conversations with staff
Lucille Ball and her Hometowns: Celoron and Jamestown by Joni Blackman.
Jamestown Gazette

Sources for Christine Baranski's
Christine Baranski's Polish Buffalo roots by Steve Cichon, Buffalo News 2/16/22
In some ways, Christine Baranski is the First Lady of Buffalo by L.M. Buffalo Rising 12/7/2021
Christine Baranski. actorcontactdetails.com
Buffalo born actress Christine Baranski talks Buffalo Bills on the Late Show by Kaley Lynch, wivb.com 1/20/2022

Sources for Teressa Bellissimo
Anchorbar.com
Meet the American who invested Buffalo wings and disrupted the entire chicken industry by Kerry J. Byrne, New York Post. July 22, 2022
Buffalo Everything: A guide to eating in "Nickel City" by Arthur Bovino
National Chicken Wing Day deals for Friday by Jayme Deerwester, USA Today, July 28, 2022
Chickenwingday.com
Buffalowing.com – Buffalo Chicken Wing Festival
A Brief History of Chicken Wings by Claire Suddath, Time Magazine, September 3, 2009

Sources for Zorah Berry
Zorah Berry Collection by Sally Schaefer, Buffalo & Erie County Public Library Special Collections Dept.
History of Buffalo Music & Entertainment by Rick Falkowski

Before Kleinhans and Memorial Auditorium: The Elmwood Convention/Music Hall by Susan J. Eck, wnyhistory.org
Correspondence with Sally Ann Schaefer
Abridged version of Volume II profile created and edited by Mike Buckley

Sources for Amanda Blake

Amanda Blake, 60, Saloonkeeper on TV's Gunsmoke for 19 years, New York Times obituary 8/18/1989
Amanda Blake, excerpt from 100 Years of Buffalo Broadcasting by Steve Chichon buffalostories.com
Amanda Blake, Biography at IMDb
Amanda Blake – Bio, Facts, Family Live of Actress at thefamouspeople.com
Gunsmoke, oldradioworld.com
Performing Animal Welfare Society, Newsletter January 2023.
Walnut Grove Plantation SC, Home of a Revolutionary War Hero, pastlanetravels.com

Sources for Louise Blanchard Bethune

Louise Blanchard Bethune: Every Woman Her Own Architect by Kelly Hayes McAlonie
Louise Blanchard Bethune - Pioneering Women of American Architecture (bwaf.org)
Louisebethune.org
Buffalo Good Neighbors, Great Architecture by Nancy Blumenstalk Mingus, Arcadia Publishing 2003.
Pioneering Woman of American Architecture by Kelly Hayes McAlonie
Louise Blanchard Bethune: Buffalo Feminist and Americas First Woman Architect. Austin M. Fox. Buffalo Spree Summer 1986.
Katherine Flickinger Schweitzer revised and updated profile from Volume I

Sources for Joan Bozer

Joan Bozer, 94, Lawmaker, Preservationist and Matriarch of the Parks Conservancy by Natalie Brody, Buffalo News, 5/6/2023
Miss Joan R, Kendig John M Bozer Marry. New York Times 7/1/1951
Biographical Note – Collection: Joan Bozer papers at University at Buffalo, Archival & Manuscripts Collections
Earth Activist Joan Bozer will be missed and fondly remembered by Queenseyes, Buffalo Rising 5/22/23
Joan Bozer's Special Career Retiring Lawmaker gave Voice to Slighted Issues, Buffalo News `1/27/1995
Joan K. Bozer obituary at dignitymemorial.com
Dr. John M. Bozer, cardiologist, UB professor, obituary Buffalo News 3/4/2016
In Memoriam: Joan Bozer – Olmsted Network by Anne "Dede" Petri, olmsted.org 5/11/23

Papers of Joan Bozer by Danielle White, November 14, 2013, Archives Space Public Interface, buffalo.edu

League of Women Voters newsletter Zonta notice, lwvbn.org November 2009

Preservation Buffalo Award text in program 2014

Red Jacket Award annual program, red-jacket-aware-former-recipients.pdf, buffalohistory.org

Thomas H. Kendig, Inventor, Manufacturer by staff Buffalo News 12/12/1990

Suggestions and editing by Catherine Flickinger Schweitzer

Sources for Kate Robinson Butler

Mrs. Edward H. Butler, News Publisher is Dead, Buffalo Evening News 8/5/1974

Kate Robinson Butler is Dead, Published Buffalo Evening News, New York Times obituary 8/5/1974

The Buffalo Evening News Building, 200 Main Street by Steve Cichon, buffalostories.com

Kate Butler Wickham, 97, Buffalo philanthropist, granddaughter of News founder by Dale Anderson, Buffalo News, 11/25/2018

Profiles Volume II: Historic & Influential People from Buffalo & WNY – the early 1900s by Rick Falkowski

Sources for Taylor Caldwell

Taylor Caldwell – a short biography taylorcaldwell.com

The Romance of Atlantis, Promotion release by publisher William Morrow & Co

Taylor Caldwell, Prolific Author Dies. New York Times 9/2/1985

Taylor Caldwell by Lorne Opler in Buffalo Rising 9/7/2007

Taylor Caldwell, 75, is still Turning Out Historical Novels by George Borrelli 3/8/1976

Conversation with Caldwell's granddaughter Drina Fried

Sources for Evelyn Rumsey Cary

Buffaloah.com. Women and the Pan-American by Mary B. Mullet in Harper's Weekly 1901

Eveyln Rumsey Cary: Artist, Philanthropist and Suffragette by Marthy Neri, The Compass in Explore Buffalo, March 2020

Eveyln Rumsey Cary – Burchfield Penney Art Center. Burchfieldpenney.org

Creativity and Persistence: Art that Fueled the Fight for Women's Suffrage, National Endowment for the Arts, August 2020

Buffalo's Delaware Avenue Mansions and Families by Edward T. Dunn.

Profitable Advertising, panam1901.org

Historic & Influential People from Buffalo & WNY – the 1800s by Rick Falkowski

Sources for Mary R. Cass

National Register of Historic Places. Registration Form for F.N. Burt Co. Factory

The Preservation Exchange by Derek King, 7/27/2012

Municipality of Buffalo, New York: A History 1720-1923 Volume 3 by Henry Wayland Hill
Profiles Volume II – the early 1900s by Rick Falkowski

Sources for Shirley Chisholm
Shirley Chisholm (1924 – 2015) National Women's History Museum by Debra Michals 2015.
Shirley Anita St. Hill Chisholm, Uncrowned Community Builders website
Shirley Chisholm (November 30, 1924 – January 1, 2005) national Archives
Exploring African-American History at the Freedom Wall in Buffalo by Jim Cheney, Uncovering New York 2/14/2023

Sources for Carolyn Jewett Tripp Clement
Mrs. Clement, Long-Time Civic Leader is Dead. Buffalo News, 12/29/43
Mrs. Stephen M Clement Wins Award of University Women, Buffalo Evening News 5/5/43
Forest Lawn Facts: Carolyn Tripp Clement
Carolyn Tripp Clement Residence Hall – University Archives, library.buffalo.edu
Buffaloah.com
Deal for Delaware Mansion assures BPO of its new home by Jonathan Epstein, Buffalo News 12/19/2017.
Edited & expanded by Catherine Flickinger Schweitzer

Sources for Frances Folsom Cleveland
Grover Cleveland in Buffalo, Western New York History
Frances Folsom Cleveland, 1864-1947, First Lady of the United States, buffaloah.com
White House Weddings: Grover Cleveland and Frances Folsom, livejournal.com 6/16/2019
The Bride of the White House by Francis Howard Williams 1886

Sources for Lucille Clifton
poetryfoundation.org/poets/lucille-clifton
poets.org/poet/lucille-clifton
literaryladiesguide.com/classic-women-authors-poetry/10-poems-by-lucille-clifton/
literaryladiesguide.com/author-biography/lucille-clifton/
msa.maryland.gov/msa/educ/exhibits/womenshallfame/html/clifton.html
africanamericanpoetry.org/lucille-clifton
smith.edu/academics/poetry-center/lucille-clifton
npr.org/2010/02/28/124113507/poet-lucille-clifton-everything-is-connected

npr.org/2007/05/22/10329530/poet-lucille-clifton-recalls-a-life-of-well-chosen-words

awpwriter.org/magazine media/writers chronicle view between starshine clay an interview with Lucille Clifton

poetryoutloud.org/poet/lucille-clifton/

faculty.georgetown.edu/bassr/heath/syllabuild/iguide/clifton.html

billmoyers.com/story/a-poem-a-day-wont-you-celebrate-with-me-by-lucille-clifton/

bmoreart.com/2021/05/how-baltimore-fed-lucille-cliftons-poetry.html

lithub.com/lucille-clifton-didnt-just-write-poems-she-inhabited-them/

brinkerhoffpoetry.org/poets/lucille-clifton

communityofwriters.org/bio/Lucille-clifton

Profile created by Catherine Flickinger Schweitzer

Sources for Katharine Cornell

Katharine Cornell, History of Women in Forest Lawn Cemetery by Patrick Kavanagh

Katharine Cornell is Dead at 81 by Alden Whitman, New York Times obituary, June 10, 1974

Katharine Cornell, buffaloah.com

Guthrie McClintic & Katharine Cornell, elisa-rolle.livejournal.com

Queerplaces – Katharine Cornell, elisa-rolle.livejournal.com

Guide to Katharine Cornell papers, New York Public Library, snaccooperative.org

Profiles Volume I: Historic & Influential People from Buffalo & WNY – the 1800s by Rick Falkowski

Abridged version of Volume II profile created and edited by Mike Buckley

Sources for Madeline Davis:

Madeline Davis, 80, trailblazing gay and lesbian activist and Historian by Dale Anderson, Buffalo News obituary, 4/29/2021

In Memoriam: Madeline Davis Eulogy, University at Buffalo Dept of Global Gender and Sexuality Studies

Madeline Davis, Who Spoke to the Nation as a Lesbian, Dies at 80 by Annabelle Williams, New York Times. 6/18/2021

Our Madeline Davis by Joan Nestle, lesbianherstoryarchives.org 6/8/2022

Sources for Ani DiFranco

Ani DiFranco: Righteous Babe by Raffaele Quirino

Ani Biography, Righteous Babe Records, righteousbabe.com

Ani DiFranco Awards, IMDb, imdb.com

History of Buffalo Music & Entertainment by Rick Falkowski

Discussions with Richard N. Fustino

Dale Anderson, BMHOF Class of 2003, bmhof.org

Sources for JoAnn Falletta

JoAnn Falletta, Music Director. bpo.org

JoAnn Falletta biography. joannfalletta.com

The JoAnn Falletta International Guitar Concerto Competition by Joanne Castellani and Michael Andriaccio

JoAnne Falletta: Pioneering Conductor and Champion of Unsung Music by Lisa Hirsh, Classical Voice, June 6, 2023.

The conductor's life: JoAnn Falletta's days are anything but routine, and they are decidedly up-tempo by Mary Kunz Goldman, Buffalo News, December 10, 2006

Sources for Abgail Powers Fillmore

Abgail Powers Fillmore at whitehouse.gov

History of Women in Forest Lawn Cemetery by Patrick Kavanagh

Profiles Volume I: Historic & Influential People from Buffalo & WNY – the 1800s by Rick Falkowski

Sources for Marian de Forest

Reviving a Legend Buffalo's Marian de Forest by Paula Voell, Buffalo News, May 17, 2001.

The Remarkable Life of Marian de Forest. Keeping the Promise, forest-lawn.com

Marian de Forest, History of Women in Forest Lawn Cemetery by Patrick Kavanagh

Marian de Forest. Pan-American Exposition Buffalo 1901, panam1901.org

Brief History of the Zonta Club of Buffalo by Dorothy WIswall, Vivian Cody and Caren Shapiro. zontadistrict4.org

Zonta International, zonta.org

Marian de Forest. Suffragette City 100, suffragettecity100.com

Marian de Forest. National Women's Hall of Fame, womenofthehall.org

Journalism, drama, and a legacy of service, spectrumlocalnews.com 3/22/22

Woman's History Month -Charlotte Mulligan, wbfo.org 3/6/2013

Where it all began A feature on Marian de Forest Buffalo, New York, USA Special thanks to Vivian Cody, member of the Zonta Club of Buffalo, NY, USA, past."

Marian de Forest, WNY Heritage Magazine, Summer 2019

Abridged version of Volume II profile created and edited by Mike Buckley

Additional information added by Catherine Flickinger Schweitzer

Sources for Mabel Ganson Dodge Luhan

Mabel Dodge Luhan 1879 – 1962, encyclopedia.com

Mabel Ganson Evans: First Marriage by Elizabeth Cunningham, mabeldodgeluhan.com

Mabel Dodge Luhan, theflorentine.net

Abridged version of Volume II profile created and edited by Mike Buckley

Sources for Minnie Gillette

Biography for Minnie Gillette in Uncrowned Community Builders

Buffalo in the '80s: Minnie Gillette, grassroots community pioneer by Steve Cichon, buffalostories.com

Ellicott Town Center Part 1 – Minnie Gillette: Be the First African-American County Legislator, Get a Street Named After You. One Street at a Time by Angela Keppel, buffalostreets.com

Minnie Gillette Dies at 62: First Black Woman Legislator by Carl Allen & Dave Ernst, Buffalo News obituary 1/8/1992

Minnie Gillette, buffaloakg.org

Suggestions and editing by Catherine Flickinger Schweitzer

Sources for Ella Portia Conger Goodyear

Bogalusa Story by C.W. Goodyear

Buffalo's Delaware Avenue: Mansions and Families by Edward T. Dunn

Buffaloah.com

The Life & Times of 888 Delaware Avenue by Ellen Zelasko, hellobuffalohikes.com

Sources for Anna Katherine Green

The New York Genealogical and Biographical Record. Volume XXXVIII, 1907

Anna Katherine "Kitty" Rohlfs Green, by Patrick Kavanagh. History of Women in Forest Lawn Cemetery.

The Mother of the Modern Detective Story: Anna Katherine Green Rohlfs. Forest Lawn Cemetery.

Anna Katherine Green and Charles Rohlfs: Artistic Collaborators. The Magazine Antiques. 2008

Onlinelibrary.wiley.com

Anna Katherine Green – Recovering 19th Century American Women Writers, Volume 1, Stockton.edu

No Mystery: Anna Katherine Green Invertor of the Detective Novel, gateway-longview.org

The Pioneering, Bestselling Anna Katherine Green – Sara Farmer, diymfa.com

Anna Katherine Green, encyclopedia.com

Profile expanded by Catherine Flickinger Schweitzer

Sources for Sara Hinson

Sara Hinson – Founder of Flag Day. Forest Lawn Cemetery. 6/10/2018

Wisconsin Wins This One, Chris Carosa. Chriscarosa.com 6/14/2015

History of Flag Day includes connection to Erie County. Observer Today. Dunkirk NY June 14, 2015

Historic & Influential People from Buffalo Y WNY – the 1800s by Rick Falkowski

Betsy Ross likely didn't sew the first U.S. flag by Erin Blakemore, National Geographic 7/1/2021

Sources for Maud Gordon Holmes

Buffaloah.com
Explore Buffalo: E&B Holmes in Buffalo Rising, 10/21/2020.
Resurgence Brewing Company website.
Maud Gordon Holmes Arboretum, arboretum.buffstate.edu
SUNY Buffalo State University Archives

Sources for Katherine Pratt Horton

Buffalo's Delaware Avenue Mansions and Families by Edward T. Dunn
Birge-Horton House (Katherine Pratt Horton Buffalo Chapter, National Society
Daughters of the American revolution. theclio.com
Women of America – part of the American History & Genealogy Project:
Katherine Lorenz Pratt Horton 1848-1931.
Buffalo Federation of Women's Clubs, University of Buffalo.
buffalo.academicworks.com
About Us - Daughters of the American Revolution-Buffalo NY at dar-buffalo.com
Historic & Influential People from Buffalo & WNY – the 1800s by Rick Falkowski

Sources for Mary Jemison

Pioneer History of the Holland Purchase of Western New York by O. Turner
A Narrative of the Life of Mary Jemison by James Seaver
The taking of Mary Jemison by Robert Griffing in History of American Women,
womenhistoryblog.com
Historic & Influential People from Buffalo & WNY – the 1800s by Rick Falkowski

Sources for Beverly Johnson

Beverly Johnson Biography. Encyclopedia of World Biography
Beverly Johnson, Britannica Online Encyclopedia
Supermodel has Super Time visiting Old Friends by Juan Forero and Karen Brady,
Buffalo News 11/24/1997
Icon Beverly Johnson Reveals a Pool was once drained after a Fashion Shoot
because she's Black by People Staff 7/17/2020
CommUNITY spotlight: Model Beverly Johnson has Fond Memories of Buffalo
by Claudine Ewing, wgrz.com 4/7/21

Sources for Doris Jones

Women in Buffalo Television interview by John DiSciullo on WBBZ
60 Years of women making history at WKBW, wkbw.com 11/15/2018
The Women of early TV in Buffalo by Steve Cichon, buffalostories.com
100 Years of Broadcasting by Steve Cichon
Conversations with Doris Jones

Sources for Mary Seaton Kleinhans

Kleinhans Music Hall and the BPO: A Story in Stereo by Raya Lee and Edward
Yadzinski, WNY Heritage, April 15, 2012

Esther Emig Dies: Store Co-Founder Championed Design of Music Hall, obituary in Buffalo News 1/26/1990.

Before Kleinhans and Memorial Auditorium: The Elmwood Convention/Music Hall. wnyhistory.org

Profiles Volume II: Historic & Influential People from Buffalo & WNY – the early 1900s by Rick Falkowski

Community Foundation for Greater Buffalo. cfgb.org

Kleinhans Music Hall. buffaloah.com

Sources for Grace Millard Knox

Buffalo's Delaware Avenue Mansions & Families by Edward T. Dunn

Find a Grave – Grace Millard Knox

Grace Millard Knox House, buffaloah.com

The House is Selected the 21st Decorators' Show House by Queenseyes, Buffalo Rising, 12/26/2020

Ross Cellino bought Knox Mansion for new firm's offices by Jonathan D. Epstein, Buffalo News, 12/15/2020

St Joseph's New Cathedral, wnyhistory.org

S.H. Knox biography, woolworthsmuseum.co.uk

Seymour H. Knox Is Dead at 92; Buffalo Banker Was Art Patron - The New York Times (nytimes.com)

Seymour Knox | Discovering Buffalo, One Street at a Time (buffalostreets.com)

UB People, library2.buffalo.edu/archives

Profile expanded by Catherine Flickinger Schweitzer

Sources for Belva Lockwood

Belva Lockwood, archives.gov/publications/

Lady Lawyers, supremecourt.gov

Belva Lockwood, Suffragists, lawyer and presidential candidate, blogs.loc.gov

Belva Ann Lockwood, Biography, nwculaw.edu

Belva Lockwood, inductee, womenofthehall.org

Belva Lockwood, womenhistoryblog.com

Maryann Saccomando Freedman, buffaloah.com

Profile created by Catherine Flickinger Schweitzer

Sources for Mary Johnson Lord

Dr. John Chase Lord Farmhouse – Buffalo, preservationready.org

John Chase Lord, DD, McClintock and Strong Biblical Cyclopedia. biblicalcyclopedia.com

John Chase Lord, Class of 1819. Kimball Union Academy – From the Archives.

Discover the Stories of 7 Buffalo Women Who Made History by Rebecca Justinger, Buffalo History Museum, buffalohistory.org 3/22/23

Famous Residents – Forest Lawn – Buffalo NY

A Brief History of the SPCA Serving Erie County by Gary Willoughby, yourspca.org

Sources for Maria Love

Delaware Avenue Mansions by Edward T. Dunn
Buffaloah.com
Marialovefund.org
Maria M. Love – Charity Ball, cfgb.org/donors/client stories
A legacy of Love more than a century later, wgrz.com
Maria Love Fund, flowersbynature.com
Continuing Maria Love's Legacy – Creator of the first daycare in the U.S., spectrumlocalnews.com
Maria M. Love Life, archive.org
Who was the real Maria Love, wnyheritage.org
The Fitch Creche of Buffalo, buffalohistorygazette.net
trinitybuffalo.org
buffaloresearch.com
profile expanded by Catherine Flickinger Schweitzer

Sources for Carmelita Merriweather

UncrownedCommunityBuilders.com
BuffaloNews.com/obituaries
Information from Buffalo Criterion
Evelyn Patterson Merriweather, 98, longtime publisher of Buffalo Criterion, Buffalo News obituary 11/17/2021

Sources for Ann Montgomery:

Little Harlem Collection by Alison Fraser
Ann Montgomery: Matron of the Little Harlem by Barbara A. Seals Nevergold, February 25, 2015, buffalorising.com
BN Chronicles: Dan Montgomery's and Ann Montgomery's Little Harlem by Steve Cichon, February 24, 2021, buffalonews.com
History of Buffalo Music & Entertainment by Rick Falkowski
Abridged version of Volume II profile created and edited by Mike Buckley

Sources for Nina Morgana

Nina Morgana, Great Singers of the Past, greatsingersofthepast.wordpress.com
Clever Child Vocalist, 1901 Buffalo Newspaper clipping
Nina Morgana Zirato Dies at 94, Served as Caruso's Assisting Artist, Buffalo News obituary 7/10/1986
Caruso Told Her That She'd be a Great Singer by Harvey Elsasser, Buffalo News 5/3/1969
Nina Morgana, Opera Star comes home to Buffalo after Triumph on Stage, Buffalo Courier 5/18/1924
Genia Las biography. Bach Cantatas Website. bach-cantatas.com
Helen Oelheim Michel, 87, Dies; Mezzo Soprano Sang with Met. Buffalo News obituary 6/30/1992

Sources for Charlotte Mulligan

Forest Lawn: The Remarkable Life of Charlotte Mulligan, forest-lawn.org
New Phoenix Theatre website newphoenixtheatre.org
The Twentieth Century Club of Buffalo website history written by Philip Nyhuis of Buffalo Spree Magazine
The Most Prestigious Club You Probably Never Heard of in Moxie Gardner blog
Buffalo Seminary History, buffaloah.com
Women's History Month – Charlotte Mulligan, wbfo.org 3/6/2013
Women's Chapter House, wnyhistory.org
Charlotte Mulligan in Bethune book by Joanna Hays

Sources for Barbara Ann Seals Nevergold

Barbara Ann Seals Nevergold bio at Uncrowned Community Builders
Remarkable Women 2023: Dr. Barbara Seals Nevergold by Jordan Norkus, WIVB 3/22/2023
Barbara Seals Nevergold bio in The History Makers – repository for the Black Experience
Willie Brown Seals biography in Uncrowned Community Builders
Uncrownedcommunitybuilders.com
Legislature of Erie County proclamation honoring receipt of 2019 Medgar Evers Award

Sources for Joyce Carol Oates

Joyce Carol Oates revisits her childhood by Carmela Ciuraru in USA Today 10/3/2015
Joyce Carol Oates's Life, Career and Notable Novels by MasterClass, masterclass.com
Joyce Carol Oates and her dark and haunting WNY childhood by staff, Buffalo News, 9/12/2015
Katz, Oates awarded National Humanities Medal by Jennifer Greenstein Altmann, Princeton University, 3/2/2011
Joyce Carol Oates Goes Home Again by Joyce Carol Oates, Smithsonian Magazine, March 2010
Joyce Carol Oates' Memoir Revisits The Farm and The Family That Shaped Her, by Lynn Neary, WBFO NPR, 9/14/2015
Heritage Moments: Farm Girl at the Lockport Library, a 7-year-old Joyce Carol Oates discovers books by Jeff Z. Klein, WBFO/NPR wbfo.org 8/1/2016
profile researched and written by Catherine Flickinger Schweitzer

Sources for Margaret Evans Price

Margaret Evans Price, meibohmfinearts.com
Margaret Evans Price, Burchfield Art Center, burchfieldpenney.org
The Margaret Evans Price Murals, Aurora Theatre, theauroratheatre.com
Profiles Volume II – the early 1900s by Rick Falkowski

Sources for Keziah Ransom

History of the City of Buffalo and Erie County by Henry Perry Smith
Historic & Influential People from Buffalo & WNY – the 1800s by Rick Falkowski
Keziah Keyes Ransom findagrave.com
The Mystery of Ransom's tavern by Heath J. Szymczak, erie.gov

Sources for Anna Reinstein

Anna Reinstein Memorial Library, History of Anna M. Reinstein
Cheektowaga Public Library at nyheritage.org
Dr. Anna M. Reinstein Memorial Scholarship Fund, buffaloacademicworks.com
Find a Grave- Anna Reinstein. findagrave.com – obituary from 1948
Profiles Volume II – the Early 1900s by Rick Falkowski

Sources for Julia Reinstein

Find a Grave – Julia Agnes Boyer Reinstein
The Julia Boyer Reinstein Library (Documenting Libraries) susanmarie.info
Julia Boyer Reinstein, Historian, Philanthropist Known as Cheektowaga's "Great Lady" Dies. By staff, Buffalo News obituary 7/19/1998
Town Bids Farewell to Julia Reinstein by Jay Rey, Buffalo News 7/22/1998
Julia Boyer Reinstein on Wikipedia
Reinstein Library Opens to the Public by Jay Rey, Buffalo News 2/26/1996
History of the Julia Boyer Reinstein Center, Buffalo History Museum Blog

Sources for Margaret St. John

Recollections of the Burning of Buffalo and Events in the History of the Family of Gamaliel and Margaret St. John. By Mrs. Jonathan Sidway, published in the Buffalo Historical Society Publications, Vol. 16.
Historic Plymouth Avenue in the Kleinhans Neighborhood, Kleinhans Community Association, May 2008.
Profiles Volume I – the 1800s by Rick Falkowski

Sources for Charlotte N. Shedd

The Early History of Hospice Buffalo edited by Abel K. Fink and Donald P. Shedd, published by The Center for Hospice & Palliative Care, 2003.
Charolotte N. Shedd, 84, nurse who co-founded Hospice Buffalo, obituary Buffalo News 4/30/2007
Dr. Robert Milch, 78, co-founder of Hospice Buffalo by Harold McNeil, Buffalo News 6/5/2021
Hospice Buffalo Our History, hospicebuffalo.com
At 86, Head & Neck Surgeon still contributes to medicine and Hospice because he helped Found, Yale Medicine Magazine, 2009 Autumn

Sources for April Stevens

April Stevens Dies at 93; Her "Deep Purple" Became a Surprise Hit by Daniel E. Slotnik, New York Times, April 26, 2023.
Ninoandapril.com. Nino Tempo and April Stevens web site

Nino Tempo & April Stevens Biography. By Linda Dailey Paulson, musiciansguide.com

45 Friday: Nino Tempo & April Stevens – All Strung Out by Bob "The Record Guy" Paxon, wnyfm.wordpress.com

History of Buffalo Music & Entertainment by Rick Falkowski

Sources for Mary Burnett Talbert

Initial draft of this profile was researched and written by McKinley Falkowski

Culp, Daniel Wallace. *Twentieth Century Negro Literature, or, A Cyclopedia of Thought on the Vital Topics Relating to the American Negro*. Toronto, Canada, Georgia: J.L. Nichols & Co., 1987.

Davis, LaQuantae. Mary B. Talbert (1866-1923). Blackpast, February 7, 2020. blackpast.org

LaChiusa, Chuck. "Mary Burnett Talbert - Chronology." Mary Talbert. Ingenious Inc. buffaloah.com.

Okazawa-Rey, Margo, and Sylvia M. Jacobs. *Encyclopedia of African-American Education*. Westport, Connecticut: Greenwood Publishing Group, 1996.

Sears, Stephen W. BIG DAY AT OBERLIN. The New York Times. The New York Times, May 20, 1990.

Michigan Street Baptist Church. Visit Buffalo Niagara. visitbuffaloniagara.com

"The Negro Exhibit" at the Pan-Am by Sarah Ruth Offhaus, Buffalo Rising, July 15, 2010

Walser, Lauren. Mary B. Talbert: The Preservation Champion You Might Not Have Heard Of: National Trust for Historic Preservation. May 21, 2014. savingplaces.org/stories/mary-b-talbert-preservation-champion.

White, Deborah G. *Too Heavy a Load: Black Women in Defense of Themselves, 1894-1994*. New York: W.W. Norton, 2000.

Mary Burnett Talbert -. Archives of Women's Political Communication. awpc.cattcenter.iastate.edu

Talbert, Mary Burnett. National Women's Hall of Fame. womenofthehall.org

University Archives. Mary B. Talbert Hall. University at Buffalo Libraries. library.buffalo.edu

Sarah May Talbert Keelan. uncrownedcommunitybuilders.com

The Most Famous Buffalonian You May Not Have Heard Of: Mary Talbert by Angela Keppel, 8/30/2020. buffalostreets.com

Abridged version of Volume II profile created and edited by Mike Buckley

Sources for Annie Edson Taylor

Overlooked No More: Annie Edson Taylor, Who Tumbled Down Niagara Falls into Fame by Jesse McKinley, New York Times, 5/1/2019.

The First Person to go Over Niagara Falls in a Barrel (and Survive). wbur.com. 6/12/2012.

A cat was the first Queen of the Mist and other facts unbeknownst to many, posted in londonthetheatredirect.com on 8/16/2019.

Three photos leave questions swirling about the identity of a women in the pictures. Could it be daredevil Annie Edson Taylor? by Anne Neville, Buffalo News 7/7/2012.

Remembering the Queen of the Mist by Carol Rogers, nystateparks.blog, 1/12/2021.

Sources for Dorothy Thompson

Dorothy Thompson (1893-1961) in the Eleanor Roosevelt Papers Project for Columbian College of Arts & Sciences

Dorothy Thompson: Americans and the Holocaust. U.S. Holocaust Memorial Museum

Dorothy Thompson: The First Lady of American Journalism by Stan Evans, Buffalo News, 2/21/2020.

Sources for Harriet Townsend

Harriet Townsend and the Women's Union by Susan Eck, WNY History

Harriet Townsend – Discovering Buffalo, One Street at a Time by Angela Kepple

Harriet Townsend – UB People – University Archives

Townsend Hall garners LEED Gold certification, buffalo.edu

Women's Union – Townsend Hall, buffaloah.com

Sources for Harriet Tubman:

Harriet Tubman Biography edited by Debra Michals, PhD, womenshistory.org

Harriet Tubman: Facts, Underground Railroad & Legacy, history.com

Harriet Tubman's relative discusses her legacy in WNY by Karys Belger, wgrz.com 10/31/2019

Site of the Cataract House – Niagara Falls Underground Railroad Heritage Center

Tour of Niagara Falls Underground Railroad Heritage Center and discussions with Amie Whitmore

Sources for Florence Wendt

Buffaloah.com. Wendt Family in Buffalo

William F. Wendt & Henry W. Wendt, findagrave.com

Buffalo Philharmonic Orchestra: The BPO Celebrates the First 75 years by Raya Lee and Edward Yadzinski, 2010

History of Buffalo Music & Entertainment by Rick Falkowski

BPO.org BPO Archives

Edgar Forsyth Wendt, findagrave.com

Buffalo Forge Company History in vintagemachinery.org

Sources for Margaret Wendt

Buffalo: Lake City in Niagara Land

Buffaloah.com. Wendt Family in Buffalo

Margaret Wendt Foundation

William F. Wendt & Henry W. Wendt, findagrave.com

The Continuing Legacy of Margaret L. Wendt by Michael Vogel, WNY Heritage, 4/15/2002.

Sources for Carol Wincenc

Carolwincencflute.com bio from her web page

Music Notes: A Flutist Takes a Solo Flight by Raymond Ericson, New York Times 4/22/1979

No Pregnant Pauses for Wincenc by Benjamin Epstein Lost Angeles Times 12/8/1992

– Stony Brook University Artis- in-Residence, Flute

Carol Wincenc - encyclopedia.com

Carol Wincenc: Magician of the Flute by Gena Raps in persimmontree.org, Winter 2013

History of Buffalo Music & Entertainment by Rick Falkowski

Sources for Penny Wolfgang

Bio of Penny Wolfgang

Judge Penny M. Wolfgang: Professional Background and Legal Expertise, trellis.law

She has no idea how to be retired by Jeff Schober, buffalotales.net

Interview with Penny Wolfgang

Baranski, Glor headline 2023 Broadcasters Hall of Fame by Alan Pergamet, Buffalo News 7/5/2023

Sources for Christine Ziemba

Resume of Christine Ziemba

Discussions and emails with Christine Ziemba

Q&A: Christine M. Ziemba on the Cheektowaga Police Department by staff, Buffalo News 2/26/2006

Ziemba to retire after 9 years as Cheektowaga Police Chief; Force's 1st woman broke new ground by Michelle Kearns, Buffalo News 1/20/2011

Can do attitude is key says retiring Cheektowaga Police Chie Christine Ziemba by Glen Gramigna, Am-Pole Eagle 3/16/2011

Woman 'Trailblazes' her way onto Cheektowaga Police Force by John Sinclair

BIBLIOGRAPHY

The Spirit of Buffalo Women
Prominent Women who called WNY their Home

Books

Ball, Lucille. l Love Lucy. New York: G.P. Putnam's Sons, 1996.

Bovina, Arthur. Everything Buffalo: A guide to Eating in "Nickel City." Countryman Press, 2018.

Blumenstalk Mingus, Nancy. Buffalo Good Neighbors, Great Architecture. Charleston: Arcadia Publishing, 2003.

Dunn, Edward T. Buffalo's Delaware Avenue: Mansions and Families. Buffalo: Canisius College Press, 2003.

Falkowski, Rick. History of Buffalo Music & Entertainment. Williamsville: 2017.

Falkowski, Rick. Profiles Volume I: Historic & Influential People from Buffalo & WNY – the 1800s. Williamsville: 2019.

Falkowski, Rick. Profiles Volume II: Historic & Influential People from Buffalo & WNY – the Early 1900s. Williamsville: 2021.

Hajdu, David. Positively Fourth Street: The lives and times of Joan Baez, Bob Dylan, Mimi Baez Farina and Richard Farina. New York: Picador, 2001.

Hayes, Johanna. Louise Blanchard Bethune: Buffalo Feminist and Americas First Woman Architect. McFarland & Company, 2014.

Hill, Henry Wayland. Municipality of Buffalo New York: A History 1720 - 1923. New York: Lewis Historical Publishing, 1923.

Karol, Michael. Lucy in Print. Lincoln, NE: iUniverse, Inc., 2003.

Lee, Raya & Edward Yadzinski. Buffalo Philharmonic Orchestra: The BPO Celebrates the First 75 Years. Buffalo: Buffalo Heritage Unlimited, 2010.

Logan, Mrs. John A. The Part Taken by Women in American History. Wilmington Delaware: The Perry-Nalle Publishing Company, 1912.

McAlonie, Kelly Hayes. Louise Blanchard Bethune: Every Woman Her Own Architect. State University of New York Press, 2023.

Quirino, Raffale. Ani DiFranco Righteous Babe. Kingston Ontario, Quarry Press, 2000.

Smith, Henry Perry. History of the City of Buffalo & Erie County. Syracuse: D Mason & Company Printers, 1884.

Publications

Information was gathered from the following newspapers, magazines and other publications to prepare this book. The article and author are listed in the applicable profile.

- Am-Pol Eagle
- Atlantic
- Buffalo News
- Buffalo Rising
- Buffalo Spree
- Courier Express
- Democrat & Chronical, Rochester NY
- Harpers Weekly
- Jamestown Gazette
- National Geographic
- New York Post
- New York Times
- Observer Today, Dunkirk NY
- People
- Time Magazine
- USA Today
- WNY Heritage Magazine

Websites

Information was reviewed in the following websites to prepare this book. The article and author are listed in the applicable profile.

- 3407memorial.com
- actorcontactdetails.com
- anchorbar.com
- archives.gov
- babevillebuffalo.com
- bmhof.org
- bpo.org
- buffalo.edu
- buffaloacademicworks.com
- buffaloah.com
- buffaloakg.org
- buffalohistorygazette.net
- buffalostories.com
- buffalostreets.com
- buffalotales.net
- buffalowing.com
- burchfieldpenney.org
- cfgb.org
- carolwincencflute.com
- chickenwingday.com
- dignitymemorial.com
- encyclopedia.com
- findagrave.com
- gateway-longview.org
- hellobuffalohikes.com
- imdb.com
- joannfalletta.com
- joanbaez.com
- lesbianhistoryarchives.org
- library.buffalo.edu

- louisebethune.com
- lwvbn.org
- mabeldodgeluhan.com
- meiborhmfinearts.com
- ninoandapril.com
- nyheritage.org
- nystateparks.blog
- oldradioworld.com
- olmsted.org
- panam1901.org
- pastlanetravels.com
- preservationready.org
- righteousbabe.com
- spectrumlocalnews.com
- suffragettecity100.com
- supremecourt.gov
- susanmarie.info
- taylorcaldwell.com
- theclio.com
- theauroratheatre.com
- thefamouspeople.com
- theflorentine.net
- whitehouse.org
- wbfo.org
- wgrz.com
- wikipedia.org
- wivb.com
- wkbw.com
- wnyfm.wordpress.com
- wnyhistory.org
- womenhistoryblog.com
- womenofthehall.org
- womenwritingarchitecture.org
- yourspca.org
- zontadistrict4.com

Organizations

The following and other organizations were consulted to assist in preparing this book. Reference to the organization may be found in the applicable profile.

- Buffalo History Museum
- Buffalo State University archives
- Burchfield Penney Art Center
- DAR Buffalo Chapter
- Forest Lawn Cemetery
- League of Women Voters
- National Register of Historic Places
- National Women's History Museum
- Niagara Falls Underground Railroad Heritage Center
- Uncrowned Community Builders
- University at Buffalo archives
- Zonta Buffalo

INDEX